Retirement among American Men

Retirement among American Men

Herbert S. Parnes
Joan E. Crowley
R. Jean Haurin
Lawrence J. Less
William R. Morgan
Frank L. Mott
Gilbert Nestel
The Ohio State University
Center for Human Resource Research

Lexington Books
D.C. Heath and Company/Lexington, Massachusetts/Toronto

Library of Congress Cataloging in Publication Data
Main entry under title:

Retirement among American men.

Includes index.
1. Retirement—United States—Longitudinal studies.
2. Age and employment—United States—Longitudinal
studies. 3. Aged men—United States—Longitudinal
studies. I. Parnes, Herbert S., 1919–   . II. Ohio
State University. Center for Human Resource Research.
HQ 1062.R38   1985   306'.38'0973   85–6876
ISBN 0–669–10334–9 (alk. paper)

This report was prepared under a contract with the Employment and Training
Administration, U.S. Department of Labor, under the authority of the Comprehensive
Employment and Training Act. Researchers undertaking such projects under government
sponsorship are encouraged to express their own judgments. Interpretations or viewpoints
stated in this report do not necessarily represent the official position or policy of the U.S.
Department of Labor.

Published simultaneously in Canada
Printed in the United States of America on acid-free paper
International Standard Book Number: 0–669–10334–9
Library of Congress Catalog Card Number: 85–6876

Contents

Tables

Figures

Preface and Acknowledgments

Since 1965 the Center for Human Resource Research of The Ohio State University and the U.S. Bureau of the Census, under separate contracts with the Employment and Training Administration of the U.S. Department of Labor, have been engaged in the National Longitudinal Surveys of Labor Market Experience (NLS). Four subsets of the civilian population in the United States are being studied: men who at the inception of the study were 45-59 years of age; women 30-44 years of age; and young men and young women between the ages of 14 and 24. In 1979 a new study of male and female youths 14-21 years of age was begun.

These groups were chosen because each is confronted with special labor market problems that are challenging to policymakers. For the youths these problems revolve around the process of occupational choice, and include both the preparation for work and the frequently difficult period of accommodation to the labor market when formal schooling has been completed. For the older group of women, the problems are those associated with reentry into the labor force after children are in school or grown. The special problems of the middle-aged men stem in part from skill obsolescence, from the increasing incidence of health problems, and from employment discrimination, all of which are reflected in declining labor force participation rates and in longer-than-average duration of spells of unemployment.

For each of the four population groups originally covered by the NLS, a national probability sample of the noninstitutional civilian population was drawn by the Census Bureau in 1966, and interviews have been conducted periodically by Census enumerators using schedules prepared by the Center for Human Resource Research. Originally planned to cover a five-year period, the surveys have been so successful and attrition so small that they have been continued beyond the originally planned expiration dates. Surveys of the two male cohorts were discontinued after the 1983 interviews, but surveys of the other cohorts are to continue for some years into the future.

The present book is the sixth comprehensive monograph on the NLS older men's data prepared by multidisciplinary research teams at The Ohio State University Center for Human Resource Research, which has primary responsibility for conducting the NLS. The first four books, *The Preretirement Years*, Manpower Research Monograph 15, by Herbert S. Parnes et al., were published by the U.S. Government Printing Office: volume 1 appeared in 1968, volume 2 in 1970, volume 3 in 1973, and volume 4 in 1975. Volume 5 was entitled *From the Middle to the Later Years: Longitudinal Studies of the Preretirement and Postretirement Experiences of Men* and subsequently published by The MIT Press in 1981 under the title *Work and Retirement: A Longitudinal Study of Men*. It is also available from the National Technical Information Service. The present volume is based on the data collected through the 1981 survey. Besides these books, hundreds of other studies based on the NLS older men's data have been prepared by individuals at research institutions and universities worldwide.

Without attempting to escape ultimate responsibility for whatever limitations remain in their chapters, the authors wish to acknowledge their debt to a large number of persons without whose contributions neither the overall study nor the present book would have been possible. Although personally unknown to us, the several thousand members of the sample who have generously agreed to participate in repeated interviews over the years must be mentioned first, for they have provided the raw materials for our effort.

Officials of the Employment and Training Administration have been very helpful to us over the years in providing suggestions for the design of the surveys and in carefully reviewing preliminary drafts of our reports. We wish to acknowledge the continuous support and encouragement of Howard Rosen, director of the Office of Research and Development during most of the years of the project, and to his successor, Burt Barnow. We profited also from valuable advice provided by Stuart Garfinkle, Frank Mott, Jacob Schiffman, Rose Weiner, and Ellen Sehgal, who have consecutively served as monitors of the project.

The research staff of the Center for Human Resource Research has enjoyed the continuous expert and friendly collaboration of personnel of the Bureau of the Census, who have been responsible for developing the samples, conducting all of the interviews, coding and editing the data, and preparing the initial versions of the computer tapes. The names of those who have been involved in these activities over the years are too numerous to be mentioned individually, but we should like to acknowledge especially our debt to Thomas C. Walsh, chief of the Demographic Surveys Division, and to his predecessors, Marvin Thompson, Earle Gerson, Daniel Levine, and Robert Pearl; to Ron Dopkowski, chief of the Special Surveys Branch, and to his predecessors, Chester Bowie, George Gray, Robert Mangold, and Marie Argana; and to their colleagues Cheryl Landman, Dorothy Koger, Tom Scopp, Nanette Perlman, Bill Hultgren, and Renee Jefferson-Copland. These are the individuals in the Census Bureau with whom we have had immediate contact in the recent past. In addition, we wish to express our appreciation to Larry Love, chief of the Field Division, for directing the data collection; Kenneth McKinnis, chief of the Methods, Procedures, and Quality Control Branch, for editing and coding the interview schedules; and to Kenneth Kaplan, chief of the Programming Branch, for the preparation of the computer tapes.

The process of revising the computer tapes received from the Census Bureau and of producing many of the tables and regressions incorporated in this book was the responsibility of the Data Processing Unit of the Center for Human Resource Research under the able direction of Carol T. Sheets. To Helene S. Churchill, production supervisor of the unit, and her staff, especially Mary Ann Graessle for her exceptional efficiency and effort, we express our thanks for serving so skillfully as intermediaries between us and the computer.

The authors profited from comments on earlier drafts of their work by their coauthors as well as by other members of the research staff of the center. We are also grateful to a number of persons outside the center for useful comments on earlier versions of portions of the manuscript, including Scott Beck, Alan Fox, Philip Rones, Steven Sandell, and Karen Schwab.

We thank Kezia Sproat, editor of the volume, for the skillful compromise she effected between technical integrity and clarity to the lay reader. We are also indebted to Mary Wildermuth for expediting the preparation of the volume, to Yvonne Holsinger for the preparation of the charts, and to Sherry Stoneman, Joyce Davenport, and Sue Ellen Rumstay for the exceptional skill and good humor with which they typed the several versions of the text and tables.

A Note on the Tables and Graphs

T he tables of this report indicate the number of sample cases underlying the statistics, but the statistics are invariably based upon weighted data. Because black men are overrepresented relative to white men in the NLS sample in a ratio of between 3:1-4:1, and thus have correspondingly smaller sampling weights, a statistic that is shown for the entire population will generally differ substantially from an average for whites and blacks weighted by the number of sample cases shown for each race.

In tables or graphs showing percentage distributions, percentages may not add to 100 percent because of rounding. Cases of "no data" have been eliminated from totals in computing percentages and means and also from all multivariate analyses. We do not show the number of cases of "no data" for any variable, but the number can frequently be ascertained by comparing the number of sample cases for the total sample with the sum of the numbers for the several categories of the variable in question. For example, in table 5-1, comparison of the total n (1,718) with the sum of the n's under "reason for retirement" (1,713) reveals that there are 5 sample cases that could not be classified by reason for retirement. By the same operations we discover that there are 668 cases of "no data" on "family income excluding respondent's earnings."

Several tables in the book present the results of multiple classification analyses (MCA). MCA is analogous to multiple regression analysis in which all of the independent variables are expressed in categorical form. The constant term in the MCA equation is the mean of the dependent variable, and the coefficient of each explanatory variable represents a deviation from this mean. Thus, the "adjusted" value of the dependent variable for each category of an independent variable represents what the dependent variable would have been had the members of the category been "average" in terms of all the other independent variables included in the analysis.

The MCA tables show both the unadjusted and the adjusted values. They also show the F-ratio in parentheses beside the name of each variable. The confidence level of this ratio tests the overall significance of the explanatory variable. The t-statistic tests the significance of a particular code category of the explanatory variable against the grand mean.

For example, in table 5-1 the *F*-ratio of the impairment variable tells us that there is a highly significant relationship (.01 level) between this variable and the probability of labor force participation, controlling for all other variables in the analysis. The asterisks beside the adjusted values tell us that the participation rates in the first two impairment categories are significantly higher than the overall average of 19 percent and that the participation rate for the severely impaired is significantly lower.

In tables presenting the results of ordinary least squares regressions, the *t*-statistic indicates whether the coefficient of a continuous variable is significantly different from 0, net of other factors. For categorical variables, the *t*-statistic indicates whether the mean value for a given category differs significantly from that of the omitted (reference) category.

1
Introduction and Overview

Herbert S. Parnes
Lawrence J. Less

The Issues and the Data

Retirement is essentially a twentieth-century phenomenon. In 1900 two-thirds of all males age 65 and older were in the labor force; even among the remaining one-third who were not, very few had the financial resources to permit them to retire. The vast majority of men continued to work until death, until physical deterioration prevented them from doing so, or until their employers, with or without justification, believed they were too old to be productive.

Prior to 1935 there was no public system of pensions; in that year the Social Security Act promised old age benefits to wage and salary workers in the nonagricultural private sector of the economy. Liberalization of the program has resulted in pension coverage for over 90 percent of the labor force, the availability of retirement benefits as early as age 62 (and of total disability benefits at any age), and a level of monthly benefits that replaces almost one-half of the preretirement earnings of the average (median) married man (Fox, 1982).

At the beginning of the century, additional pensions provided through specific employment affiliations existed in not more than ten establishments (Schulz, 1980, p. 124), but now such pensions are available for about one-half of all wage and salary workers (Munnell, 1982, p. 13). Because Social Security replaces a larger proportion of low than of high earnings, and because supplementary pensions are much more prevalent among high than low wage earners, they tend to equalize replacement rates across the income distribution.

By the 1980s retirement had become a commonplace phenomenon. The labor force participation rate of men age 65 and over, which had been 40 percent as recently as 1950, was only 18 percent in 1983. The age at which men retire also dropped sharply in the recent past: the age of eligibility for Social Security benefits was lowered from 65 to 62 in 1961 (a similar change having been made for women in 1956), and provisions for early retirement became much more common in employer pension plans (Davis and Strasser, 1970). Whereas 65 was the traditional retirement age well into the post-World War II period, the typical man now retires earlier than that. Three-fourths of all men and 84 percent of all women who apply for the Social Security retirement benefit do so before reaching age 65 (Thompson, 1983, p. 1429). While the male labor force participation rate is 84 percent at age 55 and 72 percent at age 60, it drops precipitously to 54 percent at age 62, to under one-half among men 63 and 64 and to one-third at age 65 (Bureau of Labor Statistics, 1981).

Along with this changed behavior—whether as cause or effect one cannot be certain—changes in attitudes toward retirement also appeared. At mid-century most people held the view that older persons should retire between the ages of 65 and 70. Twenty-five years later most middle-class men and women agreed that men should be ready to retire by 60-64 years of age (Schwab, 1983). Moreover, most retirees react favorably to their status. The best available evidence indicates that fewer than one-half of all retirements are in any sense involuntary (Parnes and Nestel, 1981); that most retirees are quite satisfied with retirement and would choose to retire at the same age if they had it to do over again; and that retirement has, on the average, no adverse effect on physical or psychological well-being (Friedmann and Orbach, 1974).

On the other hand, even today retirement is clearly not for everyone. One out of every 10 men age 55-59 who are still holding regular jobs vows that he "will never retire" (Parnes, Less, and Nestel, 1981, p. 183). Even though only a small proportion of retirees are forced unwillingly out of jobs by mandatory retirement rules, there is considerable anecdotal evidence of psychological trauma among some of those who are. Moreover, while it is impossible to differentiate with complete confidence between persons who are "forced" by poor health into retirement, and those who choose it voluntarily, it is clear that retirees who suffer poor health react quite differently to their status than healthy men who are otherwise comparable (Parnes and Nestel, 1981, p. 183). Finally, irrespective of the degree of volition involved, men enter retirement with widely varying prospective incomes. Thus, retirement is by no means a unitary phenomenon.

Along with its increased prevalence, retirement has become an important policy issue in recent years and promises to attract even greater attention over the next several decades. One important reason is the growing burden of adult dependency that would be produced by the combined effect of an increasing propensity to retire and a rising proportion of persons age 65 and older. The ratio of persons 65 and older to the total population has increased from 8.1 percent in 1950 to 11 percent in 1980 and, depending on what happens to the fertility rate, is projected to rise to between 13 and 18 percent by the year 2020. As a result, whereas today there are 3 contributors for each Social Security beneficiary, the ratio may drop to as low as 2:1 by the end of the first quarter of the next century (President's Commission on Pension Policy, 1981, p. 23). This dismal long-term outlook for Social Security (along with shorter-term problems produced by adverse economic conditions) led to the 1983 amendments to the program, which, among other things, were designed to reverse the trend toward early retirement.

Besides the issue of the level of support for adult dependency that society is able (or willing) to bear, a related question is whether the economy can "spare" older workers in the future to the same degree that it can today. Demographic trends suggest the possibility of labor shortages—especially in a full employment economy—as the proportion of the population age 18-44 shrinks from its present level of 42 to 35 percent by the end of the first quarter of the next century (U.S. Bureau of the Census, 1977).

Finally, important unresolved questions remain about the reasons for retirement and about its impact on the individual, questions with significant implications for public policy. First, there is still substantial disagreement on the role of poor health in explaining early retirement; two recent issues of the journal *Aging and Work* (1982, 1983) were devoted to debates on this question. Second, although the evidence is fairly clear that mandatory retirement rules do not force large numbers of persons out of jobs against their will (Parnes and Nestel, 1981; Schulz, 1974), it is widely believed that many are pushed into retirement by more subtle pressures of employers or by the discouragement produced by unfavorable labor market experiences (Bould, 1980; Rosenblum, 1975). Third, there is a rather widespread popular belief, bolstered by some of the literature, that retirement is not "good" for a person (Butler, 1975), even when it is completely voluntary.

The importance of retirement from these perspectives invites a careful scrutiny of its nature and consequences, as well as an examination of the experience of individuals of retirement age who choose to continue full-time participation in the labor market. There is already an extensive body of literature on the determinants of the retirement decision and on aspects of the postretirement experience, including valuable literature reviews by Friedmann and Orbach (1974), Kingson (1981), Larson (1978), Mitchell and Fields (1982), Morgan (1981), and Parker (1982).

However, many of the studies of the postretirement experience have been based on small and unrepresentative samples and/or on cross-sectional data. Those that have used longitudinal data sets—other than our own previous reports based on the National Longitudinal Surveys (Parnes and Nestel, 1981; Parnes and Less, 1983)—have tended to focus on a single aspect of postretirement experience; for instance, life satisfaction

(Beck, 1982), earnings replacement rates (Fox, 1982), and extent of postretirement labor market activity (Motley, 1978). The most comprehensive longitudinal analysis of the consequences of retirement (Streib and Schneider, 1971) is based on data that are over 20 years old and that emerged from a nonrepresentative sample of retirees.[1] The meager literature on men who have passed the conventional age of retirement (Rix, 1980; Rones, 1978) does not differentiate between full-time and part-time work (or between workers who have retired from "regular" jobs and those who have not), focuses largely on occupational and industrial affiliation, and does not examine such work in the context of the individual's employment record at earlier ages.

In this book we build upon our earlier studies to address some of these issues. For this purpose we have available for the first time the full 15-year National Longitudinal Surveys (NLS) record for a representative national sample of men who were age 60-74 in 1981.

Plan of the Book

The remainder of this chapter describes the NLS data and the characteristics of the cohort under consideration, focusing particularly on the major changes in their lives over the 15 years between 1966 and 1981. Major changes occurred for the sample as a majority of them crossed the boundary between middle and old age. From the perspective of the labor market, the most prominent change was the move into retirement: by 1981 three-fourths of the age cohort had retired. Although some of these men continued to work, the proportion of the total cohort who were neither working nor looking for work grew from an almost negligible level of 5 percent in 1966 to 61 percent in 1981.

Chapter 2 explores the extent to which factors such as health, employment, and other socioeconomic status variables predict mortality in the years immediately preceding and following retirement, and whether their importance has changed over the 15-year period covered by the studies. Black men have systematically higher mortality rates than whites, but almost all of this difference reflects differences in socioeconomic background. In contrast, the effect of marital status appears more deeply embedded. After controlling for background factors as well as for differences between the married and nonmarried in employment and health status, married men still face more favorable survival prospects. Detailed employment measures as well as self-reported health measures permit (1) documentation of the health-mortality association and (2) more effective measurement of other mortality differentials.

The generally acknowledged overall declines in mortality over the past fifteen years have affected all segments of the society; blacks and whites, the well- and the poorly educated, and the healthy and unhealthy have all apparently benefited from the general improvements in health and medical care services available in our society. One population subgroup, however, has benefited to a substantially greater extent than others—individuals not at work who frequently have reported illnesses of long duration. In this regard, it may be fair to conclude that those most in need have indeed benefited the most from the secular improvements in health care.

Chapter 3 examines the volume and pattern of retirements over the 15-year period. Of the nearly 8.5 million men age 60-74 in 1981 who had reported their retirement over the preceding 15 years, fewer than 5 percent had been unwillingly removed from jobs by mandatory retirement rules. A liberal estimate of the proportion discouraged by labor market adversity is perhaps twice as large—about 10 percent. Of considerably greater importance than both of these combined in forcing men into retirement, is poor health, which accounted for about a third of all retirements and for almost half of retirements by black men. The majority of retirements, then, appear to be voluntary, and most of these take place prior to age 65.

The timing of retirement is explored in chapter 4. The data highlight the trend toward early retirement in the 1960s and 1970s. Men age 59 were more likely to retire early at the end of the 15-year period than at the beginning; and those who subsequently retired were significantly more likely in the later than in the earlier years to have retired before age 65. The association between the expectation and the actual dating of retirement was not very close; in only about 30 percent of the cases were the retirements dated as planned at age 59; in most of the remainder of the cases, the men retired earlier than planned.

The economic aspects of the retirement experience are the focus of chapter 5, which describes and analyzes the sources of variation in the economic status and well-being of the retirees. At best only two-fifths of the 7 million men age 60-74 in 1981 who had retired between calendar years 1967 and 1979 were available for work in 1981; the remainder either had health problems that discouraged labor market activity or simply did not choose to work. Two trends are evident when median real family income of married retirees is examined over time. First, the level of 1980 income is higher for more recent than for earlier retirees. Second, for each cohort of retirees real family income moves downward over time, resulting largely from decreasing postretirement labor force participation of retirees and their wives.

Whatever their actual income, a very large majority of retirees profess to be able to "get by" on their income, although there are pronounced variations between nonmarried and married men in favor of the latter and even larger ones between blacks and whites. For the married men of both races combined, two-thirds report that they do better than just get by, and only 9 percent assert that they "cannot make ends meet."

Some of the important noneconomic facets of retirement are treated in chapters 6 and 7. The first of these examines the leisure time activities of retirees and the extent and character of their family and social support networks. Chapter 7 continues the analysis by exploring the correlates of physical and mental well-being among retirees.

Analysis of the social networks of the retirees confirms their importance. Having such a network permits the men to sustain regular social interaction outside the immediate household. Adult children increasingly become their primary source of outside interaction, but by no means the sole source. Friends and relatives also are frequent contacts, particularly among black retirees and among those currently not living with a wife. The substantial minority of retirees who are without an informal social network lack these opportunities and may be deprived of emergency help and social interaction, which are believed vital for quality of life and general well-being. Retirement does not seem to produce any negative effects on well-being, at least not in the initial years. If anything, men find that retirement is better than they thought it would be. However, retirees are not a homogeneous group. Voluntary retirees are relatively well off; those who have retired for health reasons are much more likely to register dissatisfaction with their status.

The minority of men in this age cohort who continue to work full-time beyond the age at which they can collect Social Security benefits are the subject of chapter 8. They constitute less than one-fifth of the total population of men between age 60 and 74 and are highly unrepresentative of that cohort. The men who continue full-time work into their late 60s and 70s consist disproportionately of those who are healthy enough to do so and who either (a) have to work because of limited resources or (b) want to because they enjoy work in general or what they have been doing in particular. Full-time labor market activity well beyond customary ages of retirement can be viable and satisfactory alternatives for significant numbers of older men; however, because they are so unrepresentative, this does *not* mean that the record of such workers can be used as a measure of the potential available to *all* younger men.

Chapter 9 summarizes the major findings of the NLS, covering earlier research as well as the topics included in this book. It concludes with a brief discussion of some of the important policy implications of the research.

Character of the NLS Data

Because longitudinal data, such as those from the NLS, in effect yield a "motion picture" of the same individuals over time, they permit more confident answers to certain types of questions than do conventional cross-sectional data such as those from the Current Population Survey (CPS), source of most of the official labor force data in the United States.[2] For instance, longitudinal data provide a more accurate basis than cross-sectional data for assessing the effect of aging on earnings, because comparisons of earnings of men of different ages at the same point in time are confounded by cohort differences—the fact, for example, that older men are, on the average, less well educated than younger men. The point is well illustrated by the difference between cross-sectional and longitudinal analysis of the NLS data themselves. Data for 1966 showed that men age 50-54 earned about 5 percent less than men age 45-49, which might have led one to predict a comparable *decline* as the latter group aged by 5 years. Yet, by 1971 the hourly earnings of this group (after adjustment for increases in the price level) had actually *risen* by more than 10 percent (Parnes et al., 1975, p. 259).

Longitudinal data are also superior to cross-sectional data for ascertaining the direction of causation between variables that are found to be related to one another. For example, if reported dissatisfaction with a job is offered as an explanation for having left it, one cannot be sure whether dissatisfaction actually caused the separation or whether the individual's reported attitude was merely a rationalization for what he had done. However, if reported job dissatisfaction in a given year is found to be related to voluntary job separation in some *subsequent* year, one can be much more confident of the cause and effect relationship.

The NLS data set is especially valuable for exploring questions relating to retirement. To begin with, the oversampling of black men makes possible statistically reliable estimates of racial differences in virtually all aspects of the study. Moreover, the longitudinal design means that there is periodic information on many dimensions of work activity, income, and attitudes from the time when almost all of the men in this age range were full-time workers to the time when about three-fourths were retired. Thus, for a substantial majority of the men who had retired by 1981, the records cover at least several years on either side of the retirement date. This design allows an examination of the factors leading to retirement on the basis of data that are not contaminated by the possibility of post hoc rationalization. That is, evidence on reasons for retirement does not rest exclusively on retrospective responses of men who have already retired, but can be inferred from measurements of health, attitudes, and labor market experience made while the men were still working. Finally, the longitudinal data allow the men's postretirement experience and attitudes to be related to various facets of their preretirement lives. A fuller description of the data set follows.

The Sample and the Surveys. A representative sample of the civilian population of males in the United States between the ages of 45 and 59 was drawn by the Bureau of the Census in 1966. Blacks were overrepresented in a ratio of 3 or 4:1 in order to permit reliable interracial comparisons. The total sample numbered 5,020: 3,518 whites, 1,420 blacks, and 82 men of other races (who are excluded from all of the data in this book). The study was originally intended to run for only 5 years, but was later extended, first to 10 and then to 15 years.[3] Interviews were conducted first in 1966 and again in 1967, 1969, and 1971. In 1968 a brief mailed questionnaire was administered. During each of the second and third 5-year periods there were biennial telephone interviews (1973, 1975, 1978, and 1980) and longer face-to-face interviews at the end of the period (1976 and 1981).

Attrition, 1966-1981. Of the original sample of 4,938 white and black men, 2,794 (2,039 whites and 755 blacks) were interviewed in 1981. About one-fourth (26 percent) of the original group had died, while 17 percent had disappeared from the sample for other reasons (primarily refusal to continue to participate). For some purposes—for instance, the analysis of mortality—we will be using the original 1966 sample. In most cases, however, attention will center on the population of men who in 1981 were 60-74 years of age. For this purpose the deaths that occurred between 1966 and 1981 do not bias the sample in any way. However, if attrition for other reasons departed substantially from a random pattern, the sample would have lost its representative character by 1981. It is important, therefore, to examine the extent of variation in the noninterview rate among the original members of the sample who were still alive in 1981.

Attrition is consistently higher for whites (24 percent) than for blacks (20 percent), and there are also differences according to income. For example, among white men attrition rates are 16 percent for respondents with 1965 incomes of $20,000 or more, and 23 percent for those with incomes under $3,000. However, such variations are probably not large enough to cause serious bias in the sample, especially since the sample cases have been reweighted to compensate for differential attrition by race, education, and geographic mobility.

The Data. While it is neither possible nor necessary to present a complete catalogue of the information that has been collected for each respondent, it is useful to mention the major categories of data that will play important roles in this analysis. We are able to define the respondent's *retirement status* on the basis of (1) his subjective perception, (2) the receipt of Social Security or other pension income, or (3) partial or complete withdrawal from the labor market.

In each survey all of the respondents were asked at what age they "expected to stop working at their regular job."[4] One of the precoded responses to this question was "already stopped," and men who answered in this way have been classified as subjectively retired.[5] Each survey also obtained information on sources of income, identifying specifically retirement benefits under the Social Security or Railroad Retirement systems, other pension income, and disability payments from the Social Security program or from other sources. Individuals who receive any of these kinds of benefits have been classified as retired on the basis of the income criterion.[6] Finally, each survey elicits information on number of weeks of labor force participation in the preceding 12 months and on employment. With this information it is possible to classify individuals as retired on the basis of complete or partial labor market withdrawal. We have used employment for fewer than 1,000 hours per year as the criterion for this measure of retirement.

Although it is easy to ascertain whether an individual has retired on the basis of each of these criteria, problems arise in pinpointing the date of retirement (and therefore the age at which it occurs). The procedures used to ascertain date of retirement are too complex to describe in detail; however, we have diligently used all of the clues provided by the longitudinal record to estimate this date.[7]

The detailed information on *work experience* that has been collected in each survey permits comparisons between preretirement and postretirement labor market activity. For example, occupation, industry, type-of-worker status, earnings, and length of service in the respondent's preretirement job are readily available, as is the regularity of employment in the preceding year or, indeed, over the entire fifteen-year period. Whether there is employment or unemployment after retirement can also be ascertained, and any postretirement employment can be compared with preretirement employment from the standpoint of intensity (hours per year), occupational assignment, industrial affiliation, and earnings.

The questions on *amount and sources of income* included in each survey permit a comparison of the financial circumstances of respondents and their families before and after retirement and also allow investigation of the extent to which real incomes are maintained during retirement.

More specifically, we are able to ascertain what proportion of preretirement earnings are replaced by Social Security and pension income and to analyze the sources of variation in these replacement rates among individuals as well as their trend over time. To facilitate this and similar types of analysis, *all income and asset values throughout the volume have been converted to dollars having the purchasing power of the dollar in 1980.*

A number of *noneconomic characteristics* have also been measured. In each survey the respondent has been asked whether any health condition prevents work or limits the kind or amount of work he can do. The 1976 and 1981 surveys also contained a detailed set of questions designed to ascertain the character and extent of functional limitations (e.g., walking, lifting, stooping, etc.) and whether the respondent experienced specified symptoms (e.g., fainting, shortness of breath, fatigue, etc.). Information on leisure time activities was collected in the 1978 survey for both retired and nonretired men and in the 1981 survey for retired men only; from these data it is possible to explore the extent of variation between retired and nonretired men in the amount of time spent on selected leisure activities and also to examine the changes that occur over a three-year period among men who are retired and among those who move from work into retirement. The 1981 interview schedule also contained a battery of questions that permit a description of each respondent's family and social support network.

The NLS data set includes a number of attitudinal variables that are useful in the analysis. Degree of satisfaction with one's current job has been asked in each survey, affording a measure of this variable in both the preretirement and postretirement job. A set of questions designed to measure generalized attitudes toward work and retirement was introduced in 1978, and in each survey from 1976 through 1981 retired respondents were asked several questions designed to measure their reactions to their own retirement. Beginning with the 1976 survey the respondent is asked to report the degree of satisfaction he feels with various aspects of his life; the answers permit comparisons between retired and nonretired individuals and shed light on the character of psychological adjustment to retirement. An additional measure of psychological well-being—the Bradburn Affect Balance Scale (Bradburn, 1969)—was included in the 1981 interview.

Characteristics of the Age Cohort

Every age cohort of individuals is in some degree unique—being shaped by the particular configuration of environmental influences that operated during their lifetime. This is why comparisons of two age groups at a single point in time is not a very reliable method of ascertaining the effects of aging; such comparisons do not tell us how much of discerned differences reflect age and how much they reflect cohort differences—that is, the fact that the two groups were born at different times and had different life experiences.

A longitudinal data bank like the NLS helps to some extent, since a *given* group of individuals can be observed at different times as they grow older. However, since the environment is forever changing, there is always uncertainty as to whether observed change is evidence of life cycle changes (aging) or a reflection of temporal changes (a changing environment). Finally, even if the temporal and life cycle effects could be disentangled, the changes observed longitudinally for a particular age group may not be generalizable because of cohort effects—that is, because the aging or maturation process may very well differ depending upon the total set of life experiences of the particular cohort studied.

The Socioeconomic Environment

It is for these reasons that it is desirable to fix in mind the charac-teristics of the age cohort under consideration in this volume, and the major environmental influences that shaped their lives. All of the men in the sample were born within seven years of the beginning or two years of the end of the First World War. All of them were old enough to remember the depths of the Great Depression of the 1930s, and the oldest members of the cohort were in the critical early stage of their careers during the entire depressed decade.

The total cohort was within the draftable age range (18-44) in World War II, and 46 percent served in the armed services during that conflict. Two-thirds of the men were in their 40s when John F. Kennedy entered the White House; the remainder were in their early 50s. Thus, the cohort were at or close to the peak of their careers during the decade of the 1960s, most of which was characterized by rates of economic growth and levels of employment opportunity that have since been unparalleled.

By the time the oldest of the men reached their early 60s, retirement under Social Security was already possible for males at age 62 (at a 20 percent reduction in benefit) and early retirement provisions had become increasingly prevalent in private pension plans. As a consequence, among that segment of the cohort still under 60 in 1976, exactly half had either already retired or expected to do so prior to reaching age 65 (Parnes et al., 1981, p. 15).

The black men in this age cohort had been born too late to profit from the civil rights movement to the same extent that their children would. Already 43-57 when the Civil Rights Act was passed, they had gone to segregated schools and, with substantial human capital deficiencies relative to whites, had entered a labor market in which racial discrimination was almost universal. As a consequence of both of these factors, their occupational distribution in the mid-1960s differed dramatically from that of white men of the same age. Relatively, only one-fourth as many of them were in professional or managerial jobs (7 vs. 29 percent of white men) and more than 4 times as many were unskilled laborers (27 vs. 6 percent). Median annual wage and salary income for blacks was only 57 percent of the median for whites (Parnes, Less, and Nestel, 1980, pp. 60, 102).

Early Formative Influences

Only slightly more than 5 percent of the cohort were foreign born; about half were at least third-generation Americans, while the remainder had parents or grandparents who had immigrated to the United States, primarily from northern or western Europe. Agriculture involved a considerably larger proportion of the American population when these men were growing up than it does today. About two-fifths of the total group and more than half of the blacks lived on farms as youngsters (figure 1-1); only one-third lived in cities with populations as large as 25,000. As adolescents, three-fourths of the whites and 58 percent of the blacks were members of intact families. Their fathers (or other heads of household in "broken homes") typically had only meager educational attainments. Almost half had not completed the eighth grade; 1 in 5 was a high school graduate, and only 6 percent held college degrees.

The men we will be studying received considerably more education than their parents, but, of course, not nearly so much as their own children. Over one-third did not go beyond the eighth grade, but 44 percent finished high school and 10 percent had college degrees. Among blacks the picture was quite different. Two-thirds had no more than an elementary school education, and fewer than 1 in 5 held a high school diploma.

Labor Market Experience Prior to Middle Age

As has already been noted, the initial interview with the NLS sample of men was conducted in 1966, when these men ranged between age 45 and 59. In that interview we explored their current labor market status in detail, but we also included retrospective questions that permitted a reasonably complete profile of their prior work experience. Some of this 1966 information provides a useful backdrop for the description of life-cycle changes between 1966 and 1981.[8]

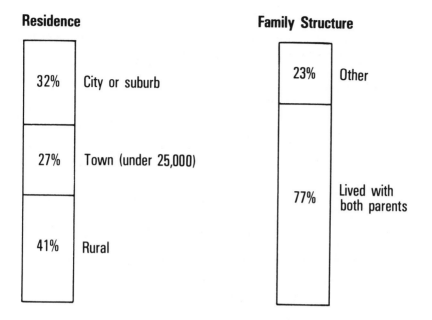

Figure 1–1. Selected Characteristics at Age 15, Men Age 60–74 in 1981 (percentage distributions)

The job held in 1966 was the longest one of their career for about three-fifths of the sample. Over two-fifths of the men had spent at least half of their work career with their 1966 employer, and as many as 1 in 10 had been in that job since leaving school (Parnes et al., 1970, p. 115). As might be expected, substantial occupational upgrading had occurred by the time the men had reached their 40s and 50s (figure 1-2). Although one-fourth had begun their careers as farm workers, this proportion had dropped to one-tenth by 1966. Nonfarm semiskilled, unskilled, and service assignments had dropped from 41 to 30 percent of the total, while the proportion of craft jobs increased from 7 to 24 percent and of managerial assignments from 2 to 16 percent. Professional assignments had also increased, but to a much smaller degree—from 8 to 11 percent of the total.

Although upward occupational mobility characterized the careers of blacks as well as whites, the blacks were far less successful than the whites in entering the better blue- and white-collar occupations. Between their first job after leaving school and the one they held in 1966, the

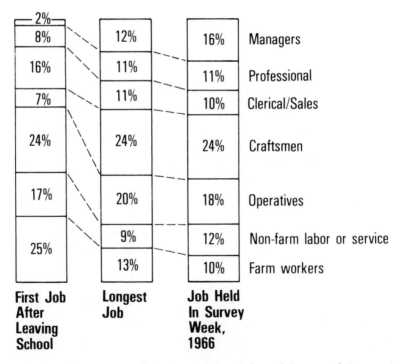

Figure 1–2. Occupational Assignment at Selected Stages of Career (percentage distributions)

proportion of black men in managerial occupational assignments grew only 2 percentage points as compared with 14 points for white men. The increase in the proportion in craft assignments was 11 percentage points for blacks and 17 for whites. Of the 28-percentage point decline in the proportion of black men in farm occupations, 21 were reflected in increases in blue-collar assignments.

Another way of seeing these changes is to note that the occupational differences between white and black men were greater in 1966 than they had been upon entering the labor market. The sum of the deviations between the 2 percentage distributions is 59 points in the case of the first job and 73 percent for the 1966 job. Blau and Duncan (1967, p. 209) had established that in the early 1960s "being a Negro in the United States has independent disadvantageous consequences for several of the factors that affect occupational careers." Thus, it is not surprising that the effects of whatever factors produced these differences (e.g., racial discrimination) should have been cumulative over lengthy work careers.

The foregoing data relate to *net* changes measured in terms of very broad occupational categories. When *gross* changes are analyzed in terms of movement up or down the occupational prestige hierarchy, 13 percent of the men were in the same 3-digit occupational category in their first and 1966 jobs; somewhat over half (57 percent of the whites and 41 percent of the blacks) had made upward occupational moves; 16 percent had made lateral shifts; and 16 percent (15 percent of the whites and 22 percent of the blacks) had slid downward. Based on their own evaluations of the various types of work they had done, most of the men in 1966 held the best occupational assignment of their careers. This was true of two-thirds of the whites and almost three-fifths of the blacks (Parnes et al., 1970, p. 132).

A majority of the men had been quite immobile geographically. As many as one-fourth had resided all their lives in the community in which we found them in 1966, and an additional one-third had lived there for at least 20 years. At the other end of the continuum, 1 in 9 had arrived within the previous 5 years. Racial differences in this regard were not pronounced, although black men were somewhat less likely than whites to be recent arrivals (Parnes et al., 1970, p. 135).

In short, when we first observed our sample of men, their labor market circumstances were, on the average, quite favorable. Summarizing our report on the initial survey, we observed that if all segments of the population fared equally well in the labor market, society's human resource problems would be less serious than they were.

> Their labor force participation is very high: nineteen out of twenty were in the labor force at the time of the survey and over 16 out of 20 were

continuously in for 52 weeks in 1965. The rate of unemployment is quite low—less than 1.5 percent in the survey week. Those who are employed are, by and large, in better jobs than the average of all males. A large majority of them are in different occupations from those in which they started their work careers, and a majority of these occupational changes appear to have been for the better. In any case, two-thirds regard their current occupational assignment to be the best of their career. The employment relationship appears to be quite stable for a large majority of the men: three-fifths have served their present employer (or have been self-employed) for ten years or more; two-fifths profess an unwillingness to consider another job at any conceivable wage rate; and more than nine out of ten claim that they like their jobs (Parnes et al., 1970, p. 238).

However, this stability and satisfaction should not obscure the very real problems that plagued a significant minority of the men.

For one thing a large majority of those out of the labor force appear to be there not by choice; most of them left their last jobs for health reasons, and most report that their health or physical condition currently prevents their working. Second, the low rates of unemployment that exist in any given week grossly understate the amount of unemployment experienced during a year; moreover, unemployment is by no means evenly distributed throughout the total age cohort.

A by no means negligible proportion of these men are in jobs at the very bottom of the occupational hierarchy, either because they started and remained there or because they slipped down during their working lives. One in twelve is an unskilled laborer . . . almost one in six is in an occupation of lower socioeconomic status than that of his first job. In addition, not all of the men have the stable work attachments described above. About a fifth claim that they would not work except for financial necessity; a tenth have served less than a year with their current employer; and although only two out of a hundred admit to an intense dislike of their current job, as many as one in eight would accept another at the same or lower wage rate (Parnes et al., 1970, p. 239).

From Middle- to Old Age; Major Changes, 1966-1981

The remaining chapters of this book use the 15-year longitudinal records of the sample for specific analytical purposes. A context for those more detailed and analytical presentations is provided by a systematic description of the changes in the lives and work experience of the men under consideration as they aged by 15 years.

However, longitudinal records of labor market experience are not an unambiguous indicator of the effects of aging, because, as we have seen, changes in the socioeconomic environment may alter behavior over time even for men of the same age. For example, some of the decrease in labor force participation over the period was almost certainly attributable to liberalization of public and private pension plans and to the increased "respectability" of retirement rather than merely to the changed circumstances of the men resulting from their having grown older. Thus before examining the 15-year longitudinal record, it is useful to have a look at some cross-sectional data for a given age group at different times during the 15-year period.

Trends in Labor Market Experience of Elderly Males: Cross-Sectional Evidence

Table 1-1 sheds some light on this matter by presenting for the periods 1966-1971, 1971-1976, and 1976-1981 selected measures of labor market behavior and experience of men who were 55-59 years of age at the beginning of each period. The most notable trends are the decrease in labor force participation and the increasing difficulty of maintaining real incomes.

With respect to labor force participation, not only did the rate for men age 55-59 drop between 1966 and 1971 and between 1971 and 1976, but the decrease as the men aged 5 years was greater during the second two time periods than during the first. The same phenomenon is evident in the data on number of weeks out of the labor force. The proportion of men with no weeks out of the labor force dropped, and the proportion who were out for at least 10 weeks doubled from 1966-1971 to 1976-1981.

Changes in the overall level of the national unemployment rate are only very imperfectly reflected in the data for men age 55-59. Whereas national unemployment averaged 4.2 percent during the first of the periods and 6.4 and 6.9 percent during the second and third, respectively, neither the unemployment rates nor the data on weeks of unemployment in table 1-1 display the same pattern; according to them, the middle period is less favorable than either the first or the third. Of course, it is conceivable that part of the observed decline in labor force participation is actually disguised unemployment.

Patterns of mobility are remarkably similar over the three time periods. There is no discernible trend in the proportion of men who remained with the same employer and in the same occupation, and the proportions who climbed up and slipped down the occupational ladder were remarkably constant for each of the cohorts as a whole, although

Table 1–1

Selected Measures of Labor Market Experience of Men 55–59 Years of Age at the Beginning of 3 Five-Year Time Periods, 1966–1981

Measure	1966–1971	1971–1976	1976–1981
Sample n[a]	1,139	1,177	1,120
Percent in labor force, beginning of period	93	91	86
Percent in labor force, end of period	73	62	57
Unemployment rate, beginning of period	2.2	1.5	2.8
Unemployment rate, end of period	4.1	6.4	3.5
Percent with no unemployment[b]	84	82	88
Percent with 10 or more weeks of unemployment[b]	8	13	8
Percent with no weeks out of labor force[b]	49	47	41
Percent with 10 weeks or more out of labor force[b]	23	39	45
Percent with same employer at beginning and end of period	76	78	76
Percent with same occupation at beginning and end of period	63	61	59
Percent with upward occupational movement[c]	16	17	18
Percent with downward occupational movement[c]	15	16	18
Percent with decrease in real hourly earnings[d]	32	49	63
Percent with decrease in real annual wages and salary income	44	52	62
Percent change in median family income (1980 dollars)	−5	−22	−18

[a]For each time period, sample consists of men interviewed both at beginning and end of period.

[b]Data cover a total of 36 months within each 5-year period.

[c]Upward or downward occupational movement refers to occupational changes involving a change of at least 3 points in the Duncan Index of Socioeconomic Status (see Blau and Duncan, 1967, pp. 117–128).

[d]Data include only men employed as wage or salary workers at beginning and end of the relevant 5-year period.

among black men the proportion experiencing downward occupational mobility almost doubled between 1966-1971 and 1976-1981—from 12 to 22 percent.

Real average hourly earnings in the total private nonagricultural economy in the United States rose by 8.8 percent between 1966 and 1971, by less than 1 percent between 1971 and 1976, and fell by 5.6 percent between 1976 and 1981 (U.S. President, 1982, p. 276). These trends help to explain the data on average hourly earnings shown in table 1-1, but the movement of some of the 55-to-59-year-old men into lower-paying postretirement jobs is almost certainly another factor. In any case, the proportion of the cohort that experienced shrinking real wages over the 5-year period grew. The fact that changes in real annual wage and salary income became less favorable over time reflects both the behavior of wage rates and the declining labor force participation of the successive cohorts of men.

Finally, median total family income was lower at the end than at the beginning of each five-year period, but the difference was considerably greater in the second and third periods than in the first. This trend incorporates all of the factors mentioned thus far, but is affected also by others—principally the labor force participation and earnings of wives and the substitution of pension for earned income.

Thus we see that cross-sectional data from three points in time for men approaching retirement age provide evidence of environmental changes that tended to reduce labor force participation and to retard the growth of real earnings. As we trace the labor market experience and behavior of the total cohort of men between 1966 and 1981, the patterns we observe will reflect these influences as well as the life cycle changes attributable to the aging of the cohort.

Changes in Demographic Characteristics

Marital Status. The proportion of men who were married and living with their wives dropped from 91 to 84 percent over the 15-year period, four-fifths of the decrease reflecting the increasing numbers of widowers. Among black men the decrease was larger—from 85 to 70 percent—and marital dissolution accounted for a larger part of the total than among whites. Of all the men who were married in 1981, four-fifths had been married only once, and a majority of the remainder had remarried prior to 1966. Thus, fewer than one in 10 of the married men in 1981 had not been with the same mate over the entire 15-year period (figure 1-3).

Family Structure. There is a dramatic change in the living arrangements and the financial responsibilities of men in their 40s and 50s as they age by 15 years. While almost two-thirds had children in the home in 1966, by 1981 this was true of only 1 in 5. At the beginning of the period fewer than two-fifths had no dependents other than wives; by 1981 the proportion had risen to 84 percent. Black men, however, were less likely than whites to be free of dependents both at the beginning and at the end of the period. Not many men lived with no other family members, but the proportion in 1981 (10 percent) was twice as great as it had been 15 years earlier, and was one-fourth among black men.

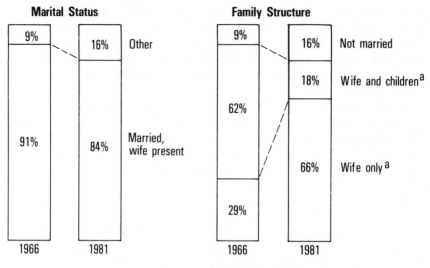

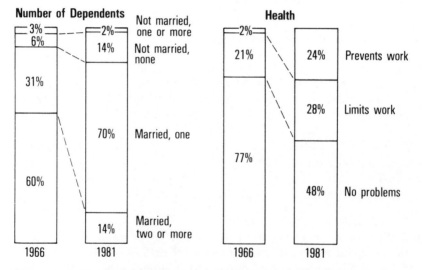

Figure 1–3. Selected Demographic Characteristics, 1966 and 1981 (percentage distributions)

Health. While substantial improvement was occurring in their circumstances relating to dependency, on the other side of the ledger was a marked deterioration in health, especially among black men. For the cohort as a whole, four-fifths reported no health problems affecting work in 1966, but by 1981 fewer than one-half could make the claim. What is worse, one-fourth of the white men and one-third of the blacks reported in 1981 that their health completely prevented their working, as contrasted with 1 and 3 percent, respectively, in 1966.

This measure of health status is regarded by many to be suspect because it focuses on the behavioral consequences of ill health and is "not necessarily independent of the labor force behavior that (it is) supposed to explain" (Chirikos and Nestel, 1981, pp. 94-95). According to this view, since work is the principal social role of adult males, the apparent deterioration in health based on responses to this type of question may not be *causing*, but simply be *reflecting* to some unknown degree the decreased labor market activity of the men. While we do not have superior measures of health covering the entire 15-year period, we do have self-reported measures of specific functional limitations (e.g., walking, standing, lifting, etc.) and of specified symptoms (e.g., pain, shortness of breath, fatigue, etc.) for 1976 and 1981. When scores on these measures are compared with responses to the question on work-limiting health problems, the same pattern is discernible. Thus, over just this 5-year period the proportion of men reporting minor or no impairments shrank from 56 to 39 percent. Over the same 5 years, the corresponding percentages of men reporting no health problems affecting work were 58 and 46.

Changes in Labor Market Activity

The most dramatic reflection of the aging of the cohort lies in the sharp decline in labor market activity between 1966 and 1981. As the age range of the men increased from 45-59 to 60-74, the proportion who were working or looking for work dropped from over 95 percent to under 40 percent. As an additional indicator, whereas 83 percent of the cohort had worked at least 50 weeks in 1966, by 1981 this proportion had dropped to 30 percent. A decline occurred also in the extent of labor market activity by the wives of married men, although this was not as precipitous as for the men themselves. For the total age group of married men, the proportion of wives with some work activity during the year dropped from about one-half to one-third between 1966 and 1981.

That labor force participation and retirement status are by no means equivalent concepts is indicated by the fact that of the three-fourths of the men who were "retired" in 1981 in the sense that they had "stopped working at a regular job," one-fifth were working or looking for work. This accounts for the fact that the labor force participation rate (39 percent) is 14 percentage points higher than the proportion of men who had not retired (25 percent).

Occupation, Industry, and Type of Worker. Very little net change occurred in the occupational distribution of the men between 1966 and 1981 or the time of their retirement, at least as measured by the major occupation groups, none of which showed a net change of more than 2 percentage points. However, the stability of the distribution conceals a considerable amount of occupational mobility: when gross changes are observed, each of the major occupation categories lost at least one-fourth of its 1966 incumbents to others over the 15-year period—from 54 percent in the case of nonfarm laborers, to 29 percent in the case of professional and managerial workers.

The same pattern is evidenced in industrial affiliation—relatively little net change was produced by a rather substantial volume of offsetting industrial shifts. Considered jointly, the occupational and industrial data do suggest small net shifts out of jobs in manufacturing and construction and into finance (real estate, primarily) and service industries as the men aged.

Net changes in type-of-worker status were also small—a slight decrease in the proportion of private wage and salary employment in favor of government work and self-employment, but even here there were substantial offsetting movements. About 7 percent of the 1966 wage and salary workers had moved into self-employment, while about 30 percent of the self-employed had moved in the opposite direction.

Average Hourly Earnings: Wage and Salary Workers. The data on average hourly earnings shown in Figure 1.4 are eloquent reminders of the fallacy in using moment-of-time cross-classifications of earnings by age to draw conclusions about the effect of aging on earning capacity. As the cohort aged by 15 years—or until retirement—there was a slight improvement (2 percent) in median real hourly wages, despite the fact that in 1966 men in their 50s received hourly earnings 6 percent below those of men in their late 40s. The patterns for black and white men are very similar except that the rise between 1966 and 1981 is somewhat greater for blacks—4 percent versus 2 percent for whites. In each year, of course, the median wage of black men is well below that of whites— the differential being over 25 percent for the total cohort and even somewhat larger for men who were between age 65 and 74 at the end of the decade.

Changes in Financial Status

Because of the large proportion of men who withdrew from the labor market over the 15-year period, it is not surprising that total family income dropped sharply in real terms. For the total cohort the median

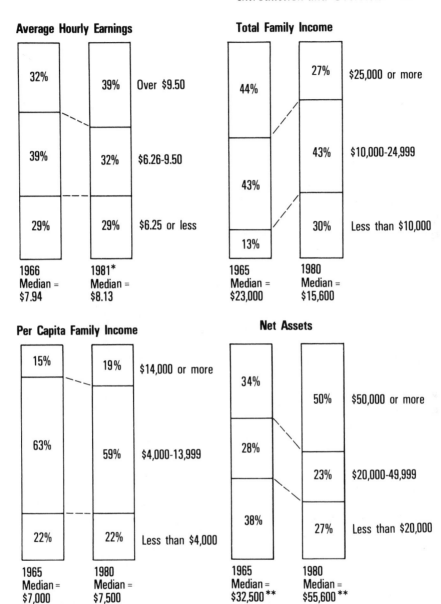

Average Hourly Earnings

1966	1981*	
32%	39%	Over $9.50
39%	32%	$6.26-9.50
29%	29%	$6.25 or less

1966
Median =
$7.94

1981*
Median =
$8.13

Total Family Income

1965	1980	
44%	27%	$25,000 or more
43%	43%	$10,000-24,999
13%	30%	Less than $10,000

1965
Median =
$23,000

1980
Median =
$15,600

Per Capita Family Income

1965	1980	
15%	19%	$14,000 or more
63%	59%	$4,000-13,999
22%	22%	Less than $4,000

1965
Median =
$7,000

1980
Median =
$7,500

Net Assets

1965	1980	
34%	50%	$50,000 or more
28%	23%	$20,000-49,999
38%	27%	Less than $20,000

1965
Median =
$32,500**

1980
Median =
$55,600**

* On pre-retirement job

** Median net value of home rose from $15,200 to $37,000.
Median value of all other assets (except automobiles) rose from $9,000 to $13,000

Figure 1–4. Selected Financial Characteristics, 1965–1966 and 1980–
1981 (1980 dollars)

(expressed in terms of 1980 dollars) fell from $23,000 in 1966, to $15,600 in 1981, a decrease of 32 percent. The greater incidence of retirement among those who had reached age 65 by the end of the period produced a larger decrease (42 percent), but the decline was substantial even for those in their early 60s (19 percent). For both age groups the decline for black men was smaller than for whites, primarily because the Social Security retirement benefit formula yields a proportionately larger pension for low-wage than for high-wage workers.

The decrease in real family income should be viewed in the light of the substantial decrease in family responsibilities that we have already described. Real per capita family income actually increased for the total cohort by about 7 percent—slightly less for black men because of the lesser decline in family size among them. In both racial groups there is a substantial difference between men in their early 60s and those age 65-74. The greater decrease in number of dependents among the older group did not compensate for the larger drop in income that they experienced. As a consequence, real income per family member fell by 16 percent among them in contrast with a rise of 56 percent among men age 60-64.[9]

The increase in median net assets over the 15-year period was very large for the total cohort, for both races, and for the older as well as the younger group of men. For blacks and whites combined, the increase was 71 percent—from $32,500 in 1966 to $55,600 in 1981. From a base less than one-fifth as large, the increase for black men was 130 percent. For both races combined, men age 65-74 fared less well in this regard than the men in their early 60s, the increases in median assets being 104 percent and 41 percent, respectively. For the entire cohort the increase in net assets was primarily—but not exclusively—the result of appreciation in value of homes, an increase of 143 percent. However, median net assets exclusive of homes also rose by 44 percent, although this phenomenon was confined exclusively to men age 60-64; among those 65-74 years old nonhome assets were virtually unchanged (+2 percent) (figure 1-4).

Life Satisfaction, 1976-1981

In the 1976 survey respondents were asked for the first time how happy they were with several aspects of their lives and with life in general, and the questions were repeated in 1981. Only a small minority of the total age cohort (6 percent) expressed any degree of unhappiness in either year, and the proportion was no higher than 10 percent in any age-race group.

Somewhat over half of the men profess to be "very happy;" this proportion declined by only 4 percentage points between 1976 and 1981.

In both years black men display a somewhat lower degree of happiness with life than whites, but the racial difference is not nearly so large as would be expected if black and white men were using the same standards to evaluate their objective circumstances. The same is true of age differences; despite their poorer health and their inferior economic status, the older group of men are just as likely as the younger to profess the highest degree of happiness and only slightly more likely to report some unhappiness. These patterns, incidently, are consistent with the findings of attitude surveys of the general population (Campbell, Converse, and Rogers, 1976).

Summary

The National Longitudinal surveys sample of white and black men who were age 45-59 when the study began in 1966 shrank from its initial level of 4,938 to 2,794 in 1981. Three-fifths of the attrition was attributable to death, which does not affect the representativeness of the 1981 sample of men age 60-74. Analysis of the characteristics of members of the original sample who dropped out for other reasons leads to the conclusion that there is not likely to be significant nonresponse bias in analyses based on the reweighted 1981 data.

Major changes occurred in the lives of members of the sample as a majority of them crossed the boundary between middle and old age. Number of dependents decreased sharply, but health problems increased. From the perspective of the labor market, the most prominent change was the move into retirement. By 1981 three-fourths of the age cohort had retired. Even though some of these men continued to work, the proportion of the total cohort who were neither working nor looking for work grew from an almost negligible level of 5 percent in 1966 to 61 percent in 1981.

Until retirement, real average hourly earnings were not only maintained as the men aged, but actually increased slightly, despite economy-wide trends that made such an increase less likely than during earlier 15-year periods (e.g., 1950-1966). However, wholesale withdrawals from the labor force caused median family income to decrease drastically in real terms—by about one-third for the total age cohort and even more for men who had reached 65, among whom retirement was more prevalent. For evaluating economic welfare, these decreases in income need to be interpreted in the light of the decrease in the burden of dependency that occurred over the same period. Real income per family member actually increased for the age cohort as a whole, but declined by 16 percent for men 65-74 years of age.

The picture presented here has been painted with an extremely broad brush, and has attempted merely to describe the major life cycle changes experienced by the cohort as a whole, with little attention either to differentiation or to explanation. The ensuing chapters present a more detailed and analytical examination of the longitudinal record.

Notes

1. A comprehensive report on the causes and consequences of retirement utilizing data from several longitudinal data sets appeared after this was written. See Palmore et al., 1985.

2. For a more complete description of the National Longitudinal surveys, see the Center for Human Resource Research (1984).

3. This fact accounts for some of the limitations of the data from the perspective of our present objectives. Because the interviews were expected to end when the oldest members of the sample would have been 64 years of age, not much thought was given at the outset to issues relating to postretirement behavior (although questions on retirement expectations were included from the beginning). Indeed, the first four volumes of reports on the data appeared under the title *The Preretirement Years*. Nevertheless, much of the information collected in the early years is useful for purposes of the present study, and questions relating to retirement experience were included in later surveys as it became clear that many respondents would retire before data collection ended. U.S. Department of Labor, Manpower Administration, Manpower Research Monograph No. 15. Washington, D.C.: U.S. Government Printing Office, vol. 1 (1970); vol. 2 (1970); vol. 3 (1972); vol. 4 (1974).

4. In a few of the telephone surveys, individuals were not asked this question if they had indicated that they were "retired" in response to the lead question designed to establish labor force and employment status. ("What were you doing most of last week—working, looking for work, or something else?")

5. In addition to this group and those who described themselves as "retired" (see footnote 4), there were two other small groups who have been included among the subjectively retired: those who at some other point in the interview attributed some event (e.g., leaving a job) or condition (e.g., absence from the labor force) to retirement and those who, in response to retrospective questions in the 1978 and 1981 surveys, indicated that they had retired at some point in the past.

6. In some of the surveys, men receiving disability income are not distinguishable from pension recipients.

7. As an example, we have made use of the date of separation from the last job reported in the survey in which the retired status is first observed. Also, use has been made of the retirement date reported retrospectively in the 1978 survey unless this is inconsistent with the longitudinal records. The complete set of decision rules are available on request from the authors.

8. In the remainder of this section, some of the data are drawn from our intial report on the cohort (Parnes et al., 1970), and are based on the total 1966 sample.

9. We have also calculated total family income per *dependent* of the respondent, and the trends are identical to those shown for income per family member.

References

Aging and Work. 1982. Vol. 5, no. 2.
————. 1983. Vol. 6, no. 2.
Beck, Scott H. 1982. "Adjustment To and Satisfaction With Retirement." *Journal of Gerontology* 5: 616-624.
Blau, Peter M., and Duncan, Otis Dudley. 1967. *The American Occupational Structure.* New York: Wiley.
Bould, Sally. 1980. "Unemployment as a Factor in Early Retirement Decisions." *American Journal of Economics and Sociology* 39: 124-136.
Bradburn, N.M. 1969. *The Structure of Psychological Well-being.* Chicago, Aldine.
Bureau of Labor Statistics. 1981. Base tables, August.
Butler, Robert. 1975. *Why Survive: Being Old in America.* New York: Harper.
Campbell, Angus, Converse, Philip E., and Rodgers, Willard L. 1976. *The Quality of American life.* New York: Russell Sage Foundation.
Chirikos, Thomas N., and Nestel, Gilbert. 1981. "Impairment and Labor Market Outcomes: A Cross-sectional and Longitudinal Analysis." In Herbert S. Parnes, ed., *Work and Retirement: A Longitudinal Study of Men.* Cambridge, Mass.: MIT.
Davis, Harry E., and Strasser, Arnold. 1970. "Private Pension Plans, 1960-1969: An Overview." *Monthly Labor Review* 93: 45-56.
Fox, Alan. 1982. "Earnings Replacement Rates and Total Income: Findings from the Retirement History Study." *Social Security Bulletin* 45: 3-23.
Friedmann, Eugene A., and Orbach, Harold L. 1974. "Adjustment to Retirement." In Silvano Arieti, *American Handbook of Psychiatry*, 2d ed., vol. 1. New York: Basic Books, Chap. 30.
Kingson, Eric. 1981. *The Early Retirement Myth: Why Men Retire Before Age 62.* Report by the Select Committee on Aging. U.S. House of Representatives. Ninety-seventh Congress. Washington, D.C.: U.S. Government Printing Office.
Larson, R. 1978. "Thirty Years of Research on Subjective Well-being of Older Americans. *Journal of Gerontology* 33: 109-125.
Mitchell, Olivia S., and Fields, Gary S. 1982. "The Effects of Pensions and Earnings on Retirement: A Review Essay." In R. Ehrenberg, ed., *Research in Labor Economics*, vol. 5. Greenwich, Conn.: JAI Press.

Morgan, James N. 1981. "Antecedents and Consequences of Retirement." In Martha S. Hill, Daniel H. Hill, and James N. Morgan, eds., *Five Thousand American Families: Patterns of Economic Progress.* Ann Arbor, Mich: Institute for Social Research, chap. 60.

Motley, D.K. 1978. "Availability of Retired Persons for Work: Findings from the Retirement History Study." *Social Security Bulletin* 41: 18-27.

Munnell, Alicia. 1982. *The Economics of Private Pensions.* Washington, D.C.: Brookings Institution.

Palmore, Erdman B., Burchett, Bruce M., Fillenbaum, Gerda G., George, Linda K., and Wallman, Laurence M. 1985. *Retirement: Causes and Consequences.* New York: Springer.

Parker, Stanley. 1982. *Work and Retirement.* London: Allen & Unwin.

Parnes, Herbert S. et al. 1970. *The Preretirement Years, Vol. 1.* U.S. Department of Labor Manpower Administration. Manpower Research Monograph No. 15. Washington, D.C.: U.S. Government Printing Office.

———. 1975. *The Preretirement Years, Vol. 4.* U.S. Department of Labor Manpower Administration. Manpower R & D Monograph 15. Washington, D.C.: U.S. Government Printing Office.

———. 1981. *Work and Retirement: A Longitudinal Study of Men.* Cambridge, Mass: MIT.

Parnes, Herbert S., and Nestel, Gilbert. 1981. "The Retirement Experience." In Herbert S. Parnes, ed., *Work and Retirement: A Longitudinal Study of Men.* Cambridge, Mass: MIT.

Parnes, Herbert S., Less, Lawrence, and Nestel, Gilbert. 1980. *Work and Retirement Data: National longitudinal Surveys of Middle-aged and Older Men, 1966-1976.* Columbus, Ohio: Center for Human Resource Research, The Ohio State University.

Parnes, Herbert S. and Less, Lawrence. 1983. *From Work to Retirement: The Experience of a National Sample of Men.* Columbus, Ohio: Center for Human Resource Research, The Ohio State University.

President's Committee on Pension Policy. 1981. *Coming of Age: Toward a National Retirement Income Policy.* Washington, D.C.: President's Committee on Pension Policy.

Rix, Sara E. 1980. *Retirement Age Workers.* Washington, D.C.: American Institute for Research, Inc.

Rones, Philip L. 1978. "Older Men—The Choice Between Work and Retirement." *Monthly Labor Review* 101: 3-10.

Rosenblum, Marc. 1975. "The Last Push: From Discouraged Worker to Involuntary Retirement." *Industrial Gerontology* Winter, 14-22.

Schulz, James H. 1974. "The Economics of Mandatory Retirement." *Industrial Gerontology* Winter, 1-10.

———. 1980. *The Economics of Aging.* 2d Ed. Belmont, Calif.: Wadsworth Publishing Co.

Schwab, Karen. 1983. *A Normative Model of Retirement Timing.* Unpublished manuscript, chap. 2.

Streib, Gordon F., and Schneider, Clement J. 1971. *Retirement in American Society: Impact and Process.* Cornell U.P.

Thompson, Lawrence H. 1983. "The Social Security Reform Debate." *Journal of Economic Literature* 21: 1425-1467.

U.S. Census Bureau. 1977. *Projections of the Population of the United States: 1977 to 2050.* Current Population Reports, Series P-25, No. 704. Washington, D.C.: U.S. Government Printing Office.

U.S. President. 1982. *Economic Report of the President.* Washington, D.C.: U.S. Government Printing Office.

2
Factors Affecting Mortality in the Years Surrounding Retirement

Frank L. Mott
R. Jean Haurin

Overall mortality in the United States has declined significantly during the 1970s (Siegel, 1980) and this decline has pervaded most age groups. Has this decline occurred among all major demographic and socioeconomic segments of the society? The longitudinal nature of the NLS data set permits us for the first time to follow a nationally representative cohort of men as they approach and pass retirement age. Other studies of mortality have been typically limited to a small number of demographic explanatory variables, but the NLS allows us to clarify the extent to which standard demographic variables like race and education may mask the effects of other factors. Background as well as more proximate factors can be determinants of mortality.

We consider several dimensions of male mortality. First, we examine the extent to which a variety of background and more proximate factors are independent predictors of male mortality in the years immediately preceding and following normal retirement age. Next we look at the extent to which mortality differentials have changed over the period: we compare the prospective 5-year mortality record of men age 55-59 in each of these years—1966, 1971, and 1976.

Has the association between mortality and socially determined explanatory variables such as health and employment altered over the period 1966-1981? If there has been an increase in the availability of health care for those with well-defined health problems during this decade and a half, the strength of the relationship between poor health and mortality would be expected to diminish over the period. Furthermore, because of the trend toward early retirement for reasons other than health, one would expect to find a reduced association between nonemployment and mortality in the 1976-1981 period as compared with 1966-1971.[1] We consider both these issues.

The Methodology

Each of our analyses requires a reference group of surviving respondents for comparision with those who die. For the 5-year mortality estimates, the reference group is derived as follows: The decedents in a given 5-year interval are distributed according to the last survey in which they were interviewed, and in almost all instances their characteristics as of that survey are used as explanatory variables in the models. Nondecedent respondents have been randomly distributed in the same proportions as the decedents according to the survey year, and have been assigned the characteristics they held at that survey.[2]

The decedent and survivor groups for the 15-year analysis were defined analogously. That is, decedents were assigned the characteristics they held at the date of their last interview. Respondents who are known to have survived to 1981 have been assigned reference years according to the distribution of survey years assigned to the decedents. Thus, for example, if 10 percent of the decedents (in a particular 1966 5-year age group, e.g., 45-49) died between 1969 and 1971, then 10 percent of the survivors were randomly selected and their characteristics measured as of 1969, and so on.[3]

We use multiple classification analysis (MCA) to estimate the independent predictors of mortality. This technique determines for each category of a given independent variable the proportion of survivors over the time period being considered (either 5 or 15 years), assuming that members of that category have an average value on all other variables included in the model. For example, the MCA "adjusted" survival rate for men with 12 years of schooling is the rate that would prevail for men with that amount of education if they were average with respect to all other characteristics in the model.[4]

The Determinants of 15-Year Survival

Our first analysis follows the total original sample as well as the separate cohorts age 45-49, 50-54, and 55-59, to examine the determinants of their surviving over the 15-year period. Our overriding objective is to find out if the general decrease in mortality over the period was pervasive or selective of particular population subgroups. Some earlier studies suggest that the influence of factors such as education on mortality levels may be sensitive to the age of an individual: mortality differentials by educational level have been found to narrow with increasing age (e.g., Kitagawa and Hauser, 1973, chapter 2), as have racial differentials.[5] We consider whether there is any systematic narrowing in mortality differentials with increasing age.

In all of the models in this section, a respondent is coded 1 if he has survived and was interviewed in 1981, and zero if he is known to have died by the time the survey was conducted. Respondents who left the sample for reasons other than mortality are excluded. We assume throughout that mortality for the group that attrited for reasons other than death is equivalent to that for the group that remained in the sample, an assumption consistent with matched NLS-life table survival estimates. Overall, 80 percent of men age 45-49, 69 percent of those age 50-54, and 60 percent of those age 55-59 survived to 1981—70 percent of the total group.[6]

The explanatory variables in these models include (1) a group of demographic and socioeconomic background factors whose relation to mortality has frequently been examined only in "uncontrolled" tabular associations and (2) two employment and health-related variables less commonly available. The demographic and socioeconomic background variables include race, educational attainment, geographic residence (central city, suburb, or nonmetropolitan), marital status, and family income.[7]

Demographic and Socioeconomic Background Variables. Race has usually been found a significant predictor of mortality at most ages: black men have lower survival probabilities than their white counterparts. But do significant racial differentials remain after controlling for other socioeconomic and demographic background factors? Although it is likely that the racial differential will narrow in a "controlled" situation, it is not clear whether all racial differences will vanish; black men have major differences from whites in patterns of morbidity (U.S. Dept. of Health and Human Services, 1981, table 1-8; Chase, 1965), and whether or not these reflect only socioeconomic differentials is an unanswered question (Siegel, 1980).

For a variety of reasons, education (e.g., Kitagawa and Hauser, 1973; Sauer, 1980) and income (e.g., Kitagawa and Hauser, 1973; Lerner and Stutz, 1975, 1976, 1977) have frequently been positively associated with the probability of survival in both individual and aggregate level analyses. Explanations for the lower mortality associated with more education include general life-style considerations such as living a less strenuous life and following a less risky occupational path. Other rationales for the relationship frequently are confounded with income-related considerations: better-educated individuals typically have higher family incomes and may thus be better able to avail themselves of required medical care.

In contrast, higher-income families may follow better health practices (Belloc, 1982). However, this association may in reality reflect the influence of education. Kitagawa and Hauser, in their analysis of 1960 data, found that both education and income had significant independent associations with mortality; our more recent data will clarify whether these relationships still prevail. We view the education variable for these men as a stable long-term status measure, not subject to change during the time interval under investigation. Although the family income variable is admittedly less stable in this regard, we view it also as a reasonable measure of "permanent income."[8]

The association between marital status and survival has interested many researchers. Numerous theories purport to explain why married individuals should live longer: married couples have more social support to combat stress and each partner has someone on whom to rely for care when ill. Also, the ability to find a spouse may be selective of certain physical, mental, and emotional characteristics associated with longer survival. Each of these considerations points to greater survival probabilities for married individuals, particularly at ages where mortality is beginning to have a major impact.

Most previous research supports the thesis that married individuals have better survival probabilities (Kitagawa and Hauser, 1973; Mott and Haurin, 1981; Ortmeyer, 1974; U.S. Dept. of Health, Education and Welfare, 1970). Our analysis will clarify to a considerable degree whether the "selection process" accounts for a significant portion of the mortality differential between married and nonmarried individuals. In addition, because we control for differences in overt health conditions and in employment (which undoubtedly proxies for other unmeasured differences in health status), remaining mortality differentials between the married and unmarried can perhaps be attributed to more subtle differences that may have social-psychological origins.

A number of other studies suggest that individuals residing in rural areas have better survival probabilities, although these studies typically have used only limited socioeconomic controls (Kitagawa and Hauser, 1973; Sauer, 1974). Presumably, these geographic differentials reflect differences in personal and occupational life-styles between urban and rural residents. We test whether a significant *independent* geographic differential exists for an age group for whom rural residence is more extensive than for younger age cohorts and for whom it has in all likelihood been of long duration.

Our final "longer-term" background variable measures the respondent's occupational status on his current or last job (Blau and Duncan, 1967). In most instances, this occupation is a good proxy for the longest job the respondent has held during his work life.[9] It is generally hypothesized that higher occupational status is associated with greater survival because higher-status occupations involve less physical risk, may carry with them better health benefits, are less stressful, and certainly are associated with higher income. Whether occupational status can be expected to have an independent effect on mortality after controlling for education and income is not clear. It has been suggested that occupational differentials in mortality have been narrowing in the past decade and that the remaining differentials are most pronounced between the lowest occupational status and all those above it (Antonovsky, 1979; Kitagawa and Hauser, 1973).

Health and Employment Variables. Our second model includes, in addition to the variables just described, direct health and employment measures (1) to determine whether these factors have strong independent effects after the other factors are controlled; (2) to find out the extent to which more commonly available status measures such as race and education are associated with mortality only because of their eventual impact on employment and health; and (3) to see whether the association between health, employment, and mortality is sensitive to age. That is, does above-average mortality for less healthy individuals at younger ages ultimately result in a weaker association between a particular health status and mortality at older ages? It is worth reiterating that we view the employment variable as an important supplementary indicator of health, one that helps compensate for the inadequacy of the self-reported health measure. Our measure of employment is the estimated number of hours worked by the respondent in the survey year; the health measure is a self-report by the respondent as to whether he had a health problem affecting the amount or kind of work he could do, and if so, how long the condition had existed.[10] The health measure includes three categories—no health problem, problem of under 5 years duration ("acute"), and problem of 5 years' duration or longer ("chronic").

Findings. The variables and the full 15-year survival models are presented in tables 2-1 through 2-4. The unadjusted coefficients are raw survival probabilities (all groups begin at 1.000 in 1966) not controlling for any of the other factors. The adjusted probabilities in the "background" model control for the variables that are considered to be relatively unchanging; they are meant in a very general way to represent the life-style of the respondent in the long run. The "total" model controls additionally for health problems and for the recent intensity of employment.

Whereas substantial unadjusted racial differences in survival appear for all age groups, the differences narrow dramatically when controls are added, to the point where they are not significant in the background model—although the direction of the differences that remain are consistent with expectations. Thus, we may conclude that after taking into account socioeconomic and demographic background factors known to be associated with race, black men in this age range are about as likely to survive over the 15-year period as white men. It is also important to note that racial differentials in survival probabilities are *not* further reduced by adding the health and employment variables. The first of these two findings suggests that observed racial differences in mortality—at least by middle age—do not have a significant genetic component. It appears that variables proxying for social and economic phenomena account for the bulk of the racial differential in mortality.

Controlling for other factors similarly reduces the importance of the educational differential in mortality, although the difference remains sig-

Table 2–1
Fifteen-Year Survival Probabilities by Age in 1966 for Selected Characteristics: Total Sample
(MCA[a] results)

			Total sample	
			Adjusted (F-ratio)	
Characteristic	*n*	Unadjusted	Background Model	Total Model
Total sample	3,962	.700	(23.011)[c]	(35.250)[c]
Race			(2.610)	(4.913)[b]
White	2,786	.711	.704	.705[b]
Black	1,176	.598	.665	.653[b]
Educational attainment			(3.633)[b]	(2.366)
Less than 9 years school	1,860	.634	.678[b]	.683[d]
9–11 years	740	.699	.707	.703
12 or more years	1,362	.765	.719[d]	.716
Duncan index of occupational status (current or last job)			(11.698)[c]	(3.836)[b]
Less than 20	1,754	.663	.698	.700
20–49	1,129	.692	.691	.688
50 or more	916	.789	.738[c]	.725[d]
NA	163	.451	.510[c]	.607[b]
Area of residence			(7.766)[c]	(9.796)[c]
Central city	1,377	.666	.669[c]	.666[c]
Suburb	1,279	.714	.693	.693
Outside SMSA	1,306	.715	.738[c]	.740[c]
Marital status			(16.741)[c]	(12.238)[c]
Married, spouse present	3,273	.721	.712[c]	.710[c]
Other	689	.584	.632[c]	.644[c]

Table 2–1 continued

| Characteristic | n | Unadjusted | Total sample | |
| | | | Adjusted (F-ratio) | |
			Background Model	Total Model
Family income			(19.725)c	(5.236)c
Less than $15,000	1,407	.588	.633c	.694
$15,000–$24,999	858	.694	.683	.658c
$25,000 or more	933	.816	.771c	.724d
NA	764	.710	.720	.723d
Health status				(100.434)c
No problem	2,211	.818		.783c
Problem - duration less than 5 years	878	.546		.585c
Problem - duration 5 years or more	873	.534		.592c
Hours worked in year				(32.925)c
None	1,124	.522		.625c
Less than 1750	624	.626		.657c
1750 or more	2,214	.802		.746c
R^2			.072	.135

Note: This model describes the probability of surviving from 1966 to 1981. The model is limited to respondents who are known to have died by 1981 or who are still being interviewed as of that date. Characteristics reference the last survey before death for the deceased and a randomly selected survey for survivors. Survivor selection years are distributed across surveys in proportions identical to the decedents' last survey distribution. The total sample model includes a control for age. Adjusted age-specific death rates in the total sample model do not differ significantly from unadjusted rates.

[a]For a description of Multiple Classification Analysis see "A Note on the Tables," on page vii.

[b]Significant at .05 level for two-tailed test.

[c]Significant at .01 level for two-tailed test.

[d]Significant at .10 level for two-tailed test.

nificant for the oldest group of men. Race and education are the two factors most commonly available in other studies; but these two factors alone are not adequate for interpretative purposes. As with the race variable, the addition of health and employment does not alter in any important way the association between survival and educational attainment. Making within-cohort inferences from three successive age cross-sections, it is also important to note that the mortality differential by education does not appear to narrow as the respondents become older. Indeed, the tendency is in the opposite direction.

The large mortality differentials by occupational status that appear before controlling for other factors are also considerably reduced (and sometimes vanish) when the background variables are taken into ac-

Table 2–2
Fifteen-Year Survival Probabilities by Age in 1966 for Selected Characteristics: Subjects 45–49 Years of Age

			Age 45–49	
			Adjusted (F-ratio)	
Characteristic	n	Unadjusted	Background Model	Total Model
Total sample	1,362	.800	(7.025)[a]	(11.296)[b]
Race			(1.697)	(2.349)
White	975	.811	.805	.805
Black	387	.696	.757	.751
Educational attainment			(0.539)	(0.158)
Less than 9 years school	514	.743	.789	.795
9–11 years	269	.779	.792	.795
12 or more years	579	.846	.812	.807
Duncan index of occupational status			(8.563)[b]	(3.855)[c]
(current or last job)				
Less than 20	554	.734	.762[a]	.766[a]
20–49	397	.818	.822	.817
50 or more	375	.873	.838[a]	.830[c]
NA	36	.483	.528[b]	.661[a]
Area of residence			(0.207)	(0.345)
Central city	471	.793	.802	.792
Suburb	472	.820	.793	.797
Outside SMSA	419	.782	.809	.813
Marital status			(7.938)[a]	(4.598)[a]
Married, spouse present	1160	.818	.812[b]	.809[a]
Other	202	.684	.723[b]	.744[a]
Family income			(6.607)[b]	(4.716)[a]
Less than $15,000	347	.699	.749[a]	.807
$15,000–24,999	338	.753	.753[a]	.736[b]
$25,000 or more	424	.885	.855[b]	.831[a]
NA	253	.807	.812	.822
Health status				(28.383)[b]
No problem	898	.876		.854[b]
Problem - duration less than 5 years	252	.646		.784[b]
Problem - duration 5 years or more	212	.639		.795[b]
Hours worked in year				(10.884)[b]
None	188	.587		.707[b]
Less than 1750	179	.684		.728[b]
1750 or more	995	.855		.828[b]
R_2			.050	.108

[a]Significant at .05 level for two-tailed test.
[b]Significant at .01 level for two-tailed test.
[c]Significant at .10 level for two-tailed test.

Table 2–3
Fifteen-Year Survival Probabilities by Age in 1966 for Selected
Characteristics: Subjects 50–54 Years of Age

			Age 50–54	
			Adjusted (F-ratio)	
			Background	
Characteristic	n	Unadjusted	Model	Total Model
Total sample	1,369	.685	(5.112)[a]	(11.217)[b]
Race			(0.594)	(2.063)
White	955	.694	.688	.700
Black	414	.596	.655	.632
Educational attainment			(0.019)	(0.092)
Less than 9 years school	665	.659	.688	.690
9–11 years	247	.682	.685	.677
12 or more years	457	.713	.682	.684
Duncan index of occupational status				
(current or last job)			(4.265)[a]	(1.466)
Less than 20	615	.673	.695	.706
20–49	389	.674	.672	.667
50 or more	306	.747	.713	.690
NA	59	.441	.476[b]	.590
Area of residence			(3.799)[a]	(3.801)[a]
Central city	482	.629	.636[a]	.641[a]
Suburb	427	.707	.692	.685
Outside SMSA	460	.710	.721[a]	.724[a]
Marital status			(4.858)[a]	(3.732)[c]
Married, spouse present	1131	.704	.696[a]	.694[c]
Other	238	.573	.618[a]	.629[c]
Family income			(8.430)[b]	(1.569)
Less than $15,000	485	.584	.596[b]	.667
$15,000–24,999	323	.693	.688	.663
$25,000 or more	294	.765	.751[b]	.693
NA	267	.723	.730[b]	.723[c]
Health status				(38.508)[b]
No problem	749	.703		.775[b]
Problem - duration less than 5 years	305	.576		.598[b]
Problem - duration 5 years or more	315	.492		.540[b]
Hours worked in year				(12.863)[b]
None	395	.532		.610[b]
Less than 1750	221	.603		.626[a]
1750 or more	753	.680		.737[b]
R_2			.035	.107

[a]Significant at .05 level for two-tailed test.
[b]Significant at .01 level for two-tailed test.
[c]Significant at .10 level for two-tailed test.

Table 2–4
Fifteen-Year Survival Probabilities by Age in 1966 for Selected
Characteristics: Subjects 55–59 Years of Age

Characteristic	n	Unadjusted	Background Model	Total Model
			Adjusted (F-ratio)	
Total sample	1,223	.604	(6.373)[a]	(10.600)[b]
Race			(1.931)	(1.742)
White	853	.616	.609	.609
Black	370	.482	.542	.543
Educational attainment			(6.744)[b]	(4.867)[a]
Less than 9 years school	678	.531	.552[b]	.521[b]
9–11 years	224	.627	.636	.637
12 or more years	321	.696	.660[a]	.647[a]
Duncan index of occupational status (current or last job)			(4.497)[a]	(2.902)[c]
Less than 20	600	.596	.631	.621
20–49	321	.543	.550[a]	.556[a]
50 or more	238	.723	.651[c]	.648
NA	64	.442	.477[a]	.539
Area of residence			(5.435)[a]	(7.355)[b]
Central city	419	.561	.565[c]	.560[a]
Suburb	376	.588	.577	.573[c]
Outside SMSA	428	.656	.665[b]	.673[b]
Marital status			(3.958)[c]	(3.203)[c]
Married, spouse present	973	.623	.616[c]	.615[c]
Other	250	.512	.544[c]	.553[c]
Family income			(4.352)[a]	(0.473)
Less than $15,000	563	.524	.550[b]	.600
$15,000–24,999	206	.627	.614	.579
$25,000 or more	198	.728	.680[b]	.611
NA	256	.616	.624	.628
Health status				(36.076)[b]
No problem	556	.746		.717[b]
Problem—duration less than 5 years	324	.443		.468[b]
Problem—duration 5 years or more	343	.495		.525[b]
Hours worked in year				(5.428)[a]
None	549	.497		.560[a]
Less than 1750	220	.587		.592
1750 or more	454	.724		.655[b]
R_2			.050	.112

[a]Significant at .05 level for two-tailed test.
[b]Significant at .01 level for two-tailed test.
[c]Significant at .10 level for two-tailed test.

count. The erratic pattern for the two older age groups (lower survival rates for the middle status in comparison with the lower status group) undoubtedly reflects the inclusion in the lowest status category of farm workers, who are known to have lower mortality.

There appears to be an association between greater survival and non-metropolitan residence for the two older groups of men, although the pattern does not always attain significance and is somewhat erratic. These differentials in survival probabilities by geographic residence appear to be quite independent of all the other factors in the model; rural residents have higher survival probabilities independent of status considerations *and* independent of more proximate health or employment factors. From a social-psychological perspective, this finding suggests that something in the rural life-style per se may contribute to greater survival. An alternate interpretation is that rural residents are selective of individuals who are "inherently" less susceptible to premature mortality.

The data in tables 2-1 through 2-4 lend strong support to the hypothesis that individuals in intact marriages have significantly higher survival probabilities than their nonmarried counterparts. Although this disparity is reduced by the introduction of the background controls, it nonetheless remains substantial. Moreover, inclusion of the more proximate health and employment variables does not reduce the gap further. To the extent that the variables in the model effectively control for the mate selectivity phenomenon and for differentials by marital status in economic well-being and overt health problems, the significant remaining differential lends support to social-psychological interpretations.

The data also show that a strong association exists between family income and mortality. The unadjusted statistics show, not surprisingly, that there is a strong positive association between income and survival, a relationship equally strong for all three age cohorts. It is significant that this association remains even with the background variables controlled—although the range of survival rates between low and high income does appear to diminish.[11]

Finally, both the health and employment variables have powerful independent associations with survival; a large part of the strong employment association undoubtedly reflects the inadequacy of the health measure. Indicative of a selection process is the *relatively* increasing likelihood of survival by healthy and employed men as one moves from the younger to the older cohorts (and conversely, the relatively declining probability of survival by the less healthy and employed). Controlling for other factors, the survival probability of the "no health problem" group declines from about .85 to .72 as one moves from the youngest to oldest group—a decline of 13 points or about 15 percent. In contrast, the corresponding measure for the group with extensive health problems declines from .80 to .53—27 points or 34 percent. A similar comparison could have been made (although not quite so dramatically) contrasting the fully employed with the nonemployed. In any event, it is clear that the significance of certain factors increases greatly with increasing age. This relationship has important implications for interpretation of other behavioral findings (e.g., employment) for older in comparison with younger men. Indeed, in interpreting all findings one must be sensitive to the fact that between 1966 and 1981 the total cohort moved from a life cycle stage in which mortality is relatively rare to one in which it is, although not typical, nonetheless not unusual.

The Temporal Patterning of Differentials in Adult Mortality

Next we break down the survival probabilities into three 5-year periods (1966-1971, 1971-1976 and 1976-1981) in order to describe the trend of mortality in relation to particular variables of interest.

In order to describe the patterning of survival for a particular 1966 age cohort over the full 15-year period, successive 5-year unadjusted and adjusted survival probabilities for a given cohort are spliced together.[12] For example, the group age 60-64 in 1971 represents the survivors of the group age 55-59 in 1966, and those age 65-69 in 1976 are survivors of those age 60-64 in 1971. The cohort who were age 55-59 in 1966 will receive primary attention, because they had moved farthest into retirement by 1981.

For men who were age 55-59 in 1966, figures 2-1 through 2-5 describe the age pattern of survival for the respondents with respect to five background characteristics. Survival begins at 100 percent for all groups in 1966. Figure 2-1 describes the temporal pattern of survival over the 15-year period by race. Three survival curves are shown for the black respondents, representing the unadjusted rates, the rates adjusted for background factors only, and those adjusted for all the factors in the models just described. Only one curve is shown for white men because there is little difference between the white survival probabilities in the three models. As expected, the slopes of both the white and black survival curves steepen with increasing age. Also, the unadjusted survival gap between the races widens significantly between the 5- and 15-year points. Controlling for background factors eliminates all of the racial mortality differential up to 1976 and lessens it considerably for the 1976-1981 period, at the beginning of which the surviving respondents had attained ages 65-69.

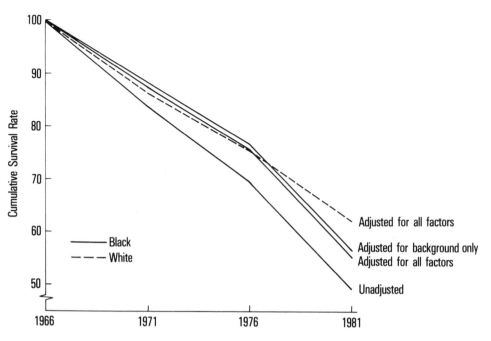

Figure 2–1. Cumulative Survival Probabilities by Race for 55–59-Year-Old Men in 1966

Figure 2-2 shows survival rates by educational attainment, contrasting men who completed 12 years or more of schooling with those having less than 9 years. While the "unadjusted" gap is by far the widest, the cumulative impact of differential education does appear to result in a significant difference in mortality at the older ages even after controlling for all of the other factors. However, after controls are added, the adjusted survival curves are esssentially parallel, rather than showing increasing disparity with advancing age.

The marital status survival pattern indicated in figure 2.3 is very similar to that described for education. Only one curve is shown for married men, as the controlled and uncontrolled survival probabilities for married men are essentially the same. Consistent with the earlier results for the 15-year model, the survival curves for married and non-married men quickly widen, then both adjusted and unadjusted follow essentially parallel courses. Controlling for background factors only, the differential narrows somewhat, but still remains substantial. The additional controls for the more proximate health and employment factors produce little further change. As noted earlier, these results provide strong

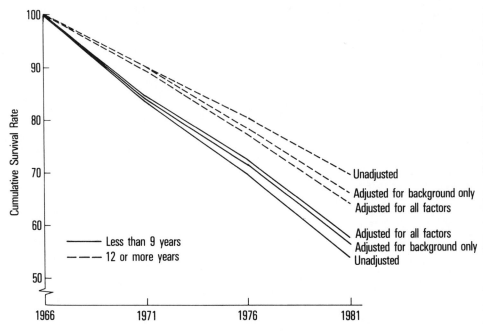

Figure 2–2. Cumulative Survival Probabilities by Year of Schooling Completed for 55–59-Year-Old Men in 1966

corroborating evidence for the thesis that marital status differentials in mortality reflect far more than the phenomenon of selection, for that effect should be captured by the education, occupation, employment, and health variables. It follows that survival is sensitive to marital status, for reasons more complex than can be accounted for by the data in this survey—and our data are far more comprehensive than those usually available to researchers!

The mortality differentials by occupational status shown in figure 2-4 are somewhat erratic. The raw data suggest that high occupational status is ultimately associated with greater survival. However, men of intermediate status are least likely to survive. In the adjusted models, the lower survival rates of this intermediate status group become even more pronounced. The more favorable mortality position of the lowest status group by the 15-year mark (when the cohort has attained age 70-74) partially reflects the tendency, noted earlier, for the group to have heavy representation of farm occupations which are known to have below-average mortality. To a great extent this phenomenon is probably an historical artifact. Indeed, the 15-year survival rate for low-status men age 45-49—a later cohort—is lower relative to their higher-status counterparts.

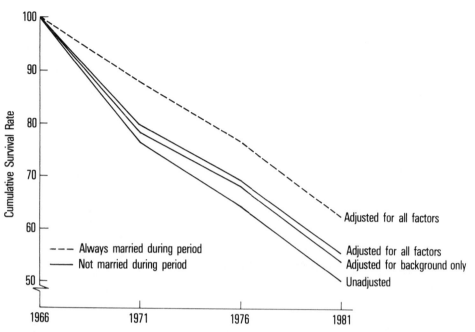

Figure 2–3. Cumulative Survival Probabilities by Marital Status for 55–59-Year-Old Men in 1966

Figure 2-5 describes the considerable unadjusted survival gap between the lowest income group and the other two groups. This gap is wide as early as 1971, and contrary to the pattern for several of the other characteristics, continues to widen over time. When background factors are controlled, however, the gap in 1971 is not nearly so large and, perhaps as importantly, it no longer widens between 1971 and 1981. Furthermore, no apparent mortality gap appears between the middle- and upper-income group after introducing *all* controls. The lowest income group, however, continues to have a slightly inferior survival profile as of the 15-year point, even after introducing the health and employment controls, which take into account differences in employment between decedents and survivors.

Period Effects on Mortality Differentials

What secular changes occurred between 1966 and 1981 in the relationship between mortality prospects and several explanatory variables, especially health and employment? To answer this question, we examine the associations between subsequent 5-year mortality probabilities and

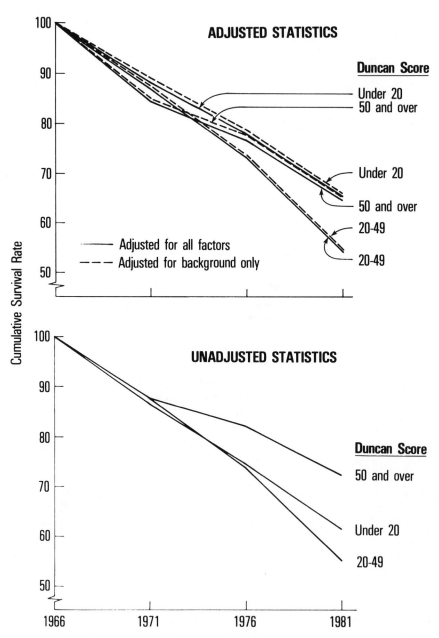

Figure 2–4. Cumulative Survival Probabilities by Occupational Status (Duncan Index) of Current or Last Job for 55–59-Year-Old Men in 1966

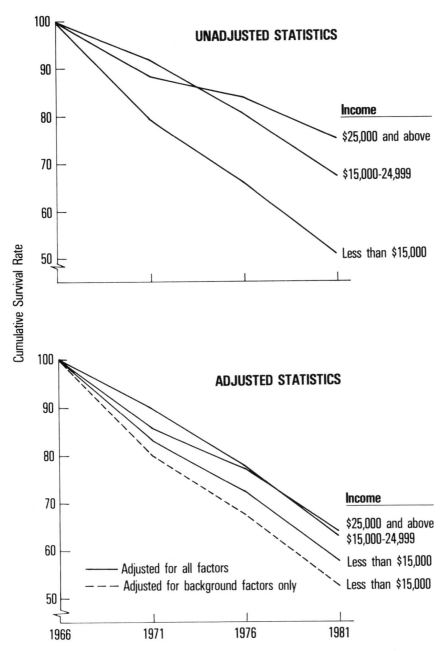

Figure 2–5. Cumulative Survival Probabilities by Family Income for 55–59-Year-Old Men in 1966

the explanatory variables for men who were age 55-59 in each of the years 1966, 1971, and 1976. Two issues frequently noted in other studies are of particular interest to us here: first, it is well-documented that overall mortality for men in this age range has shown a gradual decline during this period. Has this decline affected some more than others? Have the generally acknowledged improvements over the period in medical and health care and delivery systems, public health practices (Siegel, 1980), and perhaps life-styles, improved disproportionately the life chances of men with health problems in comparison with the rest of the population, or have the improvements been equally shared by all groups? Second, Has the increasing tendency of men to retire at an early age *independent* of overt health problems changed the "mix" of the retired compared with nonretired population in such a way as to alter their relative survival probabilities?[13]

Table 2-5 documents the extent to which the effects of health and employment and of race, education, and marital status on the mortality of men age 55-59 may have changed over the 15-year period. Whether one examines the adjusted or unadjusted statistics, no major change appears over time in the association between race or education and mortality. The mortality differentials by these two factors remain essentially the same in all three periods as mortality declines modestly over time for all education and race groups. In the case of health, a comparison of the first with the third period shows, not surprisingly, that poorer health is associated with much higher mortality in both periods, but that *within* each health category mortality decreases modestly over the decade.[14] The decline in mortality was proportionately slightly greater-than-average for those with health problems and for those in the "other" marital status. Nevertheless, the most valid generalization is that the overall decrease in mortality has been spread rather evenly among the various population subgroups—except for the differential by employment status, to which we now turn.

Perhaps the single most impressive finding of this analysis is the major secular change that has occurred in the association between employment and mortality, even *after* controlling for health status. Figure 2-6 shows that whereas the unadjusted mortality probabilities of full- and part-year workers decline gradually, the probability for nonworkers declines precipitously from a rate of about 32 percent in the first 5-year period, to about 14 percent in the third period. Also, it may be seen in tables 2-2 through 2-5 that while the mortality rate for nonworkers is much higher in all time periods before controlling for other factors, the fact remains that the *adjusted* mortality probability for that group declines about as much as the unadjusted. Thus the magnitude of the decline is not associated with changing relationships between employment and any of the other variables in the model.

Table 2–5
The Effects of Selected Variables on Mortality of 55–59 Year-Old-Men: 1966–1981[a]

Characteristic	Unadjusted Death Rate			Adjusted Death Rate			Change in Rates, 1966–1981	
	1966–1971	1971–1976	1976–1981	1966–1971	1971–1976	1976–1981	Unadjusted	Adjusted
Race								
White	.133	.105	.078	.137	.108	.080	−.055	−.057
Black	.162	.160	.124	.127	.132	.103	−.038	−.024
Difference (white-black)	−.029	−.055	−.046	+.010	−.024	−.023		
Employment								
None	.318	.288	.144	.252	.168	.103	−.174	−.149
Part year (under 1750 hours)	.195	.147	.117	.176	.128	.103	−.078	−.073
Full year (1750 or more hours)	.093	.071	.057	.108	.096	.071	−.036	−.037
Difference (full-none)	−.225	−.217	−.087	−.144	−.072	−.032		
Health problem								
None	.093	.049	.045	.113	.060	.053	−.048	−.060
Under 5 years duration (acute)	.222	.162	.148	.195	.149	.140	−.074	−.055
5 or more years duration (chronic)	.205	.318	.124	.163	.284	.108	−.081	−.055
Difference (none-acute)	−.129	−.113	−.103	−.082	−.089	−.087		
Difference (none-chronic)	−.112	−.269	−.079	−.050	−.224	−.055		
Educational attainment								
Less than 9 years school (low)	.161	.120	.124	.154	.104	.111	−.037	−.043
9–11 years	.133	.132	.077	.140	.130	.072	−.056	−.068
12 or more years (high)	.103	.089	.058	.107	.105	.068	−.045	−.039
Difference (high-low)	−.058	−.031	−.066	−.047	+.001	−.043		
Marital status								
Married, spouse present (MSP)	.119	.102	.074	.125	.107	.077	−.045	−.048
Other	.236	.163	.132	.203	.125	.113	−.104	−.090
Difference (MSP-other)	−.117	−.061	−.058	−.078	−.018	−.036		

[a]Full models available from the author. Death rates in this table are equal to 1-survival rate.

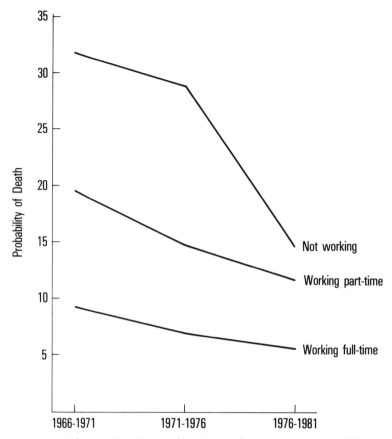

Figure 2–6. Fifteen-Year Mortality Rates for 55–59-Year-Old Men by Employment Status, 1966–1981

Table 2-6 clarifies further how the mortality declines are concentrated within the non-employed group. When health status is interacted with employment status (in models otherwise identical), the largest declines in mortality are in all instances for the nonworkers—regardless of health status, with the sharpest declines occurring among those with long-standing health problems. It seems fair to conclude that the decreases in mortality noted for all these groups—and especially for those with long-standing health problems—are related to improvements in medical and health care. In contrast, mortality remained unchanged for *full-time* workers with long-standing problems, a group which already had low mortality in 1966. This stability suggests that the kinds of long-term disabilities reported by individuals working the full year are probably not of a life-threatening nature; they clearly do not impede the

Table 2–6
The Joint Impact of Health and Employment on Mortality of 55–59 Year Old Men: 1966–1971, 1971–1976, and 1976–1981

Health and Employment	Mortality Rates						Change 66–81	
	Unadjusted			Adjusted for Background Factors				
	66–71	71–76	76–81	66–71	71–76	76–81	Unadjusted	Adjusted
No health problem								
No work	.189[a]	.000[a]	.079	.168[a]	.000[a]	.064	−.110	−.104[a]
Part-time	.142	.095	.066	.133	.096	.066	−.076	−.067
Full-time	.083	.046	.039	.089	.047	.044	−.044	−.045
Health problem under 5 years duration (acute problem)								
No work	.288	.211	.156	.265	.204	.152	−.132	−.113
Part-time	.261	.119	.199	.259	.127	.191	−.062	−.068
Full-time	.170	.158	.117	.176	.159	.121	−.053	−.055
Health problem of at least 5 years duration (chronic problem)								
No work	.373	.420	.184	.330	.388	.152	−.189	−.178
Part-time	.230	.311[a]	.090[a]	.221	.326[a]	.093[a]	−.140[a]	−.128
Full-time	.081	.198	.089	.096	.209	.093	+.008	−.003

[a]Category represents fewer than 30 respondents.

ability of the individual to maintain continuous close ties with the work force.

The sharp decline in mortality among nonemployed healthy individuals is probably related to the greater tendency for a fuller cross-section of men to retire early now than was true in the 1960s. Also, it may be that perceptions of health status have changed over the period; if individuals with marginal health problems—not of a life-threatening nature—are more likely now than in the past to report such problems, this tendency would lead to lower mortality for individuals in a specific health-nonemployment category. If the ability to retire for "disability related" reasons is more readily available at this point in history, part of the health problem-specific mortality declines could be associated with this phenomenon; the disability retired group would be "healthier" now than it was in the 1960s.

Conclusions

We have clarified the extent to which factors such as race, education, and marital status are indeed independent predictors of mortality. Whereas black men at these ages systematically have higher mortality rates than whites, almost all of this difference reflects differences between the races in socioeconomic background. In contrast, the effect of marital status appears more deeply embedded. After controlling for background factors *as well as* for differences between the married and nonmarried in employment and health status, married men still have more favorable survival prospects.

We have also demonstrated how the availability of detailed employment measures in addition to self-reported health measures enhances our ability to (1) document the health-mortality association and (2) measure more effectively other mortality differentials (such as those related to marital status) confident in the knowledge that the impact of health per se has been removed from the analysis.

Perhaps most important from a social perspective, we have shown how the generally acknowledged overall decline in mortality over the past fifteen years has impacted fairly equally on all segments of the society; blacks and whites, the well-educated and the poorly-educated, the healthy and the less healthy have all apparently benefited from the general improvements in health and medical care and services available in our society. The only population subgroup which has benefited to a substantially greater extent than others is that group which includes the most seriously at risk—individuals not at work who frequently report illnesses of long duration. Thus it seems fair to conclude that those most in need have indeed benefited most from the secular improvements in health care.

Notes

1. In 1976, 5.1 percent of men age 55-59 in the sample were employed no hours during the survey year and reported no health problem, in comparison with 1.8 percent for their counterparts age 55-59 in 1966.

2. Nondecedents in this case are not required to survive to 1981, just to the end of the 5-year period.

3. For all the weighted analyses in this study, base year weights were used to adjust for selective sample attrition and to translate the unrepresentative sample statistics into representative national proportions and numbers.

4. Before undertaking our mortality analyses, we made a careful cross-check between mortality estimates derived from our sample and those yielded by appropriate national life tables. For comparison with these survival estimates, 15-year survival rates for three 5-year age groups as of 1966 (age 45-49, 50-54 and 55-59) were derived separately by race using 1968 and 1978 life table estimates. An average of the survival rates from these two estimates was used as a "best" estimate for this 15-year period. See U.S. Dept. of Health, Education and Welfare (1971), table 5-2; and U.S. Dept. of Health and Human Services (1981), table 5-1 for the L values utilized in these computations. Implicit in survival rates derived from life tables for a single year is the assumption that the mortality experience of that year will continue into the future, a reasonably valid assumption except in periods of rapidly changing mortality. It is because mortality has in fact been declining gradually that we averaged the values derived from two life tables, one from near the beginning and one from near the end of the period under consideration. A comparison of these two approaches produce virtually identical 15-year survival rates. Indeed, in no age cohort/race category is there more than a 2-point difference in survival probabilities between the NLS and life table results. There are three important implications of this finding: (1) one can use the NLS data for mortality analyses confident that the results are in all likelihood nationally representative, (2) the nonmortality attriters are *not* selective of individuals in poor health, and (3) the surviving mature men's sample being interviewed in 1981 is still nationally representative.

5. See, for example, the literature on the black-white cross-over (Nam, Weatherby, and Ockay, 1978; Manton, Poss, and Wing, 1979).

6. The reader may note that the survival probabilities presented here differ slightly from those in table 2-1. This difference appears because the probabilities in table 2-1 were derived using the procedures described in the section on "temporal patterning of differentials in adult mortality" which follows.

7. Earlier versions of the two analyses included variables measuring the wives' education and employment status; the respondent's retirement status and south-nonsouth residence. In the interest of parsimony these variables were deleted either because they were generally not significant (wives' education and employment and south-nonsouth residence) or because they made interpretation of variables already in the model difficult (respondent's retirement status). Also, the collinearity between the "N.A." category in the wives' education and employment variables and the "other" marital status category confounded any possible interpretation of the marital status effects.

8. The validity of this approach is supported by the fact that in the next section, where family income is used at the beginning of each of the three 5-

year periods, we get results essentially similar to those reported in this section for the entire 15-year period. Also, the full models in this section include an employment variable which should remove the effect of short-term declines in family income associated with illness and declining hours of employment in the period preceding death.

9. When the current or last job held by all respondents in the mature men's cohort as of 1976 was cross-tabulated by the *longest* job held by the respondents in 1966, there was a 71 percent correspondence at the 1-digit Census occupation level. In addition, a significant portion of the remaining 29 percent were in major occupation groups not dissimilar to the one reported as the longest occupation (e.g., laborer compared with operative, and manager with professional).

10. It is acknowledged that health self-reports are less than perfect proxies for actual health. However, their association with mortality and employment in this and earlier (Mott and Haurin, 1981) research certainly support the notion that self-reports are sensitive indicators. In this regard, it is important to note the close correspondence between self-reported health differentials and health behavior differentials found in a number of Public Health Services Reports. See, for example, U.S. Dept. of Health and Human Services (1983), Collins (1983), and Wilder (1983).

11. It is of some interest to note that the addition of the health and employment variables to the model reduces the income differential to the point where it is insignificant and frequently erratic. Indeed, other models, not presented here, show that the employment and health variables each eliminate the income effect. This finding is consistent with the notion that higher income translates into greater survival through mechanisms associated with improved health.

12. The ultimate 15-year survivals derived this way and the 15-year survivals generated in the earlier section are very similar.

13. It is useful to consider first the extent to which the overall characteristics of men age 55–59 have changed over the 15 years, for to the extent that mortality is sensitive to these characteristics, it may have altered over time simply as the result of this changing mix. Men age 55–59 in 1976 were significantly more educated than their 1966 counterparts and were less likely to be employed. Otherwise, no major change appears in their reported characteristics. The net impact of these changes on mortality is unclear, as the change in educational attainment may simply have changed the meaning of "low education" so far as mortality is concerned. The significance of a high school diploma—even from the standpoint of subsequent mortality—may be quite different when high school graduation is exceptional from what it is when graduation becomes the norm.

14. The reader may note that in the middle 5-year period mortality showed an inexplicably sharp increase for the chronic health condition group.

References

Antonovsky, Aaron. 1979. "Implications of Socioeconomic Differentials in Mortality for the Health System." *Proceedings of the Meeting on Socioeconomic*

Determinants and Consequences of Mortality, Mexico City, June 19-25, 1979. 483502.

Belloc, Nedra B. 1982. "Personal Behavior Affecting Mortality." In Samuel H. Preston, *Biological and social aspects of mortality and the length of life*. Liege, Belgium: Ordina Editions, chap. 20.

Blau, Peter M., and Duncan, Otis Dudley. 1967. *The American Occupational Structure*. New York: Wiley.

Chase, Helen C. 1965. "White-Monwhite Mortality Differences in the United States." *Health, Education and Welfare Indicators*, June: 27-36.

Collins, John Gary. 1983. *Physicians' Visits: Volume and Interval Since Last Visit, United States, 1980*. Department of Health and Human Services. Series 10, No. 144. DHHS Pub. Number (PHS) 83-1572. Washington: U.S. Government Printing Office.

Kitagawa, E.M., and Hauser, P.M. 1973. *Differential Mortality in the United States*. Cambridge, Mass.: Harvard U.P.

Lerner, Monroe, and Stutz, Richard N. 1975. "Mortality Differentials Among Socioeconomic Strata in Baltimore, 1960 and 1973." *Proceedings of the Social Statistics Section, 1975 American Statistical Association*. 517-522.

———. 1976. "Socioeconomic Differentials in Mortality in Maryland, 1959-61 and 1969-71." *Proceedings of the Social Statistics Section, 1976. American Statistical Association*. 513-519.

———. 1977. "Have We Narrowed the Gaps Between the Poor and the Nonpoor?" *Medical Care* 15:8 (August): 620-635.

Manton, K.G.; Poss, S.S.; and Wing, S. 1979. "The Black-White Mortality Crossover: Investigation from the Perspective of the Components of Aging." *The Gerontologist* 19: 291-300.

Mott, Frank L., Haurin, R. Jean. 1981. "The Impact of Health Problems and Mortality on Family Well-Being." In Herbert S. Parnes, ed., *Work and Retirement, a Longitudinal Study of Men*. Cambridge, Mass.: MIT, chap. 7.

Nam, C.B.; Weatherby, N.L.; and Ockay, K.A. 1978. "Causes of Death which Contribute to the Mortality Crossover Effect." *Social Biology* 25: 306-314.

Ortmeyer, C.E. 1974. "Variations in Mortality, Morbidity, and Health Care by Marital Status." In C.L. Erhardt and J.E. Berlin, eds., *Mortality and Morbidity in the United States*. Cambridge, Mass.: Harvard U.P., chap. 7.

Sauer, Herbert I. 1974. "Geographic Variation in Mortality and Morbidity." In C.L. Erhardt and J.E. Berlin, eds., *Mortality and Morbidity in the United States*. Cambridge, Mass.: Harvard U.P., chap. 5.

———. 1980. *Geographic Patterns in the Risk of Dying and Associated Factors Ages 35-74 Years*. U.S. Dept. of Health and Human Services. Analytical Studies Series 3-Number 18. Washington, D.C.: U.S. Government Printing Office.

Siegel, Jacob S. 1980. "On the Demography of Aging." *Demography* 17: November, 345-364.

U.S. Department of Health, Education, and Welfare. 1970. *Mortality from Selected Causes by Marital Status, United States - Parts A and B*. National Center for Health Statistics Series 20 Numbers 8A and 8B. Washington, D.C.: U.S. Government Printing Office.

———. 1971. *Vital Statistics of the United States, 1968, Volume II — Section 5 Life Tables*. Washington, D.C.: U.S. Government Printing Office.

U.S. Department of Health and Human Services. 1981. *Vital Statistics of the United States, 1978, Volume II — Section 5 Life Tables*. Washington, D.C.: U.S. Government Printing Office.

———. 1982. *Vital Statistics of the United States, 1978, Volume II, Part A.* DHHS Pub. Number (PHS) 83-1101. Washington, D.C.: U.S. Government Printing Office.

———. 1983. *Americans Assess Their Health: United States 1978*. National Health Survey Series 10 Number 142. DHHS Pub. Number (PHS) 83-1570. Washington, D.C.: U.S. Government Printing Office.

Wilder, C.S. 1983. *Disability Days, United States 1980*. U.S. Department of Health and Human Services. Series 10 Number (PHS) 83-1571. Washington, D.C.: U.S. Government Printing Office.

3
The Volume and Pattern of Retirements, 1966–1981

Herbert S. Parnes
Lawrence J. Less

T his chapter has two purposes: the first is to explore alternative definitions of retirement, noting how the numbers and characteristics of retirees vary depending upon the operational definition that is used. Our second purpose is to classify retirements according to the circumstances under which they occur (i.e., the "reasons" for retirement), utilizing for this purpose the entire longitudinal record for each respondent prior to his retirement. Such a classification is useful not only for ascertaining the relative quantitative importance of the several reasons for retirement, but also for analyzing the experiences of retirees, because there is reason to believe that the quality of retirement will vary depending upon the factors that lead to it.

Alternative Measures of Retirement, 1966-1981

At one extreme the term *retirement* implies complete cessation of all labor market activity at some reasonably advanced age; at the other it connotes simply the receipt of Social Security or other pension income.[1] No matter how the term is defined, the extent of retirement in the 15 years after 1966 can be quantified from several perspectives. First, one can view the sample *prospectively* as of 1966 and inquire how many men between the ages of 45 and 59 in that year had retired by 1981. Alternatively, one can view the sample *retrospectively* as of 1981 and ask how many men 60-74 in that year had retired over the preceding 15 years. The difference between these two counts, of course, reflects the number of retired men who had died subsequent to their retirement by the time of the 1981 survey. From each perspective, we can (1) examine the retirement status of the men in each of the survey years or (2) classify them by retirement status "cumulatively"; that is, regarding as "retired" anyone who had satisfied the criterion of retirement at any time during the period. Because estimates of these kinds have not been available, we present the data in all these forms.

Figure 3-1 shows the size of the sample classified by race and age. Of the original 1966 sample of 5,020, 82 persons represented races other than black or white, leaving a total of 4,938 black and white men who were interviewed in 1966. Of these, 869 had disappeared from the sample by 1981, either because they refused to be interviewed or could not be traced. An additional 1,275 men had died, leaving 2,794 respondents who were interviewed in 1981. Because they are representative of the noninstitutionalized civilian population of white and black men age 60-74, the data should reflect rather faithfully both the incidence of retirement and the character of the retirement experience of men in that age range in 1981.

Figure 3-2 and table 3-1 summarize the retirement status of the 1966 sample in each survey year,[2] according to the three criteria described in chapter 1—(1) the individual's own perception of having stopped working at a regular job (subjective); (2) receipt of pension income (pension); and (3) working less than 1,000 hours during the year (participation). Several aspects of the data, some of which are not shown, deserve comment.

1. The proportion of the sample that is retired increases continuously and very substantially irrespective of which of the three criteria is used, from 12 percent or less in 1966 to about two-thirds in 1981.

2. In most years the pension criterion yields the highest measure of retirement and the subjective measure the lowest. The differences fluctuate somewhat erratically; between 1976 and 1981 the subjective and participation criteria produce almost identical proportions of retirees, while the proportion retired by the pension criterion is 4 or 5 percentage points higher.

3. There is a strong downward trend after 1973 in the ratio of men retired by one or two criteria to those retired by any criterion. The implication is that the passage of time strengthens the "signs" of retirement for many individuals, although we cannot be certain how much this reflects reality and how much it simply reflects lags in some of the data.

4. Subjectively reported retirement is almost never the sole indicator of the retired status. In no year did the proportion retired by their own perception but by no other criterion exceed 6 percent of those who were retired by any criterion. In contrast, the corresponding percentage for men retired only by the pension criterion exceeded 30 in 4 years and was never below 7; the percentage for men who were retired only by the labor force withdrawal criterion fell between these two values.

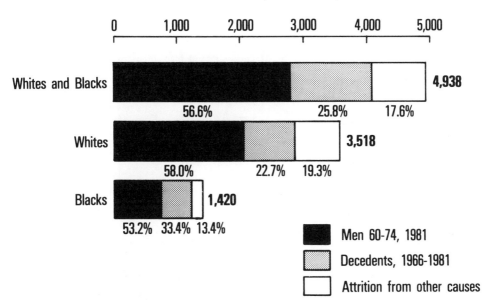

Figure 3–1. Components of NLS Sample in 1966, by Race and Status in 1981

We turn now to an examination of the "cumulative" retirement status of the men over the full 15-year period. In the first two bars of figure 3-3 each individual is classified according to whether he met any of the retirement criteria *at any time* during the period under review. The difference between the bar labeled "1966 sample" and the bar labeled "1981 sample—cumulative status" is that the former includes the men who died between 1966 and 1981 whereas the latter do not. The third bar in the graph shows the 1981 sample classified by their retirement status as of that year rather than by their cumulative retirement status.

The retirement status of four-fifths of the men can be defined unambiguously:[3] 60 percent of the 1966 sample were retired by all three criteria, and 19 percent were not retired by any. The status of the remaining 24 percent depends on the definition of retirement. Looking at this problem of definition in a somewhat different way, we can say that of the men in the 1966 sample who were retired by any criterion, about three-fourths were retired by all three; 14 percent by only one; and 12 percent by two. As was true of the annual data, the subjective criterion is least likely to occur in isolation: of all those retired by any criterion, only 2 percent were so classified on the basis of the subjective criterion alone.

Comparison of the second and third bars of the graph demonstrates dramatically that the count of the "retired" depends not only on what criterion of retirement is used, but also on whether "retirement" is con-

Percent

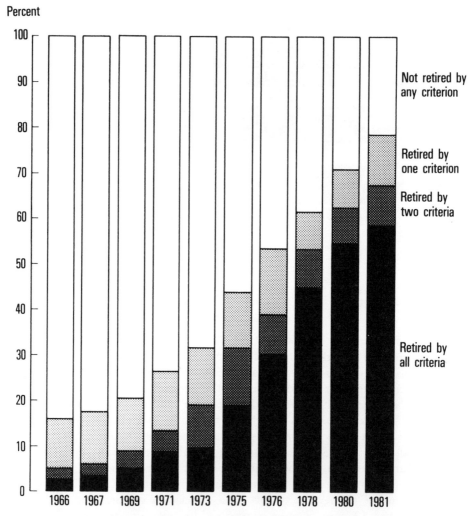

Figure 3–2. Retirement Status of Sample, by Survey Year, 1966–1981 (percentage distributions)

ceived as an event (i.e., "once retired, always retired") or a current status (i.e., "what is the individual doing in a particular year?"). From the former point of view, 86 percent of the 1981 sample had manifested retirement by at least one of our criteria at some time over the preceding 15 years, and two-thirds had retired by all three. However, if one asks how many *currently* met the retirement criteria as of the 1981 survey, the corresponding proportions are 79 and 59 percent.

Table 3–1
Percent of 1966 Sample Retired by Each Criterion and by Survey Year, 1966–1981

Criterion	1966	1967	1969	1971	1973	1975	1976	1978	1980	1981
Sample n[a]	4,083	3,961	3,793	3,653	3,488	3,328	3,221	3,051	2,871	2,794
Subjective	4.7	5.4	8.4	13.7	18.1	29.6	39.6	51.7	61.8	64.9
Participation	7.2	7.5	11.2	15.4	22.8	34.6	38.7	51.3	60.2	65.3
Pension	11.7	14.0	14.8	19.3	19.3	30.0	44.0	56.5	66.3	70.8

[a]The sample in 1966 includes all men interviewed in 1981 plus the decendents between 1966 and 1981. The reduction in sample size in the years after 1966 reflects primarily the number of deaths, but is also affected by the (relatively few) cases of men who were not interviewed in a particular year but who had reentered the sample by 1981.

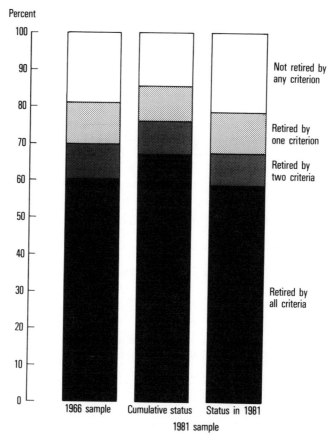

Figure 3–3. Retirement Status in 1981 of 1966 and 1981 Samples (percentage distributions)

Variations in Incidence of, and Age of, Retirement by Criterion of Retirement

Figure 3-4 breaks down the data on retirement status for the 1981 sample by race, age, and age at retirement for each of the three criteria in turn. The men are divided into two age categories, 60-64 and 65-74, to allow us to see the proportion of early retirees among a group of men all of whose members have achieved age 65. Measures of the incidence of retirement and the age at retirement differ somewhat depending on which definition of retirement is used. For retirement status, the pension criterion and the labor force withdrawal criterion produce quite comparable results. Overall, almost 70 percent of the sample is retired according to each of these criteria, and in three of the four age-race categories the two measures do not differ by more than two percentage

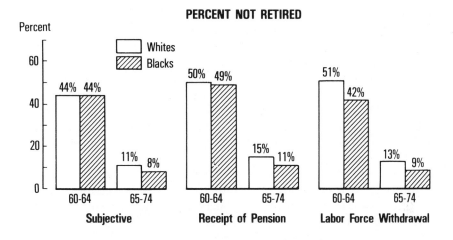

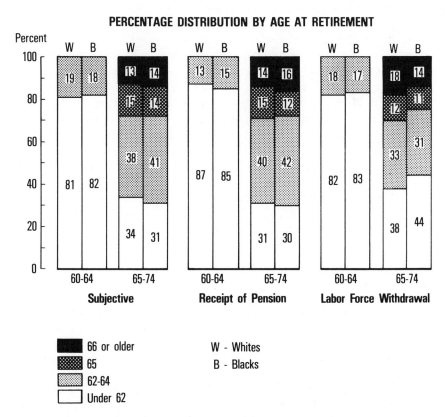

Figure 3–4. Percent of Men Not Retired in 1981 and Percentage Distribution of Retirees by Age at Retirement, by Criterion of Retirement and Race

points. Use of the subjective criterion yields a somewhat higher retirement rate—three-fourths overall. Among black men, however, the retirement rate as measured by labor force withdrawal is almost identical to that measured by the subjective criterion.

In interpreting the data on age at retirement, keep in mind that for each criterion the age at retirement is the age at which that criterion was first met. For example, consider a man who was 57 years old in 1966, who reported in 1967 that he "had already stopped working at a regular job," whose reported hours of labor force participation dropped below 1,000 for the first time in the 12 months preceding the 1973 survey, and who first received Social Security or pension income in the 12 months prior to the 1975 interview. This individual would be classified as retired by all three criteria, but his retirement age would be under 62 by the subjective criterion, between 62 and 64 by the labor force withdrawal criterion, and 65 by the pension criterion.

The receipt of pension income and the subjective criterion produce quite similar distributions of age at retirement for both white and black men. When the criterion is labor force withdrawal, a somewhat larger proportion of early retirements appears, especially among blacks. Of those members of the 1981 sample who had not yet achieved age 65, between 50 and 56 percent (depending on the criterion) had retired, but the vast majority of the retirees—four-fifths—had retired prior to age 62 by all three criteria. Depending on the criterion used, between 86 and 90 percent of those who had already reached age 65 had retired; among these the proportion of very early retirees (prior to age 62) was about one-third by the subjective criterion, a few percentage points lower by the pension criterion, and a few points higher by the labor force withdrawal criterion. All early retirements among this age group (i.e., retirement prior to age 65) accounted for between 70 and 73 percent of the total, depending on the criterion used.

Variation in Characteristics of Retirees, by Criterion of Retirement

To what extent do the characteristics of retirees differ depending upon how one defines retirement? One way to approach this issue would be to compare the characteristics of all men meeting one of the criteria with those of men meeting each of the other two in turn. The problem with this approach, however, is that the degree of overlap among the three criteria is so substantial that differences among them would be obscured. The alternative we have chosen is to compare the characteristics of men who are retired by only one criterion and by each combination of two criteria with those (the vast majority) who meet all three criteria and with nonretired men; that is, those who meet none of them (table 3-2).[4]

The disadvantage of this approach is that some of the categories have small sample sizes, making generalization hazardous; nevertheless, the smallest category contains 40 cases and the differences are generally sufficiently large that one can accept the figures with a reasonable degree of assurance.

The clearest and most striking conclusion to be drawn from table 3-2 is that men who are retired by all three criteria differ very profoundly from those who are retired on the basis of only one or two of them. They are, to begin with, an older group, and many of the other differences stem from this fact. Three-fourths of them are at least 65 years old (in 1981) as compared with proportions ranging between 23 and 58 percent for the other categories. Second, they are more likely than men in the other categories to have health problems. For instance, 2 out of every 10 report no physical or mental impairments as compared with 27 to 42 percent in the other categories of retirees.

Third, men retired by all three criteria are far less likely to be working in the postretirement period: only 6 percent worked as many as 1,000 hours in the 12 months prior to the 1981 survey, whereas the corresponding fractions in the other categories ranged between 32 and 99 percent. Median hours of work were only 640 for the all-criteria group, but not nearly that low in any other. Finally, their total family income is usually well below that of the other groups of retirees. Their median family income of $12,600 in 1980 compared with $29,620 for men retired on the basis of the subjective criterion and $19,721 for those retired on the basis of the subjective and labor force withdrawal criteria.

The impressive differences between the all-criteria retirees and those who are retired by less stringent standards should not obscure the differences within the latter group. As might be expected, those groups who meet the labor force withdrawal test—either alone or in combination with one other criterion—tend to suffer poorer health than those in other categories. Almost by definition they tend to work fewer hours[5] and consequently have lower family incomes. They also register lower degrees of satisfaction with life than the other groups. In all these respects they are closer than the men in the other three categories to the all-criteria retirees. It is at first surprising that the labor force withdrawal groups are, generally speaking, younger than the others, being closer in this respect to the nonretired men than to those who are retired by all three criteria. However, this age difference is doubtless explained by the large proportion of the group who withdraw due to disability (which can occur at any age) and whose pensions (if any are received) are in reality disability benefits.

Men retired by the pension criterion alone or in combination with subjective retirement are in the most enviable position among the retirees. They enjoy a median family income four-fifths higher than the all-

Table 3–2
Selected Characteristics of Nonretired Men and of Retired Men, by Criterion of Retirement, through Survey Year 1981

Characteristic	Not Retired by Any Criterion	Retired: All Criteria	Retired: Only One			Retired: Two Criteria		
			Pension Income	Labor Force Withdrawal	Subjective	Pension Income and Labor Force Withdrawal	Pension Income and Subjective	Subjective and Labor Force Withdrawal
Sample *n*	384	1,888	168	61	42	59	152	40
Total population (thousands)	1,606	7,456	716	191	164	221	642	142
Percent black	7	8	6	15	8	8	5	12
Percent 60–64	82	23	58	77	74	42	53	75
Percent with health limitations, 1981	20	63	34	43	38	52	32	63
Percent with no impairments, 1981	49	20	34	34	42	31	37	27
Percent with substantial or severe impairment, 1981	24	59	41	42	38	48	39	45
Median hours worked, 1981:[a] men with work experience	2,080	640	2,080	1,835	2,003	1,121	1,763	882
Percent working less than 1,000 hours, 1981[a]	1	94	1	31	3	44	11	68
Percent working more than 2,000 hours, 1981[a]	84	1	77	42	48	29	38	14

Median family income, 1980 (dollars)	26,000	12,600	22,244	19,004	29,620	17,502	22,436	19,721
Percent with family income less than $10,000, 1980	7	39	9	17	1	31	12	51
Satisfaction with life, 1981								
Percent very happy	54	50	57	50	54	49	58	50
Percent unhappy	3	8	2	8	4	5	6	3

aPast 12 months.

criteria retirees, and substantially above the other groups except those retired only by the subjective criterion. Their health is also significantly better, although perceptibly worse than that of nonretired men. They are more likely to say they are very happy with life. Interestingly, the only important differences between men retired by the pension income criterion alone and those who also acknowledge retirement (subjective criterion) is that the latter group is older than the former and is less likely to be in the labor force on a full-time, full-year basis (over 2,000 hours).

From several points of view the most curious group of retirees are those who meet only the subjective criterion—the smallest of any of the categories. They are a relatively young group and enjoy relatively good health. They are quite likely to be working: only 3 percent worked fewer than 1,000 hours in the 12 months preceding the 1981 survey, and about half worked in excess of 2,000 hours. As a consequence, even without pension income their total family income was substantially higher than that of any other group—$29,620. It seems likely that this group includes a disproportionately large number of individuals who as a result of a job (and perhaps career) change after a long period of service in a job, were able to report at some time between 1966 and 1981 that they had "already stopped working at their regular job."

Reasons for Retirement

Most studies that have attempted to ascertain the factors responsible for individual retirement decisions have simply asked retirees to explain why they retired. This approach not only risks the dangers of post hoc rationalization—for instance, the explanation of an early retirement on the basis of poor health because it is a respectable excuse for leaving the labor market—but it also risks finding differences in answers legitimately given by persons whose circumstances and motives at time of retirement were identical. Imagine two individuals covered by mandatory retirement who retire at the mandatory age, neither of whom has any desire to work any longer. If later queried about their retirement, one might legitimately respond "I had to," wheras the other might say "I was tired of working." Where health is at issue, the problem is especially complicated. Consider, for instance, three equally arthritic painters, one of whom has only Social Security to look forward to in retirement, the second of whom has additional private pension coverage, and the third of whom is identical to the second except that he detests his job. If all three retire and are asked the reason, "bad health," "good pension," and "disliked job" are, respectively, equally honest and legitimate responses.

Because of its longitudinal design, the NLS data set allows us to classify the reasons for retirement without relying on the retrospective interpretations of the respondents. Instead, the reason for retirement is based upon the longitudinal record of each respondent *prior* to his retirement. We used this approach first in analyzing retirements that had occurred by 1976, and our comparison of the results with retrospective responses of the members of the sample "reinforced our a priori view that retrospectively reported reasons for retirement are suspect" (Parnes and Nestel, 1981, p. 162). The classification used here is identical to that employed in the earlier study, with the addition of one new category, "discouraged retirees."

The basic categories of reasons for retirement are four: (1) persons who were *involuntarily* retired under a mandatory retirement plan (mandatory); (2) those whose retirement appears from the total record to have been dictated by poor health (health); (3) individuals whose retirement appears to have been attributable to labor market adversities (discouragement); and (4) the remainder; that is, men who appear to have freely chosen retirement (voluntary). The latter group is subdivided into those who retired prior to age sixty-five (early retirement) and those who retired at that age or later (normal retirement).[6]

We have included in the mandatory group only a subset of men who were covered by mandatory plans: namely, those who retired at the mandatory age *and* who had reported in the survey preceding retirement that they would have preferred to work longer.[7] In other words, in the absence of evidence that retirement was induced by poor health, we regard as voluntary retirees men under a mandatory plan who retire before they have to, or at the mandatory age if they have reported no desire to work longer. Retirees who do not qualify for inclusion in the mandatory retirement group are classified as having retired for health reasons if evidence of work-limiting health problems is found in the year preceding retirement.[8]

The "discouraged" category is the only one for which we have made some use of the retrospective reason for retirement reported by the respondents in 1981. Specifically, we have included in this group (1) men not already classified as mandatory or health retirees who reported in 1981 that "loss of job and/or no job opportunities" was the reason for their retirement and for whom the longitudinal record contained confirming evidence,[9] and (2) men who reported in the year of retirement or the preceding year a period out of the labor force attributable to inability to find work. This set of criteria eliminated approximately one-third of the persons who would have been included on the basis of their retrospective response alone, but added others, so that the total of 107 respondents is actually about 15 percent above the number yielded by the retrospective response.

Figure 3-5 shows the distribution of the retirees by reason for retirement and by year of retirement. As would be expected due to the aging of the sample, recent retirements—those between 1976 and 1981—account for about half of the total. One in 10 occurred between 1966 and 1970 and about two-fifths between 1970 and 1975. Overall, only 3 percent of the retirees were unwillingly removed from jobs by the operation of mandatory retirement plans. A somewhat larger proportion—5 percent—appear to have retired as a consequence of labor market adversity. Far more important than both of these factors combined in "forcing" individuals into retirement is poor health, accounting for 35

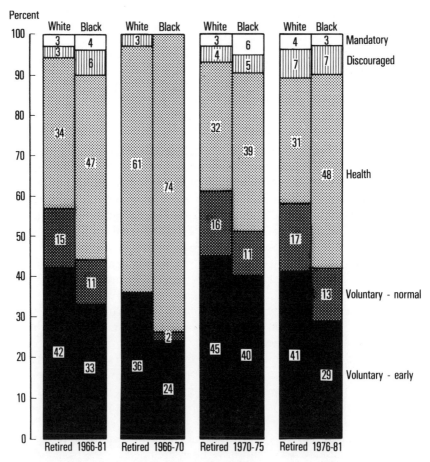

Note: Men who retired prior to 1966 are excluded because there is no basis for ascertaining the reason for their retirement.

Figure 3–5. Distribution of Retirees by Reason for Retirement, Calendar Year of Retirement, and Race (percentage distributions)

percent of the total. A majority of the retirees—almost three-fifths of the total—seem to have retired truly voluntarily. A pronounced racial difference appears, however, in reasons for retirement: Blacks are much more likely than whites to have retired for health reasons (47 vs. 34 percent), and a correspondingly smaller proportion of black retirements were truly voluntary.

Health retirements were considerably more prominent in the earliest time period than in either of the subsequent ones. The reason, of course, is the aging of the sample over time; that is, in the earliest period all of the men were still under age 65 when health problems loomed large as a reason for retirement. For the same reason mandatory retirements also were less important prior to 1970 than later, because 65 was the lowest age of mandatory retirement for 95 percent of men covered by such plans (Parnes, 1970, pp. 175-76). Finally, the same factor accounts for the substantial rise in the proportion of "normal" voluntary retirements over the 15-year period. This aging effect is shown clearly in figure 3-6, which distributes the 1981 retirees by age at retirement and reason for retirement. Whereas 47 percent of those who retired prior to age 62 did so because of poor health, the corresponding proportion of those who retired at age 62 or older was only one-fourth. Figure 3-6 also shows that even when attention is focused on the minority of men who retired at age 65 or older, only 1 in 11 was forced out of a job by mandatory retirement rules.

Several factors must be kept in mind in interpreting the distribution of retirees by reason for retirement. First, with respect to the "discouraged" category, the system of priorities used in the classification allowed individuals to fall into that group only if they did not meet the criteria for "mandatory" or "health" retirement. Of a total of 178 respondents who would have met the requirements for "discouraged" retirement, 67 were excluded because they had been classified in either the "mandatory" or "health" categories. Second, a less restrictive test of discouragement would obviously have increased the number of persons in this category. The most liberal definition that we considered—which would have classified as discouraged (in addition to those already included) all individuals with any unemployment in the year of retirement or the preceding year—would have yielded a count of 355 sample cases, slightly more than 3 times the current number. With this definition (which appears unrealistically "liberal" to us) the proportion of discouraged retirees would be increased to about 15 percent and voluntary retirements would be reduced to 46 percent of the total.

Third, a conceptual problem arises in differentiating retirement for health reasons from "voluntary" retirement. Because very few disabilities or health problems entirely preclude all types of labor market activity, retirement for health reasons is almost always in some sense "voluntary."

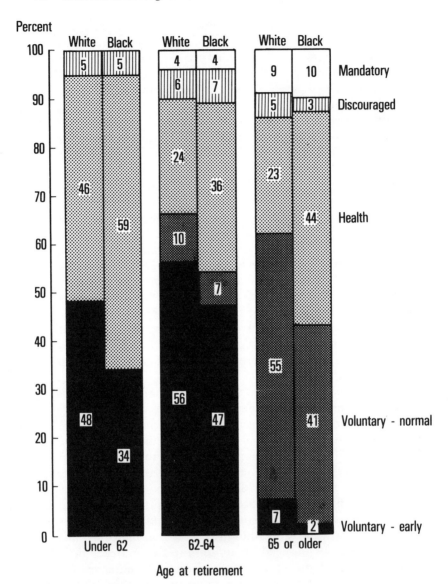

Figure 3–6. Distribution of Retirees by Reason for Retirement, Age at Retirement, and Race

This ambiguity in "reason for retirement," it should be noted, is independent of the means by which the "reason" is ascertained. Even if we were able to rely on the evidence of complete medical examinations, we would still have to decide where to draw the line between those who "had" to retire because of bad health and those who "chose to" (or should be allowed to) because of the increasing discomfort of work. If one chooses to rely on the retiree's perception of why he retired, the difficulties are even greater, because, as has been noted, different answers can legitimately be given by persons whose health conditions are identical.

Our method of differentiating the "health retirements" from the "voluntary retirements" is admittedly arbitrary. It has the advantage of relying on responses to questions asked prior to retirement and in contexts other than an explanation of the retirement decision. Nevertheless, it cannot be claimed to provide a thoroughly clean line of demarcation between the two groups of retirees, and for this reason one needs to be wary about using the percentages uncritically to indicate the proportion of retirees whose health "forced" them out of the labor market. The best that can be said is that even though there may be some overlap in objective health condition between those we have classified as the "health retirees" and the voluntary category, on average they are very distinct groups. Our analysis of postretirement experience in chapter 5 will make this clear; in the meantime, other evidence, namely the relation between the retirement categories and the detailed measures of physical and mental impairments in the 1981 interview schedule, tends to create confidence in the classification.

Figure 3-7 shows the distribution of men who had retired prior to the 1981 survey, cross-classified by our reason for retirement and by an index of impairment based on the 1981 data. Although one-third of the voluntary retirees reported no impairments, only 5 percent of those in the health retirement group reported none; and in contrast to the 73 percent of the health retirees with substantial impairment, only 26 percent of the early voluntary retirees and 24 percent of those who retired at 65 or later were so disadvantaged.

Conclusion

How many men between the ages of 60 and 74 were retired in 1981? The answer depends substantially on what "test" of retirement one uses and upon whether one views retirement as a permanent state or considers the concept as relating to *current* status, allowing individuals to move into and out of the category. That the measures vary according to the definition should not be surprising, but our data permit for the first time a quantification of these differences in the count of retirees as well as in their characteristics.

The NLS data base has permitted the use of three quite distinct cri-

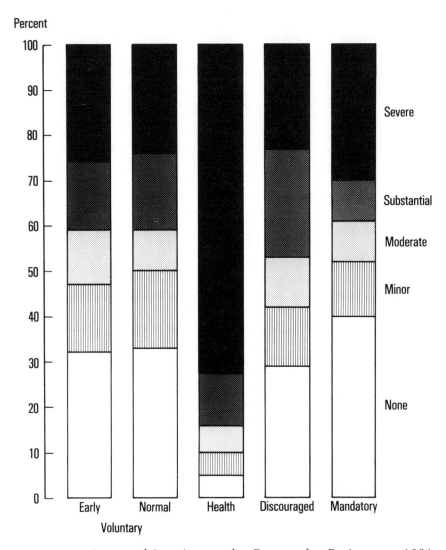

Figure 3–7. Extent of Impairment, by Reason for Retirement, 1981 (percentage distributions)

teria of retirement, either alone or in combination: (1) a response of "already stopped" to the query "at what age do you expect to stop working at your regular job?", (2) reported receipt of pension (including disability) income, and (3) partial or complete withdrawal from the labor force.

To give some idea of orders of magnitude, if one defines as retired a person who at any time during the preceding 15 years met any of these criteria, the count was about 9.5 million (85.6 percent of all men 60-74 in 1981). If, on the other hand, one requires that the individual have satisfied one of the criteria in the year in question (i.e., 1981) the number is 8.7 million (78.5 percent). If all criteria of retirement must be met, the corresponding figures are 7.5 or 6.5 million, depending upon whether retirement is viewed as an event or a status. Thus, the number of men age 60-74 who were retired in 1981 ranges from 6.5 to 9.5 million, depending on one's meaning—a spread of 44 percent on the smaller base.

Among the three criteria used as single alternatives, the differences are not nearly so great. For instance, on the cumulative basis the range was between 8.0 million and 9.0 million retirees, using the labor force withdrawal criterion and the pension income criterion respectively, and on the current status basis the spread was even smaller. As these data suggest, there is substantial overlap among the three criteria: almost 80 percent of the men who are retired by any criterion are retired by all three. Nonetheless, pronounced differences appear between those retired by all three criteria and those retired by only one or two. The former tend to be older, in poorer health, less likely to be working, and less well off both economically and psychologically.

Age at retirement varies somewhat depending upon the criterion used. For instance, among retirees between the ages of 65 and 74 in 1981, the proportion who had retired prior to age 65 ranged between 72 percent (subjective retirees) and 70 percent (labor force withdrawal). Among the subjective retirees in this age group 34 percent had retired very early (prior to 62), 15 percent at age 65, and 13 percent at higher ages.

On the basis of these findings, is it possible to suggest an optimal definition of retirement? The answer is No: the criteria of retirement necessarily depend upon the purpose of the analysis. For example, on the issue of retirement-as-an-event versus retirement-as-a-status, if one opts for the latter it becomes meaningless to ask about postretirement labor market activity. On the other hand, this concept of retirement does permit the "tracking" of individuals and the determination of the extent of movement into and out of retirement. Each of the three criteria of retirement has advantages and disadvantages. Using the pension income criterion results in excluding middle-aged individuals who are forced out of the labor market by poor health without qualifying for retirement or disability benefits, thus presenting a more sanguine view of the circumstances of retired individuals than reality warrants. Use of the labor force withdrawal criterion understates the extent of postretirement labor market activity. Using a subjective criterion perhaps relies too heavily upon self-perception and gives insufficient weight to objective conditions.

In the remainder of this book, we have chosen to view retirement as an event rather than as a current status. Moreover, the criterion of retirement will be the subjective one. In other words, the distinction between the retired and the nonretired will hinge on whether the respondent ever reported having "stopped working at a regular job." Our choice rests on several considerations. First, of all the single criteria, the subjective measure has the greatest overlap with the others. Of men classified as retired by the subjective criterion, less than 3 percent are not also retired by one or both of the other criteria. Second, we believe that the self-perceived status is the most meaningful criterion of retirement in a study that aims to determine the adequacy of postretirement income and the extent of postretirement labor market activity: to use receipt of pension income and/or withdrawal from the labor market as a criterion would be to define the criterion variable in terms of the outcome measure.

Reasons for (subjective) retirement have been ascertained on the basis of the total longitudinal records of the retirees. Although our methods and criteria are admittedly to some degree arbitrary, they have a distinct advantage over retrospective responses of the retirees.

Of the nearly 8.5 million men age 60-74 in 1981 who had retired over the preceding 15 years, fewer than 5 percent had been unwillingly removed from jobs by mandatory retirement rules. A liberal estimate of the proportion who were discouraged by labor market adversity is perhaps twice as large—about 10 percent. Of considerably greater importance than both of these combined in forcing men into retirement is poor health, which accounted for about one-third of all retirements, and almost half of retirements by black men. The majority of retirements, then, appear to be voluntary, and most of these take place prior to age 65. These categories will be used in subsequent chapters to explore variations in the postretirement experience.

Notes

1. Although the problems that this ambiguity creates for measuring and analyzing retirement have been recognized (Atchley, 1976, p. 7; Gustman and Steinmeier, 1981, p. 11), only two empirical studies (Gustman and Steinmeier, 1981; Murray, 1979) have come to our attention that deal with the matter, and neither of these focuses primarily on the effects of alternative definitions on the numbers and characteristics of retirees.

2. The 1968 survey year is omitted, since the brief mailed questionnaire used in that year does not permit classification by all of the criteria.

3. It is interesting that in a somewhat comparable study based on the Social Security Administration's Retirement History Study, Murray (1979, p. 3) found a roughly comparable proportion (about 70 percent) of cases in 1975 in which there was consistency among the three criteria of retirement (defined somewhat differently from the definitions in this study).

4. Because of small sample size, race and age breakdowns are not particularly meaningful. Although table 3-2 presents only the totals for each category of retirees, we have examined tabulations with race-age breakdowns and find no basis for concluding that the patterns differ substantially from those manifested by the aggregates.

5. It should be recalled that men in this category are not necessarily withdrawn (wholly or partly) from the labor force in 1981; it is necessary only for them to have met this criterion at some time between 1966 and 1981.

6. The early retirees also include men covered by a mandatory plan who retired prior to the prescribed age; normal retirements include men who retired at the mandatory age and who had previously indicated no desire to work longer.

7. In each survey respondents were asked if they were covered by a mandatory retirement plan. Those who responded affirmatively were asked what the mandatory age was and "would you work longer than that if you could?" Persons who responded "yes" were classified in the mandatory retirement group if they retired at the mandatory age.

8. Specifically, this category includes men who (a) reported poor health as the reason for having left their preretirement job, (b) reported poor health as the reason for absence from the labor force in the 12-month period prior to the report of retirement, (c) revised their expected age of retirement downward for health reasons in the survey preceding retirement, (d) specified poor health as the reason for not seeking work either in the year of retirement or in the preceding year, (e) reported an inability to work in the survey in which retirement was first reported or in the preceding survey, or (f) reported a work-limiting health problem in each of the *two* surveys preceding the survey in which retirement was reported. Very few respondents fell into the health retirement category solely by virtue of this last criterion.

9. Specifically, we required that the longitudinal record show either an involuntary separation from preretirement job or some unemployment in the year of retirement or in the preceding year.

References

Atchley, Robert C. 1976. *The Sociology of Retirement*. New York: Schenkman Publishing Co.

Gustman, Adam L. and Steinmeier, Thomas L. 1981. "Partial Retirement and the Analysis of Retirement Behavior." Working Paper No. 763. Cambridge, Mass.: National Bureau of Economic Research.

Murray, Janet. 1979. "Subjective Retirement." *Social Security Bulletin*. 42: 20-25.

Parnes, Herbert S., et al. 1970. *The Preretirement Years, Vol. 1*. U.S. Department of Labor Manpower Administration. Manpower Research Mimeograph No. 15. Washington, D.C.: Government Printing Office.

Parnes, Herbert S. and Nestel, Gilbert. 1981. "The Retirement Experience." In H.S. Parnes, ed., *Work and Retirement: A Longitudinal Study of Men*. Cambridge, Mass.: MIT.

4

Retirement Expectation and the Timing of Retirement

Gilbert Nestel

Introduction

The 15 years during which men in the NLS sample were making decisions about their work lives was also a period in which legislative changes were altering their retirement benefits and access to jobs. The erosion of Social Security benefits because of unanticipated inflation was halted by increases in benefits in 1968, 1970, and 1974. The net effect of this legislation was to increase benefits between 1966 and 1981 by 23 percent more than the rise in consumer prices: a $1.00 benefit in 1966 increased to $3.46 in June 1981 (Social Security Administration, 1982) while consumer prices rose to 2.8 times their 1966 level in the same period (U.S. Department of Labor, 1982). Major Social Security legislation passed in 1972 and 1977 further affected the amount these men would contribute and expect to receive in the future. Men eligible for private pension income were more certain of receiving these benefits because of the Employee Retirement Income Security Act enacted in 1974 which safeguarded the solvency of their plans and established guidelines for eligibility and benefits. The period was marked, however, by heated discussions about the adequacy of the Social Security Trust funds. Questions about shortfalls surfaced and were debated in Congress and in the media, thereby introducing some uncertainty about the amount of future benefits.

These men were also making decisions about work in a period of limited growth in real output and high levels of joblessness. Unemployment rates exceeding 6 percent became the norm in the late 1970s, with an impact on almost all economic subgroups in the society. However, workers could no longer be discharged solely because of age with the passage of the Age Discrimination in Employment Act of 1967.

The increase in the labor force participation rate of married women in this 15-year period also affected men's work decisions. Whereas about 31 percent of married women age 55-64 were employed or sought employment in 1966, by 1981 their rate of participation had risen to 36.5 percent, a 14-percent increase. Labor force participation increased even

The expert programming assistance of Karin Tracy is warmly appreciated.

more dramatically among married women in the 45-54 age range; their rate rose by 30 percent—from 44.9 to 58.0 percent.

Changes in life expectancy were also significant. Health care coverage continued to expand, and advances in the quality of medical care and in the pre-vention of disease led to further improvement in longevity. In 1966 a male age 60 could expect to live about 15.8 additional years, but by 1981 the expected life span of a 60-year-old man was 17.5 years, an increase of 1.7 years, or more than 10 percent (Social Security Administration, Office of the Actuary, 1982).

Against this ever-changing environment and changes in personal circumstances the men under consideration here made decisions about retirement. The net effect of their choices was to reduce the labor force participation rate of men age 55-64 from 84.5 to 70.6 percent between 1966 and 1981. This decline was even more substantial for nonwhites in the same age range: their participation rate declined from 81.1 to 63.3 percent (U.S. Department of Labor, 1982). Here we document the trend toward earlier retirement of this age cohort of men, and examine the relationship between their expected age of retirement and the ages at which retirement actually occurred.

The reliability of expectation as a predictor of actual retirement is related to the age at which the expectation is measured. Men who are relatively young when asked when they expect to retire report earlier ages, on the average, than older men. Part of this difference is explained by the tendency of men at younger ages to discount completely the uncertain future and to assume that personal circumstances will continue to be favorable for an early retirement. If these expectations are not fulfilled as the individual ages, the expected retirement age he reports is revised accordingly and the age of actual retirement is likewise affected. To reduce this dependency of expectations on age, our sample is restricted to never-retired men who are age 59 in the year in which their expectation is recorded.[1] All men interviewed in 1981 would have reached age 59 in one of the survey years; among the deceased, some would have attained it before death.

Expected Age of Retirement

Table 4-1 highlights the increasing trend toward early retirement as reflected in the expectations of men who were approaching retirement age. Fewer than 3 in 10 (27 percent) white men age 59 interviewed in 1981 expected to re-tire before age 65 when they were asked in 1966; when another cohort of 59-year-olds were asked their expectations in 1980, about 4 in 10 (37 percent) expected to retire early. The corre-

Table 4–1
Expected Age of Retirement at Age 59, by Race and Survey Year When Age 59 Was Attained—Men Interviewed in 1981
(percentage distributions)

Expectation	Total[a]	1966	1967[b]	1969	1971	1973	1975	1976	1978	1980
Whites										
Sample *n*	1,692	101	193	217	241	229	127	235	253	93
Total percent	100	100	100	100	100	100	100	100	100	100
Prior to age 62	9	4	7	7	7	10	8	15	9	7
62–64	26	23	15	21	24	26	29	33	35	30
65	31	32	37	35	41	26	30	29	24	26
66 and older	5	12	6	6	3	2	1	6	5	6
Never retire	15	15	18	18	16	17	16	10	13	12
Don't know	14	14	18	14	9	18	16	8	16	19
Mean age[d]	65.7	66.7	66.8	66.4	65.8	65.6	65.5	64.6	65.1	65.4
Blacks										
Sample *n*	605	36	61	97	78	97	41	88	81	24
Total percent	100	100	100	100	100	100	100	100	100	100
Prior to age 62	7	2	7	2	6	8	0	6	11	c
62–64	27	13	18	17	34	33	37	30	28	c
65	29	53	27	42	39	23	26	27	19	c
66 and older	3	0	6	6	2	1	0	6	6	c
Never retire	14	22	31	22	12	10	0	6	13	c
Don't know	20	10	11	12	7	25	37	25	24	c
Mean age[d]	65.5	66.9	67.8	67.1	65.0	64.5	63.2	64.5	65.3	c

[a]Includes men attaining age 59 in 1981, for whom the number of cases is too small for separate analysis.
[b]Includes men attaining age 59 in 1968.
[c]Less than 25 sample cases.
[d]Age 75 assigned to "never retire" response.

sponding rates for blacks was about 1 in 7 (15 percent) in 1966 and about 4 in 10 (39 percent) in 1978. No evidence of a racial difference appears when one considers all cohorts of age 59 men; about 1 in 3 whites and blacks expected to retire before they reached their sixty-fifth birthday.

A significant shift to an earlier retirement expectation began in the 1970s. In the middle and late 1960s, fewer than 3 in 10 men expected to retire prior to age 65. By the early 1970s, however, this proportion had exceeded 3 in 10, and by the middle of the decade it exceeded 4 in 10. This table also highlights the strong expected lifetime attachment to the work force of some 59-year-old men, as well as the considerable uncertainty of others about the dating of their retirements. At age 59 about 1 in 7 white and black men had no intention of ever leaving the work force, and about 1 in 7 whites and 1 in 5 blacks were uncertain about when they would retire. The latter finding is particularly interesting, because many of these men will have retired during the subsequent 3-to-5-year period.

Men who died after their fifty-ninth birthday were less likely at that age to expect to retire early than those who were still alive in 1981 (table 4-2). These men were also more likely than their surviving counterparts to expect never to retire. The differences were more apparent among blacks: among those blacks who died by 1981 about 1 in 5 (22 percent) anticipated working indefinitely. The corresponding proportion for those surviving in 1981 was about 1 in 7, or 14 percent. Differences in expectations among the whites were similar, but not nearly so large.

Age at Retirement

The trend toward early retirement observed in the expected age of retirement is also evident in the data on the actual ages at which these men retired. Table 4-3 summarizes the retirement status by 1981 of each cohort of 59-year-old men and, for the retirees, the distribution of their retirement ages. The further restriction of this table to the 1966-1975 cohorts of 59-year-olds insures that these men would have attained the conventional retirement age (65) by their 1981 interviews and provides a more meaningful estimate of the proportion who retired at an earlier age.

Among those interviewed in 1981, blacks were as likely as whites to have retired and to have done so prior to age 65. About 7 in 10 men in each racial group reported a retirement, and about 3 in 4 of these were early. Among the early retirees whites were more likely than their black counterparts to have retired prior to age 62 (45 vs. 36 percent). These

Table 4–2

Expected Age at Retirement at Age 59: Survey Year in Which Age 59 Was Attained—Men Who Died by 1981
(percentage distributions)

Expectation	Total[a]	1966	1967[b]	1969	1971	1973
			Whites			
Sample *n*	408	67	83	89	67	60
Total percent	100	100	100	100	100	100
Prior to age 62	5	2	4	7	6	9
62–64	22	15	21	11	28	36
65	33	41	39	33	35	24
66 or older	6	9	6	8	7	0
Never retire	18	19	24	20	15	15
Don't know	16	14	6	21	9	16
Mean age[c]	66.5	67.9	67.0	67.1	66.0	65.0
			Blacks			
Sample *n*	229	38	51	51	38	26
Total percent	100	100	100	100	100	100
Prior to age 62	4	0	3	8	3	4
62–64	16	10	14	16	14	18
65	43	55	41	41	45	24
66 and older	4	6	4	3	3	0
Never retire	22	17	29	26	32	8
Don't know	12	12	9	7	4	47
Mean age[c]	67.0	67.5	67.7	67.0	67.9	65.0

[a]Includes the 1975–1981 cohorts of men attaining age 59; in 1975–1981 the sample size was less than 25 cases.

[b]Includes nonretired 59-year-old men in survey year 1968.

[c]Age 75 assigned to "never retire" response.

conclusions are not significantly altered if the universe is restricted to the 1966-1975 cohorts of 59-year-olds, all of whom reached their sixty-fifth birthdays by the 1981 interview (not shown). Blacks and whites continue to be equally likely to retire in the period (about 9 in 10) and no racial differences appear in the proportion of men who retire early. Blacks continue to be less likely than whites to retire very early.

The movement toward early retirement can be seen from table 4-3 either by noting the proportion of men who retire early or by noting their mean age at retirement. In each case we follow cohorts of 59-year-old men from the survey year they attained that age until the 1981 interview date. On the basis of each criterion it is clear that the more recent cohorts of 59-year-old men were retiring at an earlier age than men who were age 59 in the mid to late 1960s. For example, half of the white retirees in the 1966 cohort did so prior to age 65; the corresponding

Table 4–3
Retirement Status and Age at Retirement among Men Interviewed in 1981, by Race and Survey Year When Age 59 Was Attained
(percentage distributions)

Status and Age	Total[a]	1966	1967[b]	1969	1971	1973	1975	1976	1978
Whites									
Sample *n*	1,692	101	193	217	241	229	127	235	253
Percent retired	71	95	90	93	91	86	66	59	35
Age at retirement									
Total percent	100	100	100	100	100	100	100	100	100
58–61	33	8	21	32	26	33	40	57	78
62–64	41	44	39	37	51	41	51	43	22
65	14	21	17	23	12	20	9	0	0
66 and older	12	26	24	18	11	6	0	0	0
Mean age	62.9	64.6	64.0	63.8	63.0	62.7	62.1	61.2	60.6
Blacks									
Sample *n*	605	36	61	97	78	97	41	88	81
Percent retired	73	97	92	91	90	88	81	57	28
Age at retirement									
Total percent	100	100	100	100	100	100	100	100	100
58–61	27	7	11	21	19	29	18	43	c
62–64	47	54	42	50	56	41	53	57	c
65	13	7	19	11	10	21	30	0	c
66 and older	14	33	28	18	15	8	0	0	c
Mean age	63.1	64.5	64.5	63.4	63.2	62.9	63.0	61.6	c

[a]Includes men attaining age 59 in 1980 and 1981.
[b]Includes men attaining age 59 in 1968.
[c]Less than 25 sample cases.

percentage for the 1973 cohort, all of whom would have reached age 65 by 1981, was more than 7 in 10—an increase of more than 20 percentage points. The black retirees in the same two years show an increase from 61 percent in 1966 to 70 percent in 1973. These differences are exaggerated to some extent because there were fewer nonretirees in 1966 than in 1973 (about 5 percent and 14 percent, respectively). However, since each of these nonretirees had attained his sixty-fifth birthday by the 1981 interview date, their age at retirement in all cases will exceed age 65. If we assign these men to the oldest retirement age category and recompute the percent who retired before age 65 in 1966 and 1973, the white percentage increases from 50 to 64 percent and for the blacks the percentages are 60 and 63 percent, respectively. On this basis convincing evidence of a strong trend toward early retirement still appears among whites, but for blacks the evidence is less conclusive.

The corresponding data for the 59-year-old men who did not survive this 15-year period indicate rates of early retirement as great as those prevailing among survivors (table 4-4). Overall about half of these men had retired before death; blacks were about 5 percentage points more likely than white decedents to have retired (55 percent and 50 percent, respectively). Of those who had retired, 3 in 4 white and black decedents retired before age 65 but blacks were somewhat more likely than whites to retire after age 65. The decedents were not any more likely than their counterparts who were alive in 1981 to have retired early; among whites the corresponding percentages are 77 and 74 percent. Among blacks about 78 percent of the decedents retired early compared to 74 percent of those who survived to 1981.

Expectations Versus Actual Retirements

Table 4-5 summarizes the retirement status of respondents in 1981 for different retirement expectation categories at age 59. Tabulations are also provided to show the proportion of men who retired as planned. The latter tables exclude nonretired men who by 1981 (last interview preceding death) were still age-eligible to retire at their expected retirement age; that is, their chronological ages at these dates were less than their expected ages at retirement. Men who were uncertain initially about when they would retire are also omitted, but those who expressed an intention to work indefinitely (never retire) and subsequently retired are included among those who changed their expectation.

A number of generalizations can be gleaned from table 4-5. First, as would be expected, there is an inverse association, particularly among whites, between the expected age of retirement and the likelihood of

Table 4–4
Retirement Status in Survey Year Prior to Death and Age at Retirement of Decedents Who Attained Age 59 between 1966 and 1973, by Race and Year in Which Man Attained Age 59
(percentage distributions)

Status and Age	Total[a]	1966	1967[b]	1969	1971	1973
			Whites			
Sample *n*	408	67	83	89	67	60
Percent retired	50	53	66	50	51	43
Age at retirement						
Total percent	100	100	100	100	100	100
58–61	40	28	27	36	52	61
62–64	37	22	48	42	33	39
65	19	38	23	19	12	0
66 and older	4	12	2	2	3	0
Mean age	62.4	63.6	62.9	62.4	61.9	61.0
			Blacks			
Sample *n*	229	38	51	51	38	26
Percent retired	55	55	70	72	49	44
Age at retirement						
Total percent	100	100	100	100	100	100
58–61	30	c	14	30	c	c
62–64	48	c	61	44	c	c
65	11	c	7	19	c	c
66 and older	11	c	19	8	c	c
Mean age	62.7	c	63.2	62.8	c	c

[a]Includes 1975 and 1976 age cohorts.
[b]Includes 1968 age cohort.
[c]Less than 25 sample cases.

being retired by 1981; for blacks the relationship is less distinct. These generalizations apply to men of all ages in 1981 as well as to those who were at least age 65 in that year. Second, more than half the men who at age 59 were uncertain about the timing of their retirements, or who expected to continue a lifetime attachment to the work force, had retired by 1981. Third, irrespective of expectations, men who died during the 15-year period were less likely than those interviewed in 1981 to have retired.

Turning to the degree of consistency between expected and actual age of retirement, we find that men who expected to retire at younger ages are the most likely to have retired as expected (table 4-6). Overall about 3 in 10 white men and 1 in 4 black men interviewed in 1981 retired as expected; that is, their retirement ages fell in the same age category as their expected ages at retirement. A similar calculation for men who expected to retire at ages 58-61 showed that 7 in 10 white

Table 4–5
Percent of Men Retired, by Expectation at Age 59, Interview Status in 1981, Age in 1981, and Race

| | Interviewed | | | | Decedent | |
| | All Ages | | Age 65 and Over | | | |
Expectation	Sample *n*	Percent	Sample *n*	Percent	Sample *n*	Percent
	Whites					
Total	1,692	71	1,110	88	408	50
58–61	141	91	81	99	20	a
62–64	450	74	255	94	87	63
65	518	72	373	90	134	51
66–70	60	59	36	85	19	a
71 and older	14	a	10	a	4	a
Never retire	256	60	188	73	74	35
Don't know	243	68	163	87	63	44
	Blacks					
Total	605	72	411	90	229	55
58–61	33	75	17	a	11	a
62–64	158	79	101	96	37	51
65	175	78	135	90	93	57
66–70	18	a	10	a	7	a
71 and older	3	a	2	a	2	a
Never retire	91	68	70	85	47	51
Don't know	117	56	70	83	30	60

[a]Less than 25 sample cases.

men and more than 4 in 10 black men had realized their expectation in this period. In contrast, fewer than 1 in 4 whites and 1 in 5 blacks who expected to retire at age 65 actually retired at that age.

The same general trend appears among the white decedents in 1981, but limited sample sizes prevent us from studying this relationship for the full distribution of expected ages. Where sample cases are adequate, such as among those age 62-64 and age 65, there is evidence that the earlier the expected age of retirement, the greater the likelihood that the retirement will have occurred as planned. Although a similar analysis for black decedents was not possible, the black decedents were the least likely to have retired as expected—only about 1 in 7 (14 percent) did so. Moreover, these men were only slightly more than half as likely (53 percent) as their surviving counterparts to have retired as planned. These differences by life status did not extend to white men, however. No evidence appears for whites that the survivors were any more likely than the deceased to have retired as expected.

A cross-classification of expected versus actual age of retirement (not shown) indicates that when expectations were not realized, retirements

Table 4–6
Percent of Men Who Retired as Expected,[a] by Expectation at Age 59, Interview Status in 1981 and Race

Expectation	Interview		Decedent	
	Sample n	Percent	Sample n	Percent
	Whites			
Total[c]	1,146	31	186	28
58–61	141	71	15	b
62–64	391	38	65	39
65	415	22	70	26
66–70	38	25	9	b
71 and older	7	b	2	b
Never retired[d]	154	0	25	0
	Blacks			
Total[c]	398	26	120	14
58–61	31	46	10	b
62–64	139	39	24	b
65	151	17	57	7
66–70	14	b	4	b
71 and older	2	b	1	b
Never retired[d]	61	0	24	b

[a]Nonretired men who had attained their expected age at retirements as of 1981 (survey year prior to death) are counted as not having retired at the expected age.

[b]Less than 25 sample cases.

[c]Excluded uncertain responses.

[d]Men assigned to "never retire" category are assumed to retire at age 75.

were more likely to occur before rather than after the expected age. This finding persists for all expected age categories except the youngest (in which case the actual retirement could not be earlier); it also applies to the decedents as well as to the men interviewed in 1981, within each of these, to the two racial groups. The net effect of these earlier-than-expected retirements was to increase the likelihood that these men would retire before the conventional retirement age.

Conclusion

Our data highlight the trend toward early retirement among different cohorts of 59-year-old men interviewed in the 1960s and 1970s. These men anticipated retiring before the conventional age with greater frequencies at the end of the period than at the beginning; and those who subsequently retired were significantly more likely in the later years than in the earlier ones to have retired before age 65. The association between the expectation and the actual dating of the retirement was not very close, however, despite the fact that the expectation was measured at an age not far from when many of the retirements were reported. Only in about 3 in 10 cases were the retirements dated as planned at age 59; otherwise, the men generally retired earlier than planned. The closest correspondence between expected and actual retirement age was found among men who expected to retire very early, suggesting that the expectation response is highly predictive of behavior that is not too distant into the future.

Note

1. Since these men were not interviewed annually, each survey year includes some men who were not 59 years of age at the time of interview. Fifty-eight-year-old men were included among the 59-year-olds if their fifty-ninth birthday fell in the same calendar year. Other 58-year-old men were also included if they reached age 59 in the subsequent survey year. In a few cases the survey year included some 60-year-old men. The sample consisted predominantly 59-year-old men if a calendar year assignment is used. Overall, 74 percent of the men were 59 years old, 22 percent were 58-year-olds, and the remaining men, about 4 percent, were 60 years of age. For simplicity of discussion we refer to this age cohort as 59-year-old men.

References

Social Security Administration. 1982. *Social Security Bulletin: Annual Statistical Supplement, 1982.* Washington, D.C.: U.S. Department of Health and Human Services.

Social Security Administration. Office of The Actuary. 1982. *Life Tables for the United States: 1900-2050. Actuarial Study No. 87.* Washington, D.C.: U.S. Government Printing Office.

U.S. Department of Labor. 1982. *Employment and Training Report of the President, 1982.* Washington, D.C.: U.S. Government Printing Office.

5
Economic Well-Being in Retirement

Herbert S. Parnes
Lawrence J. Less

ow do men fare economically in retirement? Do they continue to work or to manifest an interest in doing so? When they are employed, how do the characteristics of their jobs compare with those they held before retiring? What are the sources of their income and the relative contribution of each? How does Social Security and/or pension income compare with preretirement earnings? To what extent does the real income of retirees deteriorate as time passes? How do retirees perceive the adequacy of their incomes? How do all these factors vary according to their reasons for retiring and to other characteristics of the retirees? These are the questions to which we now turn.

In this chapter, which extends our previous work on the NLS retirees through 1976 (Parnes and Nestel, 1981), we have preserved the reason-for-retirement variable from the 1981 study and added a fourth category—"discouraged" retirees; that is, men who moved into retirement as the result of labor market adversity. The definition of these categories and the distribution of retirees among them, detailed in chapter 3, are used here in order to ascertain the degree to which postretirement experience depends on the circumstances under which retirement occurred.

The analysis is confined to men who retired (by the subjective criterion) between calendar years 1967 and 1979, inclusive, and who were interviewed in 1981. Those who retired earlier and later are excluded so that we can have an unambiguous record of at least 12 months on either side of the retirement event for purposes of measuring pre- and postretirement annual income and work experience. The resulting sample contains 1,718 individuals, who represent about 6.3 million white and somewhat over one-half million black retirees in 1981 between the ages of 60 and 74 who had been retired at least one year but not more than 15. Keep in mind that this group does not represent *all* retirees as of 1981: the oldest member of the sample is 74, so older individuals, retired for long periods of time, are not represented; nor are men who retired after 1979.

Postretirement Labor Market Activity

Labor Force Participation and Unemployment

After retiring from their "regular" job, how many were working or looking for work in the survey week of 1981? Figure 5-1 shows the labor force participation rate and the unemployment rate of the retirees classified by race, preretirement occupation, reason for retirement, and year of retirement.

Overall, 19 percent of the retirees were either working or looking for work at the time of the 1981 survey. Of these, the percentage unemployed was 4.2 percent, compared with the annual 1981 unemployment rates of 7.4 percent for all males and 3.5 percent for those 55 and older. Substantial variation appears in labor force participation according to race, preretirement occupation, and reason for retirement. White men were more likely than black men to be in the labor force (18 vs. 13 percent). The participation rate of men retired from professional or managerial positions was 10 percentage points higher than the rest of the

LABOR FORCE PARTICIPATION RATE

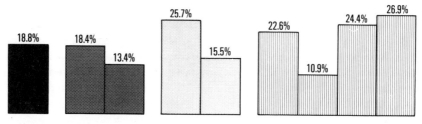

UNEMPLOYMENT RATE

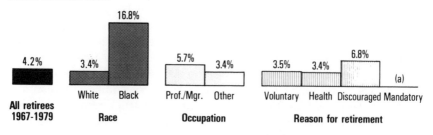

a. Percentage not calculated where base is fewer than 20 sample cases

Figure 5–1. Labor Force Participation Rate and Unemployment Rate in 1981 Survey Week by Race, Preretirement Occupation, and Reason for Retirement

sample. Men who retired for health reasons were only half as likely as the voluntary retirees to be in the labor force (11 vs. 23 percent); the other differences by reason for retirement are small and provide no basis for confident generalization because of the small number of sample cases.

Labor force participation tends to be higher immediately following retirement than it is after a number of years have elapsed. Figure 5-2 shows the labor force participation rate in the week of the first survey after retirement—23 percent as compared with the 19 percent recorded as of 1981. Analyses of the data by date of retirement (not shown on the chart) reveals no evidence of an upward trend in labor force participation over time either for the total group of retirees or for the health and voluntary retirees considered separately.

Variation in Labor Force Participation by Selected Characteristics

Most studies of the sources of variation in the labor supply of older workers (e.g., Bowen and Finegan, 1969) have not been confined to men who regard themselves as retired, but we have found two such studies. On the basis of a small ($n = 203$) and nonrepresentative sample, Fillenbaum (1971) found that the working retired differed from the nonworking retired by being less well educated, less likely to report a deterioration in health, more likely to have intended to work after retirement, and less likely to have a financial need for work. Wentworth's (1968) study of the postentitlement work experience of men drawing benefits under Social Security was based on a series of local and national surveys of male beneficiaries at various times between 1941 and 1963. She found that the probability of postretirement employment was positively related to good health and to the level of employment opportunities and negatively related to age and level of retirement income.

We investigate the factors bearing a net relationship with the likelihood of labor force participation after retirement by means of a multiple classification analysis of our sample of retirees (table 5-1). Age, extent of physical or mental impairment, character of preretirement employment, the individual's attitude toward retirement, and the employment status of one's wife all have a significant influence on the likelihood of postretirement labor market activity.

Other things equal, the retirees who had not yet reached age 65 were almost half again as likely as those age 70-74 to be in the labor force (22 vs. 16 percent), while the participation rate of men age 65-69 fell in between. Extent of physical or mental impairment in 1981 bears a very strong relationship to the likelihood of labor force participation: men with severe disabilities were only half as likely as those with minor or

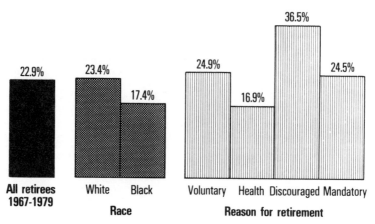

Figure 5–2. Labor Force Participation Rate in 1981 Survey Week, by Race and Reason for Retirement

no impairments to be in the labor market. It is interesting that the inclusion of this variable does not substantially weaken the net relationship between reason for retirement and labor force participation. The adjusted labor force participation rate of the health retirees is about one-third below that of the voluntary retirees. A comparable analysis (not shown) made without the impairment variable showed a 13 percentage-point difference in participation rates between the voluntary retirees and those who retired for health reasons, compared with the 8-point differential shown in table 5-1. These results suggest either that the impairment index does not measure the full extent of health problems, or that men who were forced into retirement by poor health are discouraged from seeking other employment even if it might be compatible with their health condition.

Men who had been in professional or managerial jobs before retiring were significantly more likely than others to be in the labor force in 1981, with an adjusted participation rate of 25 percent as opposed to 13-21 percent for other occupational categories. This pattern may reflect the higher wage rate available to the professional and managerial groups or the otherwise more attractive positions for which they qualify. A greater propensity to work was also manifested by the self-employed, who had an adjusted participation rate about 10 percentage points higher than that of men who had been wage or salary workers. This difference may reflect the facts that self-employed persons are less likely to be subjected to the work constraints frequently found in private pension plans, and that they are better able than wage and salary workers to arrange for part-time work or flexible work schedules after retirement (cf. Quinn, 1980).

Table 5–1
Labor Force Participation Rates of Retirees in 1981, by Selected Characteristics
(MCA[a] results)

Characteristic	n	Unadjusted Labor Force Participation Rate	Adjusted[d] Labor Force Participation Rate (F-ratio)
Total sample	1,718	19	19
Race			(0.040)
White	1,252	19	19
Black	466	16	19
Reason for retirement			(4.478)[d]
Mandatory	61	27	24
Health	650	11	13[d]
Discouraged	94	24	21
Voluntary: early	682	22	21[c]
Voluntary: normal	226	23	22
Extent of impairment[b]			(7.466)[d]
None	350	27	24[d]
Minor	164	27	26[d]
Moderate	140	23	22
Substantial	229	21	22
Severe	788	11	12[d]
Family income excluding respondent's earnings			(0.546)
$5,000 or less	693	17	20
$5,001–$10,000	160	21	20
$10,001–$15,000	96	19	14
$15,001 and over	101	24	18
Age (1981)			(3.572)
60–64	376	23	22[e]
65–69	697	20	19
70–74	645	16	16[e]
Type of worker, preretirement job			(5.909)[d]
Government	311	20	16
Private wage or salary	1,103	17	18
Self-employed	258	25	27[d]
Net assets, 1981			(0.850)
$15,000 or less	390	14	18
$15,001–$35,000	228	13	16
$35,001–$70,000	262	17	17
$70,001 and over	402	23	20
Preretirement occupation			(4.881)[c]
Professional/managerial	342	27	25[c]
Other white collar	175	21	21
Craftsmen	388	13	13[c]
All other	809	17	18

Table 5–1 continued

Characteristic	n	Unadjusted Labor Force Participation Rate	Adjusted[d] Labor Force Participation Rate (F-ratio)
Marital status			(7.039)[c]
Married: wife worked	327	27	25[c]
Married: wife did not work	1,037	16	16[c]
Nonmarried	341	17	22
Attitude toward retirement, 1978			(6.798)[c]
Favorble	498	15	14[c]
Ambivalent	685	18	18
Unfavorble	380	24	25[c]
Calendar year of retirement			(3.281)[d]
67–70	186	11	16
71–73	389	14	17
74–75	420	16	16
76–79	723	25	22[c]
R^2			.08

[a]For a description of Multiple Classification Analysis, see "A Note on the Tables and Graphs."

[b]For construction of impairment index, see table 6–4, note c.

[c]Significant at .01 level.

[d]Significant at .05 level.

[e]Significant at .10 level.

With all other factors controlled, men who retired within the past 5 years are significantly more likely to be in the labor force in 1981 than men who retired earlier. Together with the data in figures 5-1 and 5-2, this finding shows that retirees are more likely to work in the period immediately following their retirement than later. Respondents' general attitude toward work and retirement, measured in 1978,[1] proved to be a good predictor of postretirement labor market activity. Men who had expressed favorable views about retirement had an adjusted participation rate of only 14 percent, as compared with 18 percent for men with ambivalent attitudes, and 25 percent for those with unfavorable views.

Rather surprisingly, neither family income (exclusive of respondents' earnings) nor assets is significantly related to the likelihood of the retiree's labor force participation. Indeed, in the unadjusted data the highest rates of participation occur in the top category of income and assets. These results may reflect a correlation of each of these variables with a strong lifetime commitment to work, which is inadequately measured by other variables in the analysis. Thus, the income and assets variables are picking up the influence of this characteristic—which is expected to be positively related to labor force participation—as well as the influence of income and wealth—which would have the opposite influence (cf. Bowen and Finegan, 1969, p. 313).

The labor market status of the wife is a significant determinant of the husband's labor force participation. Husbands' and wives' leisure time appear to be complements: retirees whose wives work are more likely to participate than retirees whose wives do not work (25 vs. 16 percent), a finding that has also been arrived at by quite different methods on the basis of the Social Security Administration's Retirement History Study (Clark, Johnson, and McDermed, 1980). With other factors controlled, the gross differential of 3 percentage points between the participation rates of blacks and whites disappears completely.

Extent of Work Activity during Year

The pattern of employment of the retirees over the 12-month period before the 1981 survey is similar to that manifested by their labor force status in the survey week, although levels of activity are higher. For the total group of retirees, 22 percent had some employment during the year, as compared with a 19-percent labor force participation rate in the survey week. Of those who did work, half were full-year workers—11 percent of all the retirees. Employment was more likely among whites than blacks and for men who had been in professional or managerial jobs than for others. Health retirees were considerably less likely than others to be employed.

In the weeks in which they worked, most of the retirees (59 percent) worked only part-time, and almost one-fifth worked fewer than 15 hours per week. There was less variation in hours of employment per week than in weeks per year. Considering both weeks of employment and hours per week, 1 in 5 of the working retirees spent 2,000 or more hours per year on the job, while about 3 in 10 worked only 500 hours. When the number of retirees employed 2,000 or more hours is expressed as a percentage of all retirees (whether employed or not) the overall proportion is only 4 percent—as low as 1 percent among blacks and as high as 9 percent among discouraged retirees.

Retirees who had worked at any time during the 12-month period before the 1981 interview were asked the following question: "In view of the fact that you have retired from a regular job, what would you say is the main reason you have been working during the past 12 months?" An economic and a psychological stimulus to employment were the two single factors most frequently mentioned: inflation (28 percent) and boredom with retirement (21 percent). A small minority of the working retirees (1 percent) attributed employment to improved health, and about one-tenth mentioned the appearance of a job opportunity. A miscellany of other factors accounted for the work activity of the remaining men. Differences appear in this pattern both by age and by race: men 65 or older were less likely than younger men to attribute their labor market activity to the pressure of increased living costs. Black men were considerably less likely than whites to have worked out of boredom and considerably more likely to have been compelled to work by the rising cost of living.

Labor Market Propensities of Nonworking Retirees

What about the men who were not working or looking for jobs in 1981? To what extent did they plan or wish to enter the work force? We have three measures that shed light on this issue. First, men who were out of the labor force in the survey week were asked their main reason for not working or seeking work.[2] Second, they were asked whether they intended "to look for work of any kind in the next 12 months." Third, a hypothetical job offer was posed. "If you were offered a job by some employer in this area, do you think you would take it?"[3]

All three measures point to the same conclusion: that the vast majority of retirees who are out of the labor force have no interest in working. To begin with, a negligible percentage of the retirees—only 1 percent—explained their absence from the labor market by a perception that no jobs were available; among black men the proportion is 2 percent; among the mandatory and discouraged retirement groups it is 6 percent and 2 percent, respectively. Responses to the query about plans to enter the labor market in the near future are overwhelmingly negative—95 percent overall. Finally, and most persuasively, more than 8 out of 10 of the respondents categorically deny an interest in a job—35 percent because of poor health and 49 percent for other reasons. Only 2 percent respond unconditionally in the affirmative, while the remaining 14 percent indicate a conditional interest. To be sure, differences appear by reason for retirement and by preretirement occupation, but a very large majority of each group—ranging between three-fourths of the mandatory and discouraged retirees and 87 percent of the health retirees—state without reservation that they would not take a job. Even an *explicit* reference to a part-time job increased the proportion of retirees responding affirmatively to the hypothetical job offer by only 2 percentage points.

The proportion of men who expressed a categorical or conditional interest in a job is higher among those who had been professional or managerial workers than among those in other occupations (20 vs. 15 percent). Among the several reason-for-retirement categories, men who retired for health reasons have the lowest proportion expressing an interest in work—13 percent versus 17-26 percent for the other categories. However, the most substantial difference between the health retirees and the voluntary retirees is the reason the majority give for not being interested in working: three-fifths of the former mention poor health while two-thirds of the voluntary retirees provide other reasons—typically "I'm retired" or "I don't need the money."

Considering all retirees—those in and out of the labor force—what can we say about the proportion who manifest an interest in work? Adding the 22 percent of the retirees who worked at some time during the year preceeding the 1981 survey to the 16 percent of those out of the labor force in the 1981 survey week who expressed at least a conditional interest in employment yields a total of 38 percent of the total sample. Thus, on the basis of these data, the proportion of retirees in their 60s and early 70s who appear to be available for work is, at most, about two-fifths. A majority of retirees leave their jobs either because their health makes work impossible or uncomfortable or because they have tired of working and seek leisure. Although a minority—under one-fourth—continue to work (mainly part time), a very large majority of the remainder are uninterested in working, and for basically the same two reasons that led them to retire in the first place.

On the basis of very different types of data, Motley (1978) has also concluded that only a limited proportion of retirees are available for work. However, this situation apparently differs from that prevailing two or three decades ago. On the basis of national surveys of male Social Security beneficiaries conducted in 1951 and 1957, Wentworth (1968, pp. 13, 28) reports higher levels of employment than found here and concluded that "most of the beneficiaries returned to work whenever they could get a job, usually because they needed the income. The relatively few beneficiaries who were in good health but not interested in working for the most part had adequate retirement incomes."

The Postretirement Jobs of Employed Retirees

Of the minority of the retirees who were employed at the time of the 1981 survey, 24 percent of the whites and 30 percent of the blacks were serving in the same occupation as in their preretirement job (table 5-2). Of the remainder, more had moved down the socioeconomic hierarchy of occupations than had remained at the same level or moved up. Although the small number of sample cases in most of the categories preclude confident distinctions, it appears that black men were less likely to move downward than whites (probably because they had started at lower levels), and that men who had retired voluntarily at age 65 or older were more likely than those in any other category to be serving in their preretirement occupations.

Most of the postretirement jobs were in industries different from those from which the men had retired. Indeed, even using the broadest industrial categories (e.g., construction, manufacturing, and trade), almost two-thirds of the retirees had moved across industry lines. About three-fifths of the employed retirees—three-fourths of the blacks—were in wage and salary positions both before and after retirement; however almost 1 in 5 had moved from wage or salary jobs into self-employment, fewer than 1 in 10 percent had moved in the opposite direction, and 15 percent were in self-employment both before and after retirement.

Among those who were wage and salary workers at both points in time, most had reduced their weekly hours by substantial amounts, although one-fourth were working as many or more hours in their 1981 jobs as they had prior to retirement. As measured by job satisfaction, the working retirees seem, if anything, to have improved their lot: those who reported liking their 1981 job very much were a somewhat larger percentage than those reacting the same way to the job they had held at the last survey before retirement. The situation is quite different with respect to financial rewards; adjusted for changes in the purchasing power of the dollar, average hourly earnings were lower for all but about one-eighth of the men, and in over two-thirds of the cases the decrease was at least $2 per hour. In dollars of constant purchasing power, median average hourly earnings in 1981 were less than one-half of what they had been in the preretirement job. Taking into account also the reduction in annual hours, total wage and salary income in the 12 months preceding the 1981 survey was only 20 percent of what it had been in the year preceding retirement for white men, 30 percent in the case of blacks.

Postretirement Financial Status

Returning now to the total sample of retirees, we examine their financial condition, including the sources of family income, the character and amount of pension income, the relationship between pension income and preretirement earnings, and their perceptions of the adequacy of their income.

Sources of Total Family Income

As would be expected, the most universal source of income among the retirees is Social Security (or Railroad Retirement) old age benefits, which were received by 9 out of 10 of the men, with very little variation either by race or marital status (table 5-3). Other pension income went to

Table 5–2
Comparison of Current and Preretirement Job, by Race and Reason for Retirement: Retirees Employed in 1981

Characteristic	Total[a]	Race		Reason for Retirement		
		Whites	Blacks	Health	Early	Normal
Sample n	291	231	60	71	142	45
Occupation						
Total percent	100	100	100	100	100	100
Same 3-digit	25	24	30	21	22	39
Different 3-digit						
Higher socioeconomic status[b]	24	24	26	30	24	19
Same socioeconomic status[b]	11	10	19	13	10	7
Lower socioeconomic status[b]	40	41	25	37	44	35
Industry						
Total percent	100	100	100	100	100	100
Same 3-digit	27	26	39	27	24	48
Different 3-digit						
Same 1-digit	9	9	6	5	9	3
Different 1-digit	65	65	55	68	68	50
Type of worker						
Total percent	100	100	100	100	100	100
Wage and salary, both jobs	58	57	74	54	57	57
Wage and salary preretirement, self-employed in 1981	19	20	9	14	22	13
Self-employed preretirement, wage and salary 1981	8	8	4	18	7	5
Self-employed, both jobs	15	15	13	15	14	26

[a]Total includes mandatory and discouraged retirees, neither of which categories contains sufficient sample cases for separate tabulation.
[b]Based on Duncan Index of socioeconomic status. Differences of ±3 points are classified as same socioeconomic status (Blau and Duncan, 1967, pp. 117–128).

Table 5–3
Percentage of Retirees Receiving Selected Forms of Family Income, by Race and Marital Status, 1980

Source of Income	Total Race			Whites			Blacks		
	Total	Married	NonMarried	Total	Married	Nonmarried	Total	Married	Nonmarried
Sample n	1,718	1,377	341	1,252	1,039	197	466	314	144
Retiree's wages or salaries	18	18	19	18	18	20	16	17	13
Retiree's self-employment	11	11	11	12	11	12	5	6	2
Wife's earnings[a]	17	20	0	17	20	0	17	26	0
Social Security[b]	90	90	89	90	90	88	92	92	91
Retiree's pension	52	54	43	52	54	43	44	45	42
Wife's pension	10	12	0	10	12	0	5	7	0
Public assistance	8	7	18	7	5	15	28	25	34
Financial assistance from relatives	1	1	2	1	1	2	1	c	2
Income of other family members	13	12	17	13	12	15	20	17	25
Other income	69	72	55	72	74	59	32	35	26

[a]Includes self-employment income.
[b]Includes Social Security or Railroad Retirement benefits paid to retiree and/or his wife.
[c]Less than 0.5 percent.

somewhat over half of the retirees, more commonly to whites than to blacks and to married than to unmarried men of both races. Almost 1 in 5 of the retirees had earnings from wage or salary jobs and 11 percent had self-employment income. Except for the greater prevalence of self-employment income among whites than blacks (12 vs. 5 percent), only minor variations appear by race or marital status.

Among married men, wives' earnings contributed to income in one-fifth of the white and one-fourth of the black families. Additionally, 12 and 7 percent of white and black wives, respectively, contributed pension income. Income of other family members was present in 13 percent of the total sample, but more frequently among blacks than whites and among unmarried than married retirees. Over one-fourth of the black men, but under one-tenth of the whites, received public assistance. Other income (principally from property) went to almost three-fourths of the whites but to only one-third of the blacks, and in each case it was considerably less common among men who were unmarried.

The relative importance of each of these sources in contributing to the average family income of the retirees is shown in table 5-4. Average income for 1980 was $16,000 for the entire group, but ranged between $17,000 for married whites and $8,300 for unmarried blacks. The ratio of black to white family income was .60; the analogous nonmarried to married ratio was .68—somewhat higher among blacks.

Perhaps the most interesting aspect of the data is that for the retirees as a whole, retirement income from Social Security and from other pensions accounted for only 51 percent of total family income. The proportion was higher among blacks (61 percent) because the Social Security benefit formula is weighted in favor of lower wage workers. Pension benefits (other than Social Security), however, were almost exactly one-fifth of total income for all race-marital status groups except unmarried blacks. Among married men, wives' earnings represented 9 percent of income—11 percent among blacks, a proportion not much different from that contributed by the earnings of the retirees. Income of other family members accounted for 6 percent of income overall, but was as high as 9 and 18 percent, respectively, among nonmarried white and black men. Property income amounted to about one-fifth of the total for whites, but was negligible for blacks. Public assistance contributed less than 0.5 for white retirees and 2 percent for blacks.

The figures that underlie the distribution in table 5-4 reflect both the incidence of each of the sources of income and the average amount per recipient. In other words, those who did not receive a particular form of income are nevertheless included in the data, and thus reduce the average. For some purposes it is more useful to examine the average per recipient of each form of income (table 5-5). On this basis there are six

Table 5–4
Composition of Average Family Income of Retirees, by Race and Marital Status, 1980
(*percentage distributions*)

Source of Income	Total Race			Whites			Blacks		
	Total	Married	Nonmarried	Total	Married	Nonmarried	Total	Married	Nonmarried
Sample *n*	909	712	197	647	536	111	262	176	86
Average family income ($000)	16.0	17.0	11.3	16.4	17.4	11.8	9.8	10.6	8.3
Total percent	100	100	100	100	100	100	100	100	100
Retiree's wages or salaries	7	7	7	7	7	7	7	7	8
Retiree's self-employment	4	3	10	4	3	11	1	1	a
Wife's earnings or self-employment	8	9	—	8	9	—	11	14	—
Social Security or RR retirement	32	31	34	31	31	33	42	41	44
Retiree's pension	19	19	20	19	19	19	19	17	24
Wife's pension	2	2	—	2	2	—	1	1	—
Public assistance	a	a	a	a	a	a	2	2	1
Income of other family members	6	5	11	6	5	10	12	9	18
Other income	21	22	18	22	23	19	6	7	5

a Less than 0.5 percent.

Table 5–5
Mean Income per Recipient, by Source of Income, Race, and Marital Status, 1980

Source of Income	Total Race			Whites			Blacks		
	Total	Married	Nonmarried	Total	Married	Nonmarried	Total	Married	Nonmarried
Retiree's wages or salaries	$5,655	$5,901	$4,756	$5,833	$6,104	$4,826	$3,478	$3,288	c
Retiree's self-employment[a]	6,900	5,775	c	7,091	5,948	c	c	c	
Wife's earnings	7,345	7,345	0	7,512	7,512	0	5,414	5,415	0
Social Security[b]	5,469	5,795	4,175	5,589	5,887	4,292	4,168	4,531	$3,510
Retiree's pension	6,085	6,249	5,170	6,234	6,370	5,380	4,048	4,064	4,018
Wife's pension	3,132	3,132	0	3,135	3,125	0	c	c	0
Public assistance	1,168	1,197	c	1,199	1,153	c	1,089	1,336	c
Assistance from relatives	c	c	c	c	c	c	c	c	c
Income of other family members	7,106	7,006	7,465	7,132	7,082	c	6,901	6,272	c
Other income	4,702	4,926	3,571	4,826	5,028	3,763	1,029	1,032	1,023

[a]Includes self-employment income.

[b]Includes Railroad retirement as well as Social Security.

[c]Mean not calculated where number of sample cases is fewer than 20.

income sources for which the average per recipient was at least $5,000: retiree's wage or salary income ($5,655), retiree's self-employment income ($6,900), wife's earnings ($7,345), Social Security ($5,469); retiree's pension ($6,085), and income of other family members ($7,106). For all income sources the value for whites was higher than for blacks.

Social Security and Pension Income

We have seen that more than one-half of the retirees were receiving pension income other than Social Security or Railroad Retirement benefits in 1980. Private employer pensions were by far the most common, accounting for 52 percent of the total. An additional one-fourth came from civilian employment in the public sector, almost equally divided between the federal government and state and local units. One in 8 of the pensions came from unions. Only 2 percent of the retirees were receiving military pensions, but keep in mind that the NLS sample drawn in 1966 was designed to be representative only of the civilian population. Although proportionately fewer blacks than whites received pensions, no great difference appeared between the two races in the relative frequency of the various sources, except for a greater incidence of local government pensions and a smaller incidence of state government pensions among black men.

Recipients of any form of pension income other than Social Security or Railroad Retirement were asked in the 1981 interview schedule whether the reported monthly amount had increased, decreased, or remained the same over the past two years. The distribution of responses underscores one of the major problems with private pension plans during periods of inflation. Whereas virtually all of the civilian employees of the federal government (correctly) reported that their pensions had increased (federal pensions rise with increases in the Consumer Price Index, as does Social Security), only two-fifths of the pensions provided by private employers were increased. Indeed, three-fifths of the recipients of such pensions reported decreases in the recent past. The pattern was even worse in the case of union pensions and almost as bad with those provided by state and local government.

Replacement rates. A widely used measure of the adequacy of retirement benefits is their relationship to preretirement earnings—the so-called replacement rate.[4] If one takes into account the reduction in taxes that generally accompanies retirement, as well as the reduction in certain types of expenses (e.g., those related to work), it is clear that preretirement standards of living can be maintained with replacement rates less than 100 percent. A number of attempts have been made to calculate the replacement rates necessary to maintain preretirement living standards for workers at various levels of income and in different family circumstances. A recent set of such estimates for 1981 by Munnell (1982, p. 24) ranges from .86 for married couples with gross preretirement income of $6,000, to .52 for those whose incomes were $50,000. For single persons, the corresponding rates are .50 and .80.[5]

For our sample of retirees who had been employed in wage or salary jobs the average replacement rate[6] is 44 percent, but there is very substantial variation around this mean. At one extreme, about 1 in 5 has a replacement rate of 25 percent or less; at the other, 1 in 7 has a rate of 70 percent or higher. Men covered by pension plans other than (or in addition to) Social Security have higher replacement rates than those without such coverage, but the differences are considerably smaller than what might have been supposed, ranging between 3 and 13 percentage points depending on race and marital status. The reason for these relatively small differences is the intercorrelation between pension coverage and other factors affecting the replacement rate—particularly preretirement earnings. Low income workers are less likely to be covered by pension plans than high income workers; low income persons, however, have higher Social Security replacement rates because of the subsidy incorporated in the Social Security benefit formula. As the result of these intercorrelations, it is fruitless to explore the factors that affect the replacement rate except by means of a multivariate analysis. Accordingly, the results of a multiple classification analysis (MCA) of replacement rates is shown in table 5-6.

For this purpose, the sample is stratified into two groups: (1) men receiving only Social Security or Railroad Retirement benefits and (2) men who receive other pensions either along with Social Security (or Railroad Retirement) benefits, or alone. A large majority of the second group receive both Social Security and additional pension income; however, about 13 percent of the retirees (weighted)—most of whom doubtless held their preretirement jobs in government—receive no Social Security benefits.[7] In the MCA of the second group, receipt of Social Security retirement benefits is introduced as an additional explanatory variable.

The benefit provisions of the Social Security program lead one to expect the replacement rate to show a strong relationship with preretirement earnings and with marital status and age of wife;[8] both these expectations are fulfilled. Because there is a maximum earnings level subject to the Social Security payroll tax each year ($25,900 in 1980), the benefit formula yields a maximum benefit that represents a decreasing fraction of income as income rises above the maximum subject to the tax. Moreover, benefits below the maximum also represent a higher proportion of

Table 5–6
Social Security and/or Pension Replacement Rate[a] of Men Who Retired from Wage and Salary Jobs between Calendar Years 1967 and 1978, by Selected Characteristics (MCA[b] Results)

Characteristic	Retirees Receiving Social Security or Railroad Retirement Benefits Only			Retirees Receiving Pension Income Other than, or in Addition to, Social Security or Railroad Retirement		
	n	Unadjusted Replacement Rate	Adjusted Replacement Rate[b] (F-ratio) (%)	n	Unadjusted Replacement Rate	Adjusted Replacement Rate[b] (F-ratio) (%)
Total sample	399	41	(0.367) 41	610	49	(0.76) 49
Race						
White	251	40	41	460	49	49
Black	148	46	39	150	52	49
Reason for retirement			(0.537)			(5.261)[d]
Mandatory	13	c	c	36	48	45
Health	180	40	40	140	52	52[f]
Discouraged	27	43	40	27	38	37[d]
Voluntary: early	112	42	41	325	50	51[e]
Voluntary: normal	65	41	45	80	48	45[e]
Preretirement annual earnings			(50.635)[d]			(34.170)[d]
Less than $10,000	149	58	60[d]	33	66	68[d]
$10,000–$19,999	174	38	38[d]	253	54	56[d]
$20,000–$29,999	52	29	29[d]	220	47	47[d]
$30,000 or over	54	24	20[d]	104	41	38[d]
Preretirement occupation			(0.686)			(2.852)[d]
Professional/managerial	49	28	39	134	49	53[e]
Clerical or sales	36	39	46	80	55	52
Craftsmen	86	44	42	148	46	47[f]
Operatives	91	40	39	149	50	49
Laborers	53	48	40	48	51	46
Service	50	45	41	49	49	43[f]
Farm	34	53	39	2	c	c

						(5.658)[d]
Preretirement industry		(4.995)[d]				
Agriculture	37	52	43	5	c	c
Mining	3	c	c	16	c	c
Construction	51	46	44	44	44	44[f]
Manufacturing	118	35	38	250	49	48[f]
Transportation and utilities	48	50	57[d]	79	48	48
Trade	64	38	36[f]	34	45	44
Finance, insurance and real estate	12	c	c	25	47	47
Services	59	41	38	65	48	47
Public administration	7	c	c	92	56	61[d]
Year of retirement		(7.397)[d]				(10.269)[d]
1967–1970	40	37	37	40	44	39[d]
1971–1975	208	40	38[d]	296	48	48[e]
1976–1979	151	43	46[d]	274	51	52[d]
Marital status and age of wife, 1981		(5.503)[d]				(9.625)[d]
Married, wife present:						
Younger than 62	104	35	35[d]	195	44	45[d]
62–64	60	38	40	91	52	51
65 or older	138	46	47[d]	209	54	55[d]
other	94	41	39	112	46	44[d]
Recipient of Social Security/Railroad Retirement benefits						(11.770)[d]
No	—	—	—	70	41	43[d]
Yes	—	—	—	540	50	50[d]
Adjusted R²		.29				.22

aThe replacement rate was calculated by dividing the sum of Social Security (or Railroad Retirement) benefits and other pension income for the 12 months preceding the 1980 survey by the respondent's wage and salary income (expressed in terms of dollars of 1980 purchasing power) in the most recent 12-month period prior to retirement in which the respondent worked at least 1500 hours.

bFor a description of Multiple Classification Analysis see "A Note on the Tables and Graphs."

cReplacement rate not calculated where base is smaller than 20 sample cases.

dSignificant at the .01 level.

eSignificant at the .05 level.

fSignificant at the .10 level.

low than of high preretirement earnings, because of the subsidy incorporated in the benefit formula. Thus, the replacement rate varies inversely with preretirement earnings; among retirees drawing only Social Security benefits it ranges (controlling for other factors) from 60 percent for men whose preretirement wage and salary income (expressed in terms of 1980 dollars) was under $10,000, to 20 percent for those whose earnings were $30,000 or more. When attention is confined to the approximately two-thirds of the men who receive pension income other than Social Security or Railroad Retirement, the ratios are higher—ranging from 68 to 38 percent for the same categories. It should be noted that only at the low end of the income scale does the average replacement rate come close to being sufficient to maintain the preretirement standard of living. Munnell's estimates, referred to earlier, range from 73 to 86 percent for income levels between $6,000 and $10,000, but between 52 and 59 percent for incomes between $30,000 and $50,000.

Under the Social Security Act the benefit of a wife (not entitled to a higher one on the basis of her own earnings record) amounts to 50 percent of that of her husband, provided that she doesn't claim it till age 65. At earlier ages down to 62 the benefit is actuarially reduced; below age 62 the wife is not eligible for benefits. These provisions produce the expected variation in replacement rates among married men depending on the age of their wives.[9]

Although no perceptible differences appear in Social Security replacement rates among the major occupation groups of wage and salary earners, when other pensions are also included white-collar workers enjoy higher replacement rates than other categories. Industrial differentials are also discernible. Among men receiving pension income other than Social Security or Railroad Retirement, public administration has the highest replacement rate, reflecting the more liberal benefits of government employees, especially at the federal level. Among men with no supplemental pensions, those in transportation have significantly higher-than-average replacement rates, reflecting the more liberal benefits of the Railroad Retirement than the Social Security system.

Eighty-seven percent of those who receive pensions from other sources also receive Social Security, which boosts the average replacement rate by 7 percentage points. The fact that this increment is so much lower than the average replacement rate for those receiving only Social Security benefits has at least two explanations. First, some pensions are integrated with Social Security in such a way as to be reduced when recipients begin to receive Social Security benefits. Second, the group receiving other pensions doubtless includes numerous "double dippers" whose Social Security benefits are based on considerably less than full career coverage.[10]

Replacement rates are significantly higher for more recent than for earlier retirees, reflecting the liberalization of both Social Security and private pensions over the past two decades. When other factors are not controlled, the replacement rate is higher for blacks than for whites both among men receiving only Social Security and among those receiving other pensions, but this apparent disadvantage really reflects the lower earnings of blacks and the subsidy incorporated in the Social Security benefit formula. In the multivariate framework the adjusted replacement rates are, if anything, actually lower for blacks than whites, although the differences do not achieve statistical significance.

Trends in Real Family Income after Retirement

The 1970s were characterized by very substantial inflation, combined with high levels of unemployment. The consumer price level slightly more than doubled between 1971 and 1980, jumping more than 10 percent in each of three years (1974, 1979, and 1980); in the first half of the decade the annual unemployment rate dipped slightly below 5 percent in only one year; in the second half it averaged 6.7 percent. In part reflecting these trends, median real family income in the United States was virtually no higher in 1980 than it had been in 1971 ($21,023 vs. $20,926) in comparison with a rise of 32 percent over the preceding decade.[11] In this context it is interesting to examine the trend in the total family income of the retirees during the decade.

Table 5-7 presents median family income reported in the year before retirement and in each postretirement survey year for every cohort of retirees who were married as of 1981. Because the annual number of retirements was rather small between 1967 and 1974, they have been grouped into two 5-year periods. The data appear to support several generalizations. (1) Median total family income for the total group of retirees in 1980 was, in real terms, about three-fifths of what it had been in the last full preretirement year, whenever that may have been. (2) The more recent cohorts of retirees—that is, those who retired in 1975 and later—had higher levels of pre-retirement income than the earlier groups, but also higher levels of income in 1980, with the result that the ratio of 1980 to preretirement incomes was somewhat higher for the more recent group of retirees. These relationships doubtless reflect the difference in such characteristics as health and age at retirement of the different cohorts of retirees. (3) For most of the cohorts, there is a downward trend in real family income in recent years—that is, since 1976. Analysis of the levels of income by source over time indicates that the downward trend in real family income is principally attributable to the decreased labor market activity of both the retirees and their wives and to a decrease in the real value of pension income (other than Social Security).

Table 5–7
Median Real Family Income (1980 Dollars) from Year Prior to Retirement to 1981, Married Retirees, by Calendar Year of Retirement, 1967–1979[a]

Year Retired	n[c]	Preretirement Year[d]	Survey Year[b]			1981 = Preretirement Year
			1976	1978	1981	
1967–1971	121–193	$23,620	$13,481	$11,283	$11,106	.47
1972–1974	247–395	23,536	14,815	14,090	12,002	.51
1975–1976	185–292	24,029	[e]	14,012	14,216	.59
1977–1979	274–415	24,403		[e]	15,149	.62
All retirees	827–1,295	23,912			13,680	.57

[a]Tabulation includes all respondents for whom income information was provided in any year.
[b]Income figures relate to preceding calendar year in survey years 1976 and 1981 and to the 12-month period preceding the interview in 1978.
[c]Range includes the smallest number reporting in any year and the largest number reporting in any year.
[d]First full year prior to retirement for which income figure is available.
[e]Income reporting period overlaps calendar year of retirement.

Perceived Adequacy of Income

The 1981 interview schedule produced information on the subjective reaction of the members of the sample to their financial status. Respondents were asked: "Which of the following four statements best describes your ability to get along on your income: I always have money left over; I have enough, with a little extra sometimes; I have just enough, no more; I can't make ends meet." Figure 5-3 compares the responses of retirees with those of nonretired men, cross-classified by race and marital status. Overall, two-thirds of the married retirees and half of the nonmarried say they do better than "just get by" on their current incomes, while 7 percent and 13 percent, respectively, report that they cannot make ends meet. On the basis of this criterion, the differences between retired and nonretired men are not so great as the differences in their incomes would lead one to expect. Among the married men, 64 percent of the retirees and 74 percent of the nonretired do better than just get by; the proportions who can't make ends meet are 7 and 5 percent, respectively. The differences among the minority of men who are not married, however, are greater. Using questions fairly similar to ours in a survey of a national sample of all men age 65 and over (married and unmarried considered together), Harris et al. (1981, p. 72) found that 52 percent do better than "just get by."

Very profound racial differences appear in the response pattern. Indeed, the interracial differences within each retirement category are greater than the differences between retired and nonretired men of each race, and these racial differences are especially pronounced among the retirees who are married. Within this group 26 percent of the blacks and 6 percent of the whites report that they cannot make ends meet, while 6 percent and 26 percent, respectively, report that they can save regularly.

Differences in Financial Status by Reason for Retirement

Average measures of financial status of retirees conceal very wide differences according to the circumstances under which retirement occurred; men who were induced to retire for health reasons are substantially less well off than the voluntary retirees. As table 5-8 shows, 1980 median family income of married men who retired because of poor health was only two-thirds as high as that of the voluntary retirees, and the corresponding ratio for net assets was three-fifths. Eleven percent of the health retirees "can't make ends meet," in contrast with 5 percent of the voluntary retirees. The figures vary as well for the other two groups of retirees, but the small numbers preclude confident generalization.

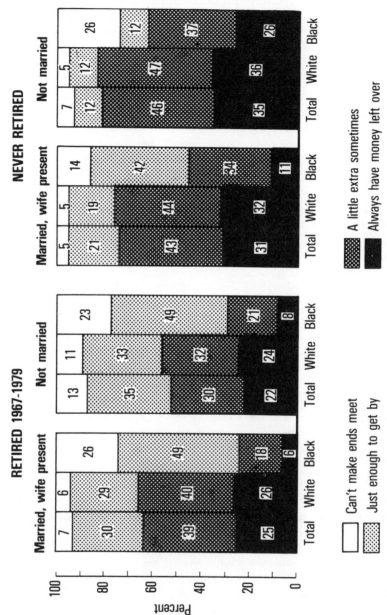

Figure 5–3. Perceived Adequacy of Income, by Retirement Status, Marital Status, and Race

Table 5–8
Selected Measures of Financial Status of Married Retirees, by Reason for
Retirement and Race, 1981

Reason for Retirement	n	Median Family Income	Median Net Family Assets	Percent Who "Can't Make Ends Meet"
		Total		
Total	1,673	$14,768	$64,449	6
Mandatory	54	20,826	83,324	2
Health	621	11,680	43,983	11
Discouraged	88	12,491	55,570	12
Voluntary, total	910	17,000	75,005	5
Early	683	17,520	74,404	5
Normal	227	15,387	79,074	6
		Whites		
Total	1,277	$15,338	$68,523	5
Mandatory	39	22,407	83,511	0
Health	435	12,265	46,300	8
Discouraged	69	12,497	63,447	3
Voluntary, total	734	17,216	78,246	4
Early	549	17,617	76,857	4
Normal	185	15,394	83,353	5
		Blacks		
Total	396	$8,790	$14,815	26
Mandatory	15	a	a	a
Health	186	7,844	9,625	39
Discouraged	19	a	a	a
Voluntary, total	176	10,514	18,528	13
Early	134	10,566	18,516	11
Normal	42	9,760	22,357	19

[a]Measure not shown where base is fewer than 20 sample cases.

Conclusion

Of the 7 million men age 60-74 in 1981 who had retired between calendar years 1967 and 1979, only a minority manifested any interest in
labor market activity in 1981. At best, only two-fifths of the total group
of retirees are available for work; the remainder either have health problems that discourage labor market activity or simply do not choose to
work.

The minority (one-fifth) of the retirees who were in the labor force
in 1980 differed significantly in a number of respects from the majority
who were not. A multivariate analysis demonstrates that the likelihood
of postretirement labor market activity declines precipitously with advancing age even within the relatively narrow span of years from 54 to

73, and with increasing severity of health problems. Men who had been in professional or managerial jobs prior to retirement and those who expressed relatively unfavorable attitudes toward retirement had above-average participation rates.

Nine out of ten retirees receive Social Security (or Railroad Retirement) benefits, and one-half receive other pensions, predominantly from private employers but also from public sector employers and from unions. Substantial proportions have one or more additional sources of income; nevertheless, Social Security and other pensions accounted for about half of the retirees' average family income of $15,300 in 1980.

The average proportion of preretirement earnings represented by public and private pensions (replacement rate, expressed in terms of dollars with 1980 purchasing power) is 44 percent, but there is considerable variation around this mean. For about one-fifth of the retirees the replacement rate is under 25 percent; for 1 in 7 it is 70 percent or higher. Replacement rates of persons who receive Social Security benefits vary dramatically with preretirement earnings levels, because of the subsidy inherent in the Social Security benefit formula. Replacement rates vary also with other characteristics of retirees. They are higher for married than for unmarried men, reflecting the benefit provisions of the Social Security program; higher among men whose preretirement jobs were in transportation, reflecting the more liberal benefits of the Railroad Retirement Act than of the Social Security Act; and higher among more recent retirees, reflecting liberalization in Social Security and private pensions over the past two decades.

When median real family income of married retirees is examined over time, two trends are evident. First, the level of 1980 income is higher for more recent than for earlier retirees. Second, for each cohort of retirees real family income has moved downward over time, resulting largely from decreased postretirement labor force participation of both retirees and their wives as time goes on.

Whatever their actual income, a very large majority of retirees say they are able to "get by" on their income, although there are pronounced variations between nonmarried and married men in favor of the latter and even larger differences between blacks and whites. Nonetheless, for the married men of both races combined, two-thirds report that they do better than just get by, and only 9 percent assert that the "cannot make ends meet." By way of comparison, the corresponding proportions for nonretired men are 74 and 5 percent. There are, however, profound differences according to both objective and subjective measures of financial status between men who retired for health reasons and those who retired voluntarily. Among the married men in each group, for example, family income in 1980 was one-third lower for the health retirees than for those who retired voluntarily, and twice as many of the health retirees say they are not able "to get by" on their income.

Notes

1. The questions were designed to measure a generalized attitude toward retirement rather than the respondent's reaction to his own retirement. On a 4-point scale, respondents were asked to indicate the extent of their agreement with each of the following statements: (1) Retirement is a pleasant time of life. (2) People who don't retire when they can afford to are foolish. (3) Older workers should retire early when they can, so as to give younger people more of a chance on the job. (4) Work is the most meaningful part of life. (5) Most people think more of someone who works than they do of someone who doesn't. Values of 1-4 were assigned to each question, with the highest score representing the most favorable attitude toward retirement. Total scores thus range from 5 to 20. Those from 5 to 11 are classified as "unfavorable"; 12 to 13, "ambivalent"; and 14 to 20, "favorable."

2. The same question was asked with respect to the weeks during the preceding 12 months that the individual was out of the labor force. Responses are so similar to those for the survey week that they are not described.

3. Precoded responses were: Yes, definitely; Yes, if it is something I can do; Yes, if satisfactory wage; Yes, if satisfactory location; Yes, if satisfactory hours; Yes (if other); No, health won't permit; No, don't want to work, retired; No, don't need the money; and No, other. The respondents who replied in the negative were asked: "What if it were a part-time job?"

4. We are grateful to Alan Fox of the Social Security Administration's Division of Retirement and Survivors Studies for helpful comments on an earlier draft of this section.

5. See, also, Schulz (1980, p. 78). Schulz's estimate for a "middle-income worker" is 65-70 percent, comparable to Munnell's estimate for the same income level.

6. The rate was calculated by dividing the total retirement benefits received by the respondent in the 12-month period preceding the 1981 survey by his average wage and salary income in the year prior to retirement, expressed in dollars of 1980 purchasing power. We also calculated replacement rates using the average of a 2-year period in the denominator. The patterns were very similar to those yielded by the 1-year income figures. The latter were used because they result in fewer cases of missing data. For other methods of calculating replacement rates and for an analysis of such rates based on the Retirement History Study, see Fox (1982).

7. About 2 percent of the retirees—23 sample cases—reported neither Social Security nor other pension income in 1980.

8. For a detailed description of the Social Security program, see Myers (1981).

9. An earlier version of the Multiple Classification Analysis (MCA) without the age breakdown showed significantly lower benefits for nonmarried than for married men.

10. To be eligible for some Social Security retirement benefits the age group of men under consideration here would have needed only 40 calendar quarters of self-employment income (of at least $400 per year) or of earnings in covered employment (of at least $50 per quarter). The earnings in covered employment might have been achieved at any time from 1937 on; the self-employment in-

come at any time after 1950. Clearly, it would not be difficult for individuals whose principal careers were in noncovered government employment (and who earned full pensions there), to have achieved eligibility for at least minimum Social Security benefits as well.

    11. *Economic Report of the President*, 1981, table B-27 p. 264.

References

Bowen, William G., and Finegan, T. Aldrich. 1969. *The Economics of Labor Force Participation*. Princeton, N.J.: Princeton University Press.

Clark, Robert L.; Johnson, Thomas; and McDermed, Ann Archibald. 1980. "Allocation of Time and Resources by Married Couples Approaching Retirement." *Social Security Bulletin* 4: 3-16.

Fillenbaum, Gerda G. 1971. "The Working Retired." *Journal of Gerontology*, 1: 82-89.

Fox, Alan. 1982. "Earnings Replacement Rates and Total Income: Findings from the Retirement History Study." *Social Security Bulletin* 10: 3-22.

Harris, Louis et al. 1981. *Aging in the Eighties: America in Transition*. Washington, D.C.: The National Council on the Aging.

Motley, D.K. "Availability of Retired Persons for Work: Findings from the Retirement History Survey." *Social Security Bulletin* 41: 18-27.

Munnell, Alicia. 1982. "The Economics of Private Pensions." Washington, D.C.: Brookings Institution.

Myers, Robert J. 1981. *Social Security*. Homewood, Ill.: Richard D. Irwin.

Parnes, Herbert S., and Nestel, Gilbert. 1981. "The Retirement Experience." In Herbert S. Parnes, ed., *Work and Retirement: A Longitudinal Study of Men*. Cambridge, Mass.: MIT.

Quinn, Joseph F. 1980. "Labor Force Participation Patterns of Older Self-Employed Workers." *Social Security Bulletin* 4: 17-28.

Schulz, James H. 1980. *The Economics of Aging*. 2nd Edition. Belmont, Cal.: Wadsworth.

U.S. President. 1981. *Economic Report of the President*. Washington, D.C.: U.S. Government Printing Office.

Wentworth, Edna C. 1968. *Employment After Retirement: A Study of the Postentitlement Work Experience of Men Drawing Benefits Under Social Security*. Social Security Administration, Office of Research and Statistics. Research Report no. 21. Washington, D.C.: Government Printing Office.

6

Leisure Activities and Social Networks

William R. Morgan
Herbert S. Parnes
Lawrence J. Less

Retirement has obvious economic consequences for the individual, and these have been explored in the preceding chapter. However, retirement has important social-psychological implications as well. Complete cessation of work means that the activity to which most men have devoted the largest portion of their waking hours no longer occupies them; not only is the familiar work routine disrupted, but the individual is also removed from the social environment of the workplace. Significant adjustments take place as the retiree seeks other uses of his time and attempts to develop other social contacts. In this chapter, after a brief description of the extent of, and reasons for, migration among retirees, we examine the use of leisure time and explore the character and determinants of the social networks they enjoy.

Migration

Press accounts have referred to increasing numbers of elderly individuals making interstate moves in recent years. Preliminary results of a study of Census data on interstate migration by persons age 60 and older show that the increase between 1970 and 1980 was 4 times as large as the corresponding increase over the preceding decade. The investigators "suspect that they are moving primarily to improve their life style" (*New York Times*, December 9, 1983, p. 20).

In the 1981 NLS interview schedule retirees were asked whether they had ever changed their city or county of residence for a year or more since first retiring. Approximately one-fifth of the retirees had done so, the proportion ranging between 12 percent of the men who had retired between 1977 and 1981 to 21 percent of those who had retired between 1967 and 1976 and 31 percent of those who had retired before 1967.

We are grateful to Kenneth Chi for assistance with the data analysis.

The migration rate for all retirees was about 3 times as high among whites as among blacks, 19 percent and 6 percent, respectively (figure 6-1).

Most of the moves were apparently made to improve the quality of the physical or social environment. Over three-fifths of the retirees reported that the most important reason for the move was to achieve a change of climate or physical environment (31 percent), to be with friends or relatives (20 percent), or for health reasons (11 percent). Seeking a lower cost of living (9 percent) or improved job opportunities (3 percent) accounted for only 1 in 8 of the moves.

Leisure Activities

Gerontological literature contains numerous studies of the leisure activities of the elderly (Bosse and Ekerdt, 1981, references; Harris et al., 1981; Longino and Kart, 1982; Roadburg, 1981, references; Weiner and Hunt, 1981, references), and some have focused on the impact of retirement (Bell, 1975; Bosse and Ekerdt, 1981; Foner and Schwab, 1981; Palmore, et al., 1979; Peppers, 1976; Simpson, Back, and McKinney, 1966). Many of the studies have aimed at testing competing theories of aging. Disengagement theory (Cumming and Henry, 1961) views aging as an inevitable period of withdrawal desired by both the individual and society. In contrast, activity theory (Havighurst and Albrecht, 1953) holds that high activity levels maintained into old age increase life satisfaction, and that if withdrawal from society occurs, the aging individual is the passive victim rather than the initiator of such disinvolvement. Kleemeier (1964) has pointed out that leisure activities may substitute for work "in creating good morale and high life satisfaction in the later years" (p. 183). Atchley (1971), in support of the "continuity theory" suggests that leisure can have a great deal of positive value as a "bridge between pre- and postretirement life" (p. 17). A comprehensive review of the literature on adjustment to retirement (Friedmann and Orbach, 1974) concludes that "there is no basis for the assumption that retirement causes or necessarily results in a constriction of life space and activity."

Despite this considerable work, what is known about the patterns of leisure activity among the elderly and, in particular, about differences in this regard between retired individuals and those who have remained at work is not entirely satisfying. Except for the single tabulation provided by Foner and Schwab (1981), the limited number of studies of the latter issue have been based upon very small unrepresentative samples. Here we attempt to overcome these shortcomings.

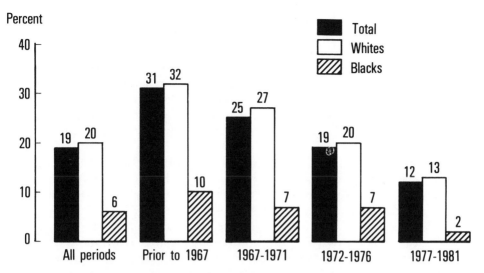

Note: From the city or county of resident at retirement.

Figure 6–1. Proportion of Retirees Making Geographic Move since Retirement, by Year of Retirement and Race

First, we describe the leisure activity of retired men and identify the characteristics associated with variation in the extent of leisure pursuits. Second, we examine the change in the pattern and extent of leisure activity as men move into retirement over a three-year period. Third, various aspects of leisure activity will be used as intervening variables to explore the character and determinants of social networks.

No definition of leisure is universally accepted, although it generally connotes time spent in activities other than work for pay or personal maintenance (Kaplan, 1961; Kleemeier, 1964; Robinson, chap. 4, 1977). This uncertainty gives rise to the question whether the meaning of leisure changes once an individual loses or abandons his primary labor market role (Hendricks and Hendricks, 1977; Roadburg, 1981). In any case, most investigations of leisure pursuits have attempted to obtain some measure of the amount of time—either in relative or absolute terms—that the individual has spent in a variety of specified activities (Harris et al., 1981; Bosse and Ekerdt, 1981).

In the case of the NLS, the 1978 interview schedule asked respondents whether they had engaged in each of six different types of activity during the preceding twelve months: (1) sports or exercise (e.g., golf, tennis, swimming); (2) reading books, magazines, or newspapers; (3) hobbies (e.g., collections, woodworking, playing a musical instrument, or gardening); (4) visiting with friends or relatives; (5) working on home maintenance or home repairs around the house; or (6) doing volunteer work. For each affirmative response, the individual was asked during how many weeks he engaged in the activity and, on the average, about how many hours per week he was thus involved. The 1981 interview schedule repeated these questions and added four additional activities: (1) attending meetings or religious services, (2) going to movies or other spectator events, (3) helping friends or neighbors without pay, and (4) watching television.[1] Because of time constraints, however, the series of questions in 1981 was asked only of individuals who had identified themselves as retired.[2] Thus, comparisons between 1978 and 1981 (for the six types of leisure activity common to both surveys) can be made only for individuals who were retired at both times or who retired between the two years.

On the basis of these questions, we have constructed two variables for each type of activity: (1) a dichotomous variable indicating whether the respondent engaged in the activity and (2) the total number of hours (weeks x weekly hours) that he spent on the activity. The latter has also been summed across the total number of activities to provide an aggregate annual figure. The limitations of the resulting data are self-evident. To begin with, this method of obtaining information on the amount of time devoted to various activities is not as reliable as the use of time diaries (Robinson, 1977). Second, we clearly cannot claim that all forms of leisure activity are included, although the 1981 list is substantially better in this regard than that used in 1978.

Findings from the 1978 Survey

Parnes and Less (1983, pp. 82-99) analyzed in detail the 1978 data for the total cohort, differentiating between men who had retired and those who had not. Before examining the 1981 activity patterns of retirees, it will be useful to review the principal findings of this earlier study.

Gross Relationships: Retirement Status and Race. For the total sample, reading and visiting were by far the most popular leisure time activities, engaged in by over 85 percent of the respondents. At the other extreme was volunteer work, which occupied only 1 in 5 of the men. Between these, in descending order of frequency, were home maintenance work (67 percent), hobbies (53 percent), and exercise (40 percent). The average amount of time devoted to the activities by those who participated in them ranged from about 485 hours in the case of reading, to about 150 each for home maintenance and volunteer work. Black men were much less likely than whites to engage in each of the activities, the difference being about 20 percentage points or more in the case of reading, exercise, and hobbies.

The relative popularity of the several types of activity was identical for retired and nonretired men and, indeed, little difference appeared between the two groups in the incidence of each activity, except for the lesser participation of the retired men in home maintenance (63 vs. 73 percent). As would be expected, however, retired men spent more time at each activity than the nonretired. Taking all of the activities together, the typical respondent estimated spending about 1,000 hours per year—in the neighborhood of 20 hours per week. For black men, however, the amount of time was only two-thirds as great as for whites.

Multivariate Analysis. With other characteristics of the men controlled (e.g., age, health, and socioeconomic status), retirement status was found to make a more substantial difference than in the simple bivariate relationships described above. Retired men devoted 47 percent more time than their nonretired counterparts to the leisure activities covered by the survey—a differential of about 7 hours a week in contrast to the less than 5-hour difference shown by the bivariate data.

The racial difference persisted with other factors controlled. Other things equal, black men devoted about 3 fewer hours per week than whites to the specified activities. This finding led us to conclude that questions on leisure time activities probably have a cultural bias, and that a serious effort to explore racial difference in leisure activities would require a different approach. Consistent with this interpretation is Neulinger's (1981, p. 126) observation that there are good theoretical reasons for expecting major differences in leisure behavior between whites and blacks. "Leisure behavior is part of one's cultural heritage, and the American black certainly had a cultural background different from the average white American . . . their job was to make leisure possible for everyone except themselves."

Leisure Time Activities of Retired Men: 1981

Table 6-1 shows, for the entire sample of retirees, the degree of participation in the 10 activities covered by the survey. Not surprisingly, TV viewing is the most universal pastime, involving all but about 4 percent of the retirees, with visiting and reading coming next in popularity (89 and 87 percent, respectively). As in the 1978 data, volunteer work is at the other end of the continuum, engaging only 1 in 5 of the men. Approximately half or more of the retirees devote time to home maintenance (72 percent), attending meetings (57 percent), helping friends or neighbors (51 percent), sports or exercise, and the proportion who attend movies, sporting events, or other forms of entertainment outside the home is about the same.

Table 6–1
Numbers of Hours Devoted during Past 12 Months to Specified Leisure Activities by Retired Men, 1981
(percentage distributions)

Number of Hours	Exercise	Reading	Hobbies	Visiting	Home Mainte-nance	Volunteer Work	Organiza-tions	Outside Entertain-ment	Helping Others	T.V.
Sample (n = 1599)										
Total percent	100	100	100	100	100	100	100	100	100	100
None	68	13	47	11	28	81	43	65	49	4
1–250	20	24	30	55	56	15	47	34	47	15
251–500	6	23	8	17	7	2	6	1	2	15
Over 500	6	40	15	17	9	2	4	1	2	66[b]
Mean[a]	288	524	379	305	186	192	166	52	73	840

[a]Excludes nonparticipants.
[b]Broken down as follows: 501–1,000 = 28 percent; 1,001–1,500 = 25 percent; over 1,500 = 13 percent.

When only the participants in each activity are considered, the average number of hours per year varies greatly, from 840 for TV viewing and 524 for reading, to 73 and 52 for helping others and for attending entertainment events, respectively. In the case of each of the activities except TV viewing and reading, relatively little variation appears in the amount of time participants spend; between three-fifths and nine-tenths of the men who engage in each of 8 activities devote no more than 250 hours per year—about 5 hours per week on average. In the case of reading and television, however, the dispersion is much greater. Somewhat over one-fourth of those who read spend as little as 250 hours per year at it, while 46 percent spend more than 500 hours. Variation in the extent of TV viewing is even more extreme: about 30 percent watch for less than 500 hours per year, an equal proportion for 500-1,000 hours, and about 40 percent for more than 1,000 hours.

As was true in the 1978 data, there are very large racial differences in the incidence of participation and in the time spent in these leisure time activities. Except for attending meetings (including religious services) the proportion of black men participating in every one of the activities is lower than that of whites, ranging from 30 percentage points for home maintenance to 4 points in the case of TV viewing. Racial differences in the amount of time spent by participants follows pretty much the same pattern. Only in the cases of attending meetings and helping friends does the average mount of time spent by black participants equal or exceed that of whites.

We also examined age differences in the patterns of leisure time pursuits. Except for an inverse relationship between age and (1) participation in exercise (40 percent for men age 60-64 vs. 29 percent for those age 70-74) and (2) home maintenance activity (79 vs. 68 percent), no regular differences appear among the three 5-year age groups.

To all of the specified activities combined, retirees in 1981 devoted an average of 2,139 hours—somewhat over 41 hours per week. The average for black men was almost 600 hours per year below that for whites. Television viewing accounted for two-fifths (39 percent) of the total. When the list of activities is confined to those included in the 1978 interview schedule, the average number of hours spent by the 1981 retiree totaled about 1,200, which compares with the 1,100 hours that were estimated in 1978.

Multivariate Analysis. What characteristics of retirees are associated with the variation in the amount of time they devote to the specified leisure time activities? This question is addressed by the data shown in table 6-2, which presents the results of a multiple classification analysis (MCA). The universe is confined to men who had been retired for at least 12

Table 6–2
Total Number of Hours per Year Devoted to All Leisure Activities, by Retired Men[a], by Selected Characteristics, 1981
(MCA results)

Characteristic	n	Unadjusted # of Hours	Adjusted[b] # of Hours (F-ratio)
Total Sample	1,344	2,253	2,253
Race			(12.133)[f]
Whites	985	2,295	2,283[f]
Blacks	359	1,722	1,853[f]
Age			(2.538)[h]
60–64	318	2,225	2,248
65–69	547	2,317	2,334[h]
70–74	479	2,200	2,167[h]
Marital status			(1.327)
Married	1,093	2,266	2,236
Nonmarried	251	2,183	2,338
Physical or mental impairment, 1981[c]			(1.137)
None	276	2,370	2,272
Minor	132	2,464	2,373
Moderate	121	2,298	2,213
Substantial	165	2,396	2,371
Severe	623	2,107	2,197
Total family income, 1981			(2.331)[g]
Less than $5,000	151	1,892	2,035[h]
$5,000–$9,999	234	2,021	2,092[g]
$10,000–$14,999	172	2,272	2,264
$15,000–$19,999	123	2,445	2,411[h]
$20,000 or more	212	2,424	2,337
Occupation			(4.438)[f]
Professional	120	2,625	2,571[f]
Managerial	160	2,463	2,416[g]
Other white collar	140	2,458	2,392
Craft	301	2,194	2,159
Other blue collar	401	2,120	2,162
Other	218	1,907	2,042[g]
Region			(0.231)
South	527	2,125	2,230
Non South	817	2,316	2,263
Size of community			(2.343)[h]
Small	530	2,113	2,171[h]
Medium	539	2,367	2,326[h]
Large	275	2,288	2,259
Work activity, 1981			(25.101)[f]
None	1,124	2,323	2,352[f]
Some	319	1,919	1,777[f]

Table 6–2 continued

Characteristic	n	Unadjusted # of Hours	Adjusted[b] # of Hours (F-ratio)
Attitude toward retirement, 1978[d]			(4.397)[g]
Favorable	408	2,484	2,387[f]
Ambivalent	518	2,227	2,269
Unfavorable	310	2,071	2,131[g]
Reason for retirement			(2.986)[g]
Forced	42	2,145	2,060
Health	513	2,030	2,117[f]
Voluntary early	538	2,376	2,306
Voluntary normal	179	2,476	2,466[g]
Discouraged	66	2,253	2,253
Adjusted R^2			.09

[a]Universe restricted to men who retired at least 12 months prior to the 1981 survey, the period to which leisure time activity questions related.

[b]For nature of adjustment see "A Note on the Tables and Graphs."

[c]For construction of impairment index see Table 6–4, note b.

[d]See text footnote 3.

[e]Not included in regression.

[f]Significant at the .01 level.

[g]Significant at the .05 level.

[h]Significant at the .10 level.

months before the 1981 survey, the period to which the leisure time activity questions relate.

The gross racial difference previously observed in leisure activity time is maintained even with other characteristics controlled. Other things being equal, black retirees devote about 8 fewer hours per week than whites to the specified activities, which reinforces our conclusion based on the 1978 data regarding cultural bias in the questions.

Both family income and occupational level of preretirement job bear positive relationships with the amount of time spent in leisure time activity. The difference between professional workers and nonskilled blue-collar workers amount to 400 hours per year, or almost 8 hours per week. With regard to income, a difference of about 375 hours a year separates those with annual incomes under $5,000 and those earning $15,000-$19,999, although the highest income group ($20,000 or more) devotes somewhat fewer hours to leisure than the next lower category. The fact that occupational level and income exert independent effects on leisure activities suggests that the kind of work men do influences leisure activities not only through the income that it generates, but also by conditioning (or reflecting) their interests.

Marital status shows no significant relationship to the measure of leisure time activity, but age does, albeit in a curious way: men age 65-69 devote significantly more time to leisure activities than those in either the older or younger 5-year age category. Health condition as measured by the impairment index is not related to the amount of time retirees devote to the specified activities. When we excluded television viewing from these activities, however, there was a statistically significant relationship for the impairment variable. Although this relationship was not completely systematic, men with minor impairments were significantly below average and men with severe impairments were significantly above average in the annual number of hours devoted to leisure activity exclusive of TV.

Significant differences also appear in the amount of time retirees devote to leisure pursuits depending on whether they have postretirement jobs, the reasons for their retirement, and their general attitudes toward work and retirement. Paid employment during the year reduces the average hours of leisure by 575, other things being equal. Men who retired for health reasons devote considerably less time to the specified pursuits than do voluntary retirees. Because this difference is net of differences in the extent of impairments, it suggests either that the impairment index does not reflect the full extent of health differences among the several groups of retirees or that, irrespective of current state of health, men forced by bad health to retire are psychologically less disposed than others to develop interests in the types of leisure activities covered by the survey. Men who retired voluntarily at age 65 or older devote an above-average number of hours to leisure activities.

The strong positive relationship between attitude toward retirement and extent of leisure time activity is difficult to interpret confidently because the direction of causation is ambiguous. However, because the attitudinal variable—obtained in 1978—purports to measure a *generalized* reaction to the idea of retirement rather than the degree of satisfaction with the retired status,[3] it seems reasonable to conclude that men who hold favorable views of retirement are more likely to develop purposeful uses of leisure when they themselves retire.

Changes in Leisure Activities, 1978-1981

By selecting from the activities covered by the 1981 interview schedule those that were also included in 1978, it is possible to learn what changes occurred (1) among retired men as they aged by 3 years and (2) among men who moved from work to retirement between the two dates.

Men Retired in Both Years. There were 1,085 men in the sample who reported themselves as retired in both 1978 and 1981. For each of these years, the extent of their involvement in the activities covered in the 1978 survey can be assessed. The incidence of participation in the six activities common to the 1978 and 1981 interview schedules is remarkably stable over the 3-year period. The largest changes are a 9-percentage-point decline in the proportion engaging in exercise or sports, a 6-point drop in the percentage involved in hobbies (including gardening), and a 4-point drop in the percentage doing home maintenance. These decreases, incidentally, were no greater for the older than for the younger half of the cohort. Excluding those who do not engage in the activity, the number of hours of participation increased in each case, by amounts ranging from 4 percent in home maintenance to 47 percent in hobbies. Even in exercise activities, hours of involvement showed an increase of 14 percent—all attributable to the younger half of the age cohort.

When the combined effect of changes in participation and intensity of involvement in all activities is calculated, the average number of hours increased by 12 percent—15 percent for those who were age 60-67 in 1981 and 9 percent among those age 68-74. As in the previous relationships, the pattern for whites and blacks differed—the average hours for blacks in 1981 remained virtually the same as when they were 3 years younger.

Men Retiring Between 1978 and 1981. A total of 243 respondents had reported themselves retired for at least 12 months at the time of the 1981 survey, although they had still been at their jobs in 1978. Except for an 11-point increase in the proportion who engaged in home maintenance activity, very little growth appeared in the incidence of participation in leisure activities as the men moved into retirement, but a large increase appeared in the *amount of time* devoted to each by those engaged in it. The smallest increase in number of hours (6 percent) was in home maintenance; in no other instance, however, was the increase under 25 percent, and the number of hours devoted to exercise and to hobbies more than doubled. Considering all the activities combined, the total number of hours increased from 866 to 1,250, or 44 percent.

Interestingly, this longitudinal estimate of the effect of retirement on the amount of time devoted to the specified leisure activities is almost identical to the estimate based on a cross-sectional analysis of the 1978 data (Parnes and Less, 1983, p. 92). With other factors controlled in a multivariate analysis, men who were retired in 1978 spent 369 more hours per year on these activities than their never-retired counterparts—a difference of 47 percent.

Social Networks of Retirees

One major implication of these expanded hours in leisure activity by retired men is an increase in their social interaction level when they are away from work. The nature of this interaction varies, of course, with the nature of the leisure. Certain of the leisure activities measured in 1981—TV viewing, reading, hobbies, and home maintenance—take place primarily at home and thus produce opportunities for interaction primarily with other household members. In 1981 retirees engaged in these four leisure activities an average of 32 hours per week, representing three-fourths of their estimated total weekly time spent in the ten measured leisure activities. This increased household interaction is primarily with wives, secondarily with children. In 1981, 84 percent of the retirees were married and living with a spouse. In addition, 24 percent of the men also had children or assorted other persons living in their households.

By contrast, the remaining leisure activities—recreational exercise, visiting friends or relatives, doing volunteer work, helping friends and neighbors, attending meetings and religious services, and attending spectator events—all take place primarily outside the household; and all but possibly the last are likely to involve intensive social interaction with nonhousehold members. The average of 11 hours per week spent in these activities is one gauge of the extent to which these men are able to avoid the psychological and physical risks of social isolation.

More generally, sustained social interaction with others outside the household, whether in the context of part-time work or leisure-related activities, constitutes the retirees' membership in a social network (Adams, 1967). Although members of one's social network, including children, friends, relatives, and neighbors, provide a crucial support system throughout the life course, gerontological research indicates this is particularly so for the elderly. The informal social network is preferred whenever possible over more formal institutional mechanisms when aid is needed (Cantor, 1980). Moreover, the subjective awareness of belonging to a social network contributes to a sense of well-being in the elderly even more than the actual frequency of contact in the network (Ward, Sherman, and LaGory, 1984). Knowing there is someone nearby who cares about you may be more important than the care itself. On the other hand, the high value placed on social and economic independence and personal autonomy in our society is a countervailing subjective force that may cause some of these men to deny any awareness of, or need for, a support network.

The Presence and Composition of Retirees' Perceived Social Networks

The retired men were asked in 1981 whether or not they had persons outside their household (1) who could give financial or personal help; and (2) to whom, other than their children, they felt "especially close." For all retirees, 57 percent reported they had someone outside their household who could give financial help. Somewhat more, 72 percent, reported that they had someone who could give personal help. Exactly half reported they had at least one person outside their household (besides their children) who was not a potential helper but to whom they felt close. Considering the three questions together, fully 85 percent of the men identified at least one person outside their household who could help either financially or personally or to whom they felt close. The 15 percent who identified no one approximate the proportion of retirees who in 1981 perceived themselves to be socially isolated.

The social composition of these networks revealed a strong preference for close relatives. The person turned to first for financial help was most frequently one of their children (58 percent), next, another relative (32 percent), and only infrequently a friend or other nonrelative (11 percent). The person selected first for personal help tended again to be either one of their children (40 percent) or another relative (25 percent), although 1 of every 3 retirees did choose either a friend (24 percent) or other nonrelative (11 percent). Even the individual named first as someone close (other than children) was equally as likely to be a relative (50 percent) as a friend (46 percent) or other nonrelative (4 percent).

These patterns of relationships became more pronounced with increasing age; that is, children were even more likely to be the primary financial and personal helpers among the older retirees. The proportions of retirees in the age categories 60-64, 65-69, and 70-74 who selected children first for financial help were 48 percent, 54 percent, and 68 percent, respectively. Similarly, the proportion who selected children first for personal help were 29 percent, 41 percent, and 48 percent, respectively. Although it is plausible and consistent with other research that aging per se increases the likelihood of dependence on one's children, particularly if one's relative and friend helpers are also elderly, the other possible interpretation for this cross-sectional correlation is that having children as one's primary helpers increases the likelihood of survival to old age. Children may care more, or at least feel more obligated, than friends or relatives, and hence may better facilitate survival.

Black retirees and retirees not currently married were more likely than white and married retirees to perceive friends as their primary financial and personal helpers; conversely, they were less likely to select children. Only 41 percent of black retirees named one of their children first for financial help, compared to 60 percent for whites. Similarly, only 22 percent identified an offspring first for personal help, compared to 44 percent for whites. Among retirees not currently married only 39 percent and 32 percent named a child first for financial and personal help, respectively. The comparable values for married retirees were 61 percent and 42 percent. The greater reliance of both these groups on friends to provide the network of support outside the household is consistent with common understandings about black-white, married-nonmarried differences in male social relations. More immediately, though, it simply reflects the greater likelihood for widowed and black retirees to live directly in the households of their children.

Proximity and Frequency of Network Contact

Respondents were asked in 1981 what they would do for help, or had done in the past, when a serious medical emergency arose. The proportion who had experienced such an emergency for themselves or their wives was 38 percent, and ranged from 33 percent of those age 60-64 to 43 percent of those age 70-74. Although these men relied predominantly on formal institutional mechanisms (emergency squad, doctor, police, or fire departments) for handling the situation, in over 10 percent of the cases the first response was to contact someone in their informal social network of neighbors, friends, and relatives. The same tendency appeared when all of the men were asked how they planned to respond to a future emergency. Planned use of the formal institutional mechanisms, particularly the emergency squad, however, was somewhat greater than the reported actual use. The approximately 20 percent of the men whose first planned response was "to get to the emergency room" were further asked how they would get there. About two-thirds, 68 percent, of the retirees age 60-64 planned to use their own cars, but this proportion steadily decreased to 53 percent for the men age 70-74. Compared with the younger men, the older men planned instead to rely more on the emergency squad (29 percent compared to 19 percent), a friend or neighbor's car (13 percent compared to 6 percent) or a taxi (4 percent compared to 1 percent). Use of both formal institutional and informal network supports apparently increases with advancing age, both serving as substitutes for former reliance on one's own means.

We next examined the physical proximity of the informal social network. For respondents naming persons who could give personal help, as in the case of a medical emergency, the median distance of the person selected first was 4 miles. This varied from only 2 miles when the primary personal helper was a friend, to 9 miles when the helper was one of their children. For financial help the median distance of the person named first was slightly greater, 10 miles, reflecting the greater tendency to rely on children over friends, and on more distant (and presumably more affluent) children also. Still, the close physical proximity of the helpers, whether personal or financial, remains striking. The median distance of the person they felt close to was also 4 miles, ranging from 2 miles for friends to 9 miles for relatives. A minority of respondents did identify persons who were some distance away. This ranged from 30 percent who identified a primary financial helper who was 100 or more miles distant, 21 percent whose primary close person was 100 or more miles distant, and 16 percent whose primary personal helper was 100 or more miles distant. The latter would be of little direct assistance during emergency situations.

Perhaps the more important use of the informal network, however, is as a source of sustained social interaction. For most retirees, having significant others outside the household with whom they regularly interact is a critical element in quality of life. Removal from former work associates can be problematic for retirees, particularly for those who have previously engaged in few leisure-time social activities. To explore this issue we examined the frequency with which retirees report having social contacts with their primary network members, both in face-to-face interaction and by telephone. Just under 1 in 5 retirees reported such interaction occurs daily. Daily face-to-face interaction occurred with 18 percent of the identified close persons, 16 percent of the personal helpers, and 14 percent of the financial helpers. Daily telephone interaction occurred with 20 percent of both the primary financial and personal helpers and with 12 percent of the close persons. Over half of the retirees reported that this contact occurs at least once a week. Contact occurred in person or by phone at least weekly with 60 and 64 percent of the personal helpers, respectively; with 58 percent and 51 percent of the financial helpers; and with 42 and 53 percent of the close persons.

The most frequent contacts were with children, over the telephone. One in 4 (25 percent) of the retirees reported having daily phone conversations with the child whom they identified as either their primary financial or personal helper. Three of 4 (71 percent) report having a telephone conversation with their children-helpers at least once a week. By contrast, face-to-face interaction occurs most frequently with friends, although even in this type of direct contact children participate almost as much. Friends identified as primary helpers were seen daily by 18 percent of the men, compared with 16 percent who reported seeing their children-helpers daily. At least weekly direct contact occurred with 65 percent of friend-helpers and 58 percent of children-helpers.

Determinants of Network Size and Composition

What background and retirement conditions determine how many persons are in a retiree's perceived network? To what extent are the primary network members predominantly adult children, friends, or relatives? After being asked to identify the relationship of their primary financial and personal helpers and other close persons, retirees in 1981 next estimated the total number of persons they could ask for financial and personal help, and how many others they regarded as close. The sum of their responses yielded possible scores ranging from zero for those who named no one in each, to 30 for those who gave the maximum of 10 or more persons in each category. The actual mean was toward the low end, at 4.6 persons (table 6-3), with a standard deviation of 4.4. This variable, our measure of network size, is analyzed with respect to two sets of determinants: a set of 9 basic and relatively fixed background conditions and a set of 4 variables describing the individual's circumstances in retirement.

The background variables include (1) years of education completed; (2) Duncan socioeconomic index of the retiree's last full-time occupation as measures of socioeconomic status; (3) ethnic minority status, measured by a dummy variable coded 1 for black, zero for whites; (4) region, a dummy variable coded 1 for South and zero for non-South, (5) residential location, a multiple dummy variable, with central city the referent category and separate dummies coded 1 for suburban and rural locations; (6) respondent's age; (7) number of children; (8) marital status coded 1 if married and living with spouse, zero otherwise; and (9) household composition. The household composition variable measures what others besides a spouse live with the respondent; it consists of four dummy terms. Contrasted with the referent category of men living alone or with a spouse are (a) men living also with dependent children, (b) with adult children, (c) with dependent others, and (d) with adult others. Children and others were classified as "dependent" rather than "adult" if they had no earnings in the past year. The few households having both children and others were assigned to the other categories.

The four variables describing retirement conditions are (1) leisure activity participation, (2) weeks of employment during the preceding year, (3) health impairments, and (4) income level.[4] Leisure activity participation in 1981 comprises three separate variables for (a) number of home-centered activities (TV viewing, reading, hobbies, and home maintenance); (b) number of social activities away from home (recreational exercise, visiting, volunteering, helping friends, and attending meetings); and (c) number of nonsocial activities away from home (going on overnight trips and attending entertainment events) the men engaged in during the past year.[5]

Column one of table 6-3 presents the regression of total network size on the nine background variables alone. Network size is positively related to the men's education level, residence in the South, and total number of children. It is negatively related to age, to being black, and to having dependent children or others in the household. Variables with no effect are the status of the retiree's last full-time occupation, marital status, having adult children in the household, and whether his residence is urban, suburban, or rural.

These background variables were expected to operate directly on network size primarily by setting opportunity constraints on the number of persons available to serve in the support network. The positive effect for the total number of children supports the traditional hope of parents having enough children to look after them in old age. Conversely, having dependent children and others still living in the household reduces network size because it eliminates the opportunity to draw upon these individuals as potential outside helpers. Living in the South, or at least the traditional South (more likely perhaps for this older generation than for others) increases the likelihood that one is a member of a large kin network and community of friends and neighbors who can be drawn on as a support network. Age also affects network opportunities to the degree that advancing age steadily reduces the number of surviving nonchildren relatives and friends. Similarly, black men's higher mortality restricts the size of their potential support network compared to white men's, particularly given black retirees' greater tendency to select friends over children.

The second way these background variables may affect network size is indirectly through their influence on the men's present retirement conditions, which in turn directly affect network size by delimiting interaction opportunities. Accordingly, a second equation (column two of table 6-3) reestimated the effect of the nine background variables net of the four basic retirement conditions—extent of participation in leisure activities, weeks of employment in past year, level of income in past year, and number of reported health impairments. Any substantial reduction in the coefficient of a previously significant background variable indicates that that variable's effect operates primarily indirectly by influencing one or more of these retirement conditions.

Two background variables do become nonsignificant in this second equation—the positive effect of education and the negative effect of age. Although it is not shown here, education is positively related to leisure activity participation, postretirement employment, and income level. Each of these retirement conditions in turn significantly increases network size, presumably by increasing interaction opportunities away from home. One's educational background thus influences network size primarily through its impact on these current retirement conditions. Similarly, the age of retirees is negatively related to postretirement employment and leisure activity. The negative effect of age on network size thus operates primarily by reducing the retiree's own employment and leisure activity, rather than by reducing the pool of network survivors, as we first thought.

Focusing now on the retirement condition effects, equation two indicates that all four substantially affect network size. As expected, the positive effect of leisure activity participation operates only for activities

Table 6–3
The Number of Nonhousehold Financial Helpers, Personal Helpers, and Other Close Persons, as Determined by the Background and Retirement Conditions of Retired Men in 1981
(OLS unstandardized regression results)

Explanatory Variablesᵇ	Total Persons				Financial Helpers	Personal Helpers	Other Close Persons
	(1) b	(t)	(2) b	(t)	(3) b	(4) b	(5) b
Retirement conditions, 1981							
Number of leisure activities:							
Social	—		0.624ᵃ	(6.77)	0.126ᵃ	0.260ᵃ	0.238ᵃ
Trips	—		0.183	(1.20)	0.102	0.041	0.040
Home	—		-0.075	(-0.72)	0.024	-0.050	-0.050
Employment weeks	—		0.019ᵃ	(3.34)	0.004	0.006ᵃ	0.009ᵃ
Health impairmentsᶜ	—		0.067ᵃ	(3.38)	0.010	0.032ᵃ	0.026ᵃ
Income ($0–$5,000)							
$5–$15,000	—		0.414	(1.23)	0.029	0.191	0.195
$15–$25,000	—		0.955ᵃ	(2.44)	0.123	0.470ᵃ	0.362
$25,000+	—		1.341ᵃ	(3.07)	0.349ᵃ	0.400	0.592ᵃ
NA	—		-0.115	(-0.33)	-0.154	-0.138	0.178
Background conditions							
Education, years	0.072ᵃ	(2.07)	0.003	(0.07)	0.001	0.028	-0.027
Occupation, Duncan SEIᵈ	0.002	(0.49)	-0.004	(-0.86)	-0.002	-0.003	0.000
Black	-0.968	(-2.40)	-1.054ᵃ	(-2.66)	-0.213	-0.361	-0.481ᵃ
South	0.917ᵃ	(4.29)	0.826ᵃ	(3.93)	0.274ᵃ	0.316ᵃ	0.237ᵃ
Residence (central city)							
Suburban	-0.005	(-0.02)	-0.158	(-0.63)	0.002	0.014	-0.173
Rural	0.083	(0.32)	-0.085	(-0.33)	-0.091	0.057	-0.051
Age	-0.060ᵃ	(-2.46)	-0.024	(-0.98)	0.003	0.000	-0.028ᵃ
Marital status	-0.145	(-0.52)	-0.382	(-1.36)	-0.233ᵃ	-0.230	0.080
Children, number	0.286ᵃ	(5.82)	0.267ᵃ	(5.52)	0.148ᵃ	0.096ᵃ	0.023

Household composition (alone or with wife only):							
Children without earnings	−1.753[a]	(−4.39)	−1.467[a]	(−3.74)	−0.652[a]	−0.584[a]	−0.231
Children with earnings	−0.527	(−1.23)	−0.771	(−1.82)	−0.297	−0.541[a]	0.067
Others without earnings	−1.404[a]	(−3.67)	−1.139[a]	(−3.04)	−0.215	−0.381[a]	−0.543[a]
Others with earnings	−0.205	(−0.34)	−0.412	(−0.68)	−0.224	−0.060	−0.127
Constant	7.202		3.716		0.461	0.751	2.504
R^2	.049		.100		.072	.069	.051
Dependent variable mean	4.56		4.56		1.34	1.92	1.31
Sample n	1959		1959		1959	1959	1959

[a]$p < .05$.

[b]Referent category given in parentheses after variable name for the three variables having multiple dummy terms.

[c]For a description of the impairment index, see note c, Table 6–4.

[d]For a description of the index, see Blau and Duncan (1967), pp. 117–128.

involving social interaction away from home. Participation in the predominant home-centered and nonsocial activities has no bearing on network size. Weeks of employment also increases network size, presumably by keeping the retiree in contact with a pool of work associates. Income level, as a general facilitator of many forms of opportunity, also acts to increase network size. The one possibly surprising finding is the positive effect of health impairments on network size. It may be that having these impairments encourages (indeed, requires) more persons to help the retiree, thereby expanding his support network.

The final analysis of network size involves looking separately at its three components—the number of financial helpers, personal helpers, and other close persons. The mean network size of 4.6 includes an average of 1.3 financial helpers, 1.9 personal helpers, and 1.3 close persons. Separate regression equations (columns 3-5 in table 6-3) were estimated for each of these components, using the same set of background and retirement variables. When summed, the three equations are equivalent to equation two—the sum of the coefficients for a given explanatory variable across the three equations equals the corresponding single coefficient in equation two. Of primary interest in this decomposition analysis is whether any particular explanatory variable operates more strongly for one of these types of persons in the support network than for another. In general, the answer is negative. Variables having significant effects on total network size operate relatively uniformly across the three components, increasing our confidence in the summary measure of network size used in equations one and two.

Finally we examine why retirees tend to select particular types of relationships over others for their primary outside helpers. Two questions are posed: (1) For all retirees in the sample who had at least one primary financial or personal helper ($n = 1563$), what background and retirement conditions influence the tendency to select children over all others? (2) For those who have at least one primary helper but do not select children ($n = 732$), what conditions influence their selection of friends over relatives? The same set of explanatory variables, including the nine background and four retirement conditions, were used in two regression equations to examine these questions (table 6-4). The dependent variable in the first equation ranged in value from zero to 2, scored zero if children were not selected for either financial or personal help, one if selected for one or the other form of help, and 2 if selected for both forms. The dependent variable in the second equation also ranged from zero to 2, scored for friends in a completely analogous manner.

The background and retirement condition variables were expected to influence network composition in the same general way they did network size—by structuring differential interaction opportunities with the possible relationship types. This expectation was only partially confirmed. The background variable having the strongest impact on the tendency to choose children over others was the retirees' total number of children. Closely related, having children or others living in the household, either adults or dependents, had the opposite effect. If the retiree and his children are living in the same household, then by definition only nonchildren are available as outside helpers. Such children would of course still be available for help, even though not as part of the network of persons outside the household. Net of these two relatively obvious effects, four other background variables also significantly affected the selection preference. Age and marital status were positively related to the tendency to select children, and being black and residing in a rural area reduced it. Background variables which had no effect were the two measures of socioeconomic position, education and former occupation, and residence in the South.

Thus, after controlling for differences due to family size and household membership, retirees who were older, currently married, white, and nonrural were more likely to rely on children for their support network. Conversely, retirees who were younger, without a spouse, black, and from rural areas were more likely to rely on friends and other relatives. This preference was independent of socioeconomic position or region of residence. Differential interaction opportunity is again the most plausible

Table 6–4
The Extent Children Are Chosen Over Friends and Relatives and the Extent Friends Are Chosen Over Relatives, for Financial and Personal Help, as Determined by Background and Retirement Conditions, for Retired Men Having Helpers in 1981
(OLS unstandardized regression results)

Explanatory Variables	Children Chosen (over Friends/Relatives)		Friends Chosen (over Relatives)	
	b	*(t)*	*b*	*(t)*
Retirement conditions, 1981				
Number of leisure activities				
Social	−0.039[a]	(−2.24)	0.091[a]	(3.94)
Trips	0.055	(1.88)	−0.134[a]	(−3.47)
Home	0.053[a]	(2.66)	−0.055[a]	(−2.17)
Employment weeks	0.001	(0.57)	0.000	(0.22)
Health impairments[c]	0.002	(0.48)	0.020[a]	(3.94)
Income ($0–$5,000):[b]				
$5–$15,000	0.074	(1.14)	0.157	(1.82)
$15–$25,000	0.079	(1.05)	0.002	(0.02)
$25,000+	0.034	(0.41)	0.144	(1.37)
NA	0.069	(1.02)	0.212[a]	(2.40)

Table 6–4 continued

Explanatory Variables	Children Chosen (over Friends/ Relatives)		Friends Chosen (over Relatives)	
	b	(t)	b	(t)
Background conditions				
Education, years	−0.006	(−0.81)	0.012	(1.36)
Occupation, Duncan SEI[c]	−0.001	(−0.86)	0.002	(1.54)
Black	−0.320[a]	(−4.18)	0.070	(0.80)
South	0.008	(0.20)	0.083	(1.55)
Residence (central city)				
Suburban	0.003	(0.07)	−0.072	(−1.14)
Rural	−0.103[a]	(−2.09)	0.044	(0.68)
Age	0.031[a]	(6.70)	0.007	(1.12)
Marital status	0.163[a]	(3.11)	−0.119	(−1.85)
Children, number	0.115[a]	(12.25)	0.032[a]	(2.53)
Household composition (alone or with wife only)				
Children without earnings	−0.380[a]	(−4.80)	−0.148	(−1.60)
Children with earnings	−0.457[a]	(−5.64)	−0.085	(−0.91)
Others without earnings	−0.183[a]	(−2.56)	−0.092	(−1.09)
Others with earnings	−0.426[a]	(−3.61)	0.255[a]	(2.05)
Constant	−1.728		−0.182	
R^2	.167		.109	
Dependent variable mean	0.79		0.65	
Sample *n*	1563		732	

[a]$p < .05$.

[b]Referent category given in parentheses after variable name for the three variables having multiple dummy terms.

[c]Each respondent was asked whether he ever had difficulty performing each of 12 specified activities (e.g., walking; stooping, kneeling or crouching; reaching; hearing) plus an "other" category and, if so, whether he could perform the activity at all. In addition, he was asked whether any of seven specified symptoms (e.g., pain, fainting spells, shortness of breath) plus an "other" category "bothered" (him) enough to be a problem." The impairment score was arrived at by assigning a 1 for each activity that could be performed only with difficulty, a 2 for an activity that could not be performed at all, and a 1 for each symptom reported by the respondent. Potential scores thus ranged from 0 through 34. A score of 1 is classified as minor, 2 as "moderate," 3 or 4 as substantial, and 5 or more as severe.

[d]For a description of the index, see Blau and Duncan (1967), pp. 117–128.

single interpretation of this pattern, but it is less convincing here than in the case of network size. The possible additional importance of attitudinal and cultural factors in this choice needs further consideration.

The likely importance of attitudinal factors in the network composition choices of retirees is further suggested by the nonrelationships of three of the four retirement condition variables which were hypothesized to act primarily by structuring interaction opportunities. Only leisure activity participation made a difference. Engaging in home-centered activities increased the likelihood of choosing children, whereas doing the away-from-home social activities increased the choice of friends and relatives other than children. Similar to the effect for network size, the relative social isolation of home-centered activities is likely to reinforce reliance on children, whereas the away-from-home activities maintain and expand retirees' contacts with friends and other relatives. By contrast, income level, employment weeks, and health impairments, all of which were also positively related to network size, were unrelated to the network composition choice of children over friends and other relatives.

For those retirees who selected either a friend or a relative who was not their child as their primary helper, the choice between these two types was structured in a manner analogous to the previous findings. Of the three types of leisure activities, the social ones increased friend choice; the home-centered and nonsocial ones reduced their selection. Having health impairments also increased the choice of friends, but the other two retirement conditions, income and employment, were unrelated. The social activities generate interaction with friends and thus increase their support; the health impairments further increase friends' support by legitimizing it. The only two background variables related to the choice of friends over other relatives were total number of children and having other adults besides the spouse living in the household. Both variables would tend to reduce contact with nonchildren relatives away from the household.

Summary and Conclusion

Leisure Activities

All of the members of the sample were queried about the extent of their involvement in 6 types of leisure time activity in the 1978 survey, and men who reported a retired status in 1981 were asked the same set of questions about those activities plus 4 additional ones, including television viewing. The 1981 retirees devoted an average of somewhat over 2,000 hours in the preceding 12 months in the 10 activities combined, with TV viewing accounting for two-fifths of the total. The most universal activities were television, visiting, and reading, which occupied 96 percent, 89 percent, and 87 percent of the men, respectively. Volunteer work was at the other end of the continuum, with a participation rate of only 19 percent.

Occupational level and family income bear independent positive relationships with the extent of leisure time activity, suggesting that the type of work men do is related to their leisure pursuits not only through income but through the types of interests associated with different categories of occupations.

The *pattern* of leisure time activity varied only slightly among retirees between 1978 and 1981, but the amount of time devoted to each activity by those who participated in it increased by amounts ranging from 4 and 47 percent—12 percent for all 6 activities combined. When the 1978 and 1981 responses are compared for men who retired between the two dates, the data support the conclusion that retirement does not alter the incidence of participation in these specified activities, but permits those who participate to devote substantially increased amounts of time to them—about 44 percent overall.

Social Networks

Our analysis of the social networks of the retirees is based on a series of questions for men who reported they were retired in 1981. Fully 85 percent of the retirees identified one or more individuals living outside their household who either could give them help or to whom they felt close. Adult children were identified most often, but friends and other relatives also were frequent contacts, particularly among black retirees and those currently not living with a wife. These network relationships did give assistance in emergencies, for example, in providing transportation to the hospital. Probably more important is the opportunity they provided for ordinary social interaction. For most of the retirees the identified members of their network lived less than 10 miles away, and were contacted either in person or by phone at least once a week. For men who have gradually and sometimes abruptly given up long-established social relationships in the workplace, having these continuing opportunities for interaction are believed vital for their quality of life and general well-being. Conversely, the substantial minority of retirees who are without an informal social network lack these opportunities and may be deprived accordingly.

The regression analyses point to the conclusion that the size and composition of the retirees' support networks are strongly conditioned by available interaction opportunities. These opportunities emerge from a set of predetermined factors, particularly one's total number of children, and from the current retirement conditions of leisure and employment activity and health and income levels.

Local and national debates are currently underway over expenditures of public funds in each of the four retirement condition areas—leisure activities (e.g., building more senior citizen centers, and raising public transit subsidies for the elderly), employment opportunities (e.g., less costly Social Security work penalties), health (e.g., possible reductions in Medicare benefits), and income (e.g., various adjustments in Social Security benefit levels). The substantial effects of each of these retirement conditions on the retirees' social network size accentuates the general importance of these policy debates in helping retirees to find alternatives to social isolation.

In future years the steady diminution in the size of the American family will increase the tendency for retirees to rely more on friends and nonchildren relatives to constitute their informal support networks. Otherwise the proportion of retirees who perceive themselves to be socially isolated from potential helpers and close persons will increase considerably from the current level of fifteen percent. In the present analysis the only retirement condition variable found to increase the selection of friends and nonchildren relatives into one's network was participation in those away-from-home leisure activities that were social in nature. Such participation will become increasingly important for the ability of retirees to build and sustain support networks.

The current tendency for children to dominate the retirees' support network may be more than a matter of their greater relative numbers and availability. It may be one further indication that the nuclear family bonds between children and their parents remain strong throughout the life cycle. Improved understanding of these bonds will become helpful in assessing the future likelihood of similarly strong bonds outside of family ties. In social interaction generally persons tend to bond together primarily on the basis of value consensus, mutual self-interest, or social obligation. None of these principles seems sufficient in itself to explain the prevalence and apparent strength of retirees' primary bonds to their children. In a rapidly changing American society value conflict across generations has been relatively common. Furthermore, social obligations have never been strongly felt or adhered to within the context of the prevailing democratic and individualistic ideology. Self-interest, and in particular the protection of inheritable family property, is probably also a relatively minor bonding factor, given the relatively small amounts of wealth available in most families and the predetermined equitable distribution formulas commonly used in intergenerational transmission. The factor that is most crucial in uniting retired parents with their adult children is what Adams (1967) calls the sense of positive concern. Such positive concern seems to be a product of the sustained and intensive interaction and emotional life of the nuclear family. How well this concern can be developed among nonfamily relations may be crucial to future generations of retired Americans.

Notes

1. There was also a question on travel that is not included in this section of the chapter because the number of hours devoted to the activity was not as clear.

2. The criterion of retirement was the individual's affirmative response in 1981 to the question: "Have you ever retired from a regular job either voluntarily or involuntarily?"

3. The statements to which respondents were asked to indicate whether they strongly agreed, agreed, disagreed, or strongly disagreed were as follows: (1) Retirement is a pleasant time of life. (2) Older workers should retire when they can, so as to give younger people more of a chance on the job. (3) Work is the most meaningful part of life. (4) Most people think more of someone who works than they do of someone who doesn't. (5) People who don't retire when they can are foolish. Each response was given a score ranging from 1 to 4, with 4 assigned to the response indicating the most favorable attitude toward retirement. The values for the 5 statements were summed and the totals were then divided into 3 approximately equal groups, which are labeled, in descending order "favorable," "ambivalent," and "unfavorable."

4. Income level was the 1981 reported income in the past year, represented in the analysis in multiple dummy variable form. The referent category was $0-$5000, with 4 dummy terms for respondents having incomes either from $5,000 to $14,999, $15,000 to $25,000, $25,000 +, and for respondents who gave no answer (NA).

5. Use of number of activities rather than hours of activities in each area permits a closer estimate of the number of different activity settings, both within and outside the household. The actual amount of time spent in a particular activity or setting was of less relevance here, given our focus of explaining variation in the size and composition of the social networks.

References

Adams, Bert N. 1967. "Interaction Theory and the Social Network." *Sociometry*, 30: 64-78.

Atchley, Robert C. 1971. "Retirement and Leisure Participation: Continuity or Crisis." *The Gerontologist*, 11: 13-17.

Bell, B.D. 1975. "The Limitations of Crisis Theory as an Explanatory Mechanism in Social Gerontology." *International Journal of Aging and Human Development*, 6: 153-168.

Bosse, R., and Ekerdt, D.J. 1981. "Change in Self-perception of Leisure Activities with Retirement." *The Gerontologist*, 21: 650-654.

Cantor, Marjorie H. 1980. The informal support system: its relevance in the lives of the elderly. In Edgar F. Borgatta and Neil G. McCluskey, eds., *Aging and Society: Current Research and Policy Perspectives*. Beverly Hills: Sage, pp. 131-146.

Collins, Glen. 1983. "Many More Elderly Migrate to New States." *New York Times*, December 9, Late Edition, Section A, p. 20.

Cumming, E., and Henry, W.E. 1961. *Growing Old: The Process of Disengagement*. New York: Basic.

Foner, Anne, and Schwab, Karen. 1981. *Aging and Retirement*. Monterey, Cal.: Brooks/Cole Publishing Co.

Friedman, Eugene A., and Orbach, Harold L. 1974. "Adjustment to Retirement." In Silvano Arieti, *American Handbook of Psychiatry*, 2d ed., vol. 1. New York: Basic. Chap. 30.

Harris, Louis et al. 1981. *Aging in the Eighties: America in Transition.* Washington, D.C.: The National Council on the Aging.

Havighurst, R.J., and Albrecht, R. 1953. *Older People.* New York: Longmans, Green, and Co.

Hendricks, J., and Hendricks, D. 1977. *Aging in Mass Society: Myths and Realities.* Cambridge, Mass.: Winthrop Publishers.

Kaplan, Max. 1961. "Toward a Theory of Leisure for Social Gerontology." In Robert W. Kleemeier, ed., *Aging and Leisure.* New York: Oxford U.P., chap. 30.

Kleemeier, Robert W. 1964. Leisure and disengagement in retirement. *The Gerontologist,* 4: 180-184.

Longino, Charles F., Jr., and Kart, Cary S. 1982. "Explicating Activity Theory: A Formal Replication." *Journal of Gerontology,* 6: 713-722.

Neulinger, John. 1981. *The Psychology of Leisure.* Springfield, Ill.: Charles C. Thomas.

Palmore, E., et al. 1979. "Stress and Adaptation in Later Life." *Journal of Gerontology,* 34: 841-851.

Parnes, Herbert S. and Less, Lawrence. 1983. *From Work to Retirement: The Experience of a National Sample of Men.* Columbus, Oh.: Ohio State University Center for Human Resource Research.

Peppers, L.G. 1976. "Patterns of Leisure and Adjustment to Retirement." *The Gerontologist,* 16: 441-446.

Roadburg, A. 1981. "Perceptions of Work and Leisure Among the Elderly." *The Gerontologist,* 21: 142-145.

Robinson, John P. 1977. *How Americans Use Time.* New York: Praeger.

Simpson, I.H.; Back, K.W.; and McKinney, J.C. 1966. "Continuity of Work and Retirement Actviities and Self Evaluation." In I.H. Simpson and J.C. McKinney, eds., *Social Aspects of Aging.* Durham, N.C.: Duke University Press.

Ward, Russell A.; Sherman, Susan R.; and La Gory, Mark. 1984. "Subjective Network Assessments and Subject Well-being." *Journal of Gerontology,* 39: 93-101.

Weiner, A.I., and Hunt, S.L. 1981. "Retirees' Perceptions of Work and Leisure Meanings." *The Gerontologist,* 21: 444-446.

7
Longitudinal Effects of Retirement on Men's Psychological and Physical Well-Being

Joan E. Crowley

This chapter explores both the psychological and physical quality of life of retired men. Two approaches are used: first, responses of retired men to questions about the retirement experience are described. Second, a multivariate analysis of data from the subsample of men who were working in 1976 is executed to ascertain the longitudinal effects of retirement on well-being, controlling for the quality of life and for the character of employment reported at an earlier time.

The transition from work to retirement can be considered either as a specific life event that creates a potential crisis of identity, or as an expected transition from one phase of life to another. The possible negative impact of retirement on the quality of life derives from the attendant loss of occupational identity and the social and other benefits obtained through work (Elwell and Maltbie-Crannell, 1981). Because work can create strain as well as satisfaction, however, retirement may actually improve health by removing work stress, if the psychological and financial needs fulfilled by employment can be met through other sources (Thompson and Streib, 1958). Loss of the work role is accompanied by a dramatic increase in leisure time—well over forty hours per week for most men, when transportation and preparation for work are added to actual work hours. Much of the growing literature on use of leisure time among retirees addresses the question of whether and how leisure is used to substitute for satisfactions once found on the job (see chapter 6).

An alternative way of looking at retirement is provided by continuity theory, which emphasizes that retirement is an accepted social role itself, anticipated by men and for which some men actively prepare (Larson, 1978). Retirement is thus considered a normatively specified transition,

Without the persistence and careful research assistance of Linda K. Tyner, this chapter would be only a shadow of what it has become. Her help is gratefully acknowledged.

and its effects should be restricted to those factors most directly associated with retirement itself, such as increased time for other activities and reduction in income. Health, happiness, and satisfaction should be largely functions of the man's total situation, including social ties, interests, and resources, which may not be substantially changed by the fact that he is retired. Thus, the effects of retirement should depend on how the retired status interacts with these more general statuses for the individual (Palmore, Fillenbaum, and George, 1984).

Research based on continuity theory has pointed out the need to look at the circumstances of retirement in order to assess its outcomes. Men who retire because of poor health (a large proportion of early retirees) will continue to report poor health after retirement. Similarly, men who are retired against their will should have more negative reactions to retirement than voluntary retirees, who should perceive themselves as having more control over their lives. Control has been associated with positive outcomes on many psychological dimensions (Walker, Kimmel, and Price, 1980-1981).

Much of the previous literature on quality of retired life has serious limitations: these stem from the lack of comparability of retired men with nonretired men on critical dimensions such as health, age, income, and prior occupation. Few previous studies have taken into account factors associated with the decision to retire. As chapter 3 has shown, very few men retire because they reach a mandatory retirement age. Retirement before the age of 65 is very common, especially among men with health problems and those with better financial resources. Thus, even with age controlled, comparing retirees with workers may show that retired men have more health or other problems, whether or not retirement itself had any effect upon health.

Several studies have asked samples of retirees to describe their experiences before and after retirement, but their responses have the usual problems of retrospective data. The longitudinal design of the NLS allows determinants of the decision to retire to be taken into account without using retrospective assessments of preretirement conditions.

The close association of retirement with age presents special analytical problems. Some differences between retirees and workers may be due to age, others to retirement; the effects on well-being of these different determinants are difficult to untangle. Older individuals tend to evaluate satisfaction by contrasting their objective life conditions with what they think is reasonable or fair to expect at their stage in life, rather than with aspirations, as is typical for younger people (Carp, Carp, and Millsap, 1982). Thus, elderly respondents may tend to report themselves as happier than would younger respondents who enjoy comparable health, financial status, and so forth.

One of the most important age-related processes affecting well-being is deteriorating physical health, both for the men and for their wives. Retirement also brings a reduction in financial resources, as wages are usually only partially replaced by pensions and inte-rest income (See chapter 5). The effect of this drop in income on quality of life is usually cushioned by reduced needs for income due to the accumulation of assets over the work life and reduction in expenses related to work and child-raising responsibilities. However, the adequacy of retirement income may deteriorate over time, due to increases in the cost of living, especially in costs of medical care. Both of these processes—the effect of aging on health and the effect of retirement on income—lead to differences in the external situations of retirees, differences which may have some effect on their perceived well-being but are not attributable to the state of retirement itself. The NLS includes a number of measures of the subjective evaluation of life after retirement, as well as measures of the health and income of the full sample at various points in time, which can be used to untangle these influences and to identify which retirees are most likely to adapt well to the transition out of the labor force.

The Conceptual Model and the Variables

The conceptual model on which most of the analysis is based takes well-being as an outcome in large part determined by the resources available to the respondent, specifically, health and financial resources that allow the individual to cope with problems and to take advantage of opportunities which might arise. The decision to retire is itself largely a function of these resources; that is, men in poor health and those whose financial situation is sufficiently secure are likely to retire earlier. Resources should be less important in the retirement decision of men compelled to retire by company rules, although the selective attrition from the labor force of men in poor health or with high assets means there will be some relationship between resources and staying in the labor force long enough to reach mandatory retirement.

Figure 7-1 formalizes the model. Essentially, well-being in retirement is seen as a function of the individual's personal attributes; for instance, education, race, and age, postretirement resources, and the circumstances surrounding the decision to retire. The decision to retire, in turn, is a function of factors affecting the individual's preretirement well-being— namely, the conditions of preretirement employment (work attributes), preretirement resources, and personal attributes. The time relationships implied in the figure are important, because they emphasize that the model represents an ongoing process. Current well-being is substantially

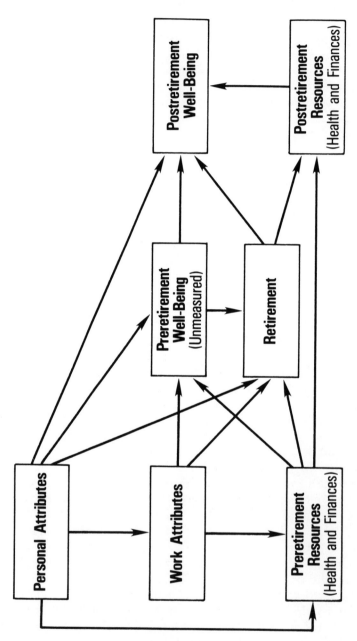

Figure 7–1. Conceptual Model of Determinants of Postretirement Well-Being

affected by the current situation and the current situation is itself a function of earlier states and events. Most importantly, the model acknowledges that retirement is a function of previous levels of (health and financial) resources, and that current resources are in turn partly a function of retirement. The time dimension is necessary to untangle the causal relationships.

Keep in mind that the individual's health is both a measure of physical well-being and a resource determining the amount of happiness obtainable from life. This duality will complicate to some extent the interpretations of the following analysis. Also, except for health, the measures of well-being are not generally available for the period prior to retirement. However, the model predicts that with preretirement well-being controlled, there would be no direct relationship between preretirement work or resources and postretirement well-being.

One aim of this research is to identify the factors that determine whether a man's retirement is a rewarding or a punishing experience. It is hypothesized that well-being in retirement is partly a function of the level of career involvement and the type of job held prior to retirement. Jobs with few intrinsic rewards should be easier to leave behind than others. Furthermore, the resources available for creating a comfortable life, namely income and health, will be important determinants of the effects of retirement. Men who retire voluntarily should report higher levels of well-being than men who retire for other reasons, due in part to better financial preparation for the transition, in part to better health and in part merely to the fact that they experience personal control over the decision to retire.

The Measurement and Meaning of Well-Being

We examine now some of the implications and meanings of the measures of well-being that will be used in the analysis. Well-being usually refers to the subjective assessment of life, either in general or in specific facets of experience. Good health is an assessment of physical well-being. Psychological well-being is the attitude an individual has about life as a whole; it is multidimensional in at least two senses. For one thing, there are obviously various aspects of life to which one may react. For another, attitudes can be broken down into three parts: affect, cognition, and behavior (Ostrom, 1969), or more colloquially, feeling, thinking, and acting. The affective component refers to the strictly emotional side of evaluation—how happy and proud, or how distressed and sad a person feels about life. The cognitive component is the intellectual response to life; it refers to beliefs about life as a whole, including specifically comparisons of one's life with perceptions of how well others are doing, or with how well one expected himself to be doing at a given age. These affective and cognitive aspects of attitudes toward life will be our primary concern. The behavioral component, which reflects intentions or actions, is beyond the scope of the current analysis.

In the context of well-being as an attitude, then, the question is how the retirement experience affects the quality of life as perceived by older men; we recognize that their attitudes will include both affective and cognitive components. Because the perception of well-being involves a complex assessment of life as a whole, a single indicator cannot be comprehensive or sufficient. Several measures of well-being are available in the NLS, each with somewhat different connotations, and each measuring a separate aspect of subjective well-being.[1]

The most purely affective measure of well-being is the Bradburn Affect Balance Scale (Bradburn, 1969; Andrews and McKennell, 1978). This instrument contains two subscales, one for positive affect and one for negative affect. The affect balance measure is the difference between the positive and negative affect scores.[2] One of the more surprising and consistently replicated findings resulting from work using the Bradburn scales is that positive well-being and negative well-being are independent of each other (Bradburn, 1969; Stock and Okun, 1982). The difference between positive and negative scores measures the degree to which an individual tends to report positive emotional experiences over negative ones, the degree to which he is more happy than unhappy. Note that two men could report the same number of positive feelings and yet each have a very different balance between happiness and sadness.

Several measures in the NLS ask directly how happy the respondents are with their lives. The global happiness measure asks for a single assessment of whether the respondent is "very happy," "somewhat happy," "somewhat unhappy," or "very unhappy" with things altogether. In addition, domain-specific happiness items use these same response categories to describe the respondent's assessment of his housing, area of residence, health, standard of living, and leisure time activities. Because factor analysis showed that all the domain specific items seemed to measure a single dimension, they were summed to form an index.

Both the index and the global measure of happiness should have a strong affective component, because they ask for an assessment of happiness. The advantage of the multiple item scale is that it may take on a much wider range of values, and is thus a more sensitive measure. On the other hand, the global measure may capture variance in happiness due to aspects of life not included among the specific items that make up the index scale.

The most cognitively oriented measure of the set asks respondents whether they were living better, worse, or about the same as their friends.[3]

This question requires not only an assessment of the respondent's situation but also an assessment of the living conditions faced or enjoyed by friends. Some research suggests that satisfaction among the elderly is a function of what they feel they can expect to have at their stage in life, whereas younger people tend to compare their current situation to their aspirations. For this reason, the elderly may be more satisfied than younger people with the same "objective" life situation.

Measures of health ask about one particular aspect of life, physical health, rather than the more global aspects presumably tapped by the psychological measures. Again, the NLS provides several related indicators, each assessing somewhat different aspects of health. The most objective measure is the index of impairments, based on responses to whether individuals have difficulty performing specific activities, or whether they experience any of a series of common symptoms "enough to be a problem."[4] The items comprising the index thus ask for a series of decisions about fairly concrete situations, with very specific and current referents.[5]

Two other health measures ask respondents (1) to evaluate their health relative to other men of their age; and (2) to report whether their health has gotten better, worse, or stayed the same over the previous five years. These comparisons are by nature subjective: men with the same objective health condition may differ on their assessment of their health relative to other men, depending on the actual health of men in each individual's reference group and on the degree to which the individual has adapted to chronic health problems. There may also be types and degrees of impairment not captured by the specific items in the impairment index that are picked up in the global assessment.

Reaction to Retirement

This section describes the subjective reaction of men to retirement. The 1981 interview included a number of questions asked only of men who reported themselves as having retired by the time of the interview date, about how well they felt they were doing in retirement. The questions are not direct measures of well-being, but they do provide a context for understanding how retirement might or might not affect perceptions of life as a whole.

Reason for Retirement. The reasons for retirement identified earlier in this volume—mandatory, health, discouraged, voluntary early, and voluntary normal—have strong conceptual links with well-being and adjustment to retirement.[6] Men who retire voluntarily should have prepared themselves, both psychologically and financially, for the transition and have a favorable evaluation of the retirement role. In contrast, men who are forced to retire when they would prefer to continue to work, either because they have reached an arbitrarily defined age or because their health will not permit them to continue, should be relatively unprepared for the transition. Some of these men may have negative attitudes about retirement, or may fear leaving the familiar world of work for the unfamiliar world of leisure. Men who retire because of their health should of course report lower levels of physical well-being, and their poor health should affect their psychological well-being. Men who leave the labor market following a spell of unemployment may also have difficulty, both due to lack of preparation for being "a retiree" and due to the problems which were associated with their unemployment—lack of resources, perhaps the experience of being terminated from a desired job, and so forth.

While dividing retirees by the reason they retired has a strong appeal as a mechanism for understanding how retirement might affect well-being, use of these categories as defined makes it harder to understand the effect of other predictors on well-being. These categories are established by the conditions under which the individual retired, but they are, at the same time, strongly related to the identified resources used to predict well-being. For instance, health retirees should be less healthy than other categories of retirees because the category is defined by the presence of health problems prior to the time of retirement. Discouraged workers have experienced unemployment, which should in itself have strong negative effects on well-being. Voluntary early retirees are both younger on the average than most other retirees (except for the health retirees) and financially better off than the other categories (certainly at the point of retirement).

Differentiations by reason for retirement can be based on two different forms of information. The categories used in earlier chapters are based on the longitudinal records of the respondents up to the time of retirement: these will be referred to as panel-based categories. Retirees were also asked in 1981 to give their own reasons for being retired, and their responses were combined to form retrospective categories that corresponded to the panel-based ones.

Most men were placed in the same category using either of the two strategies. The biggest difference in the overall distribution is that 10 percent of the men are counted as mandatory retirees by the retrospective question in contrast with only 3 percent by the panel measure, mainly because one-fourth of the men who were considered by the panel criteria to be voluntary normal retirees said retrospectively that they retired because they had reached the compulsory retirement age or because of "company policy." This discrepancy stems from the fact that such men had reported prior to retirement that they did not want to continue working past the compulsory retirement age. Apparently, some men adapt their desired retirement age to the compulsory retirement age, but still perceive themselves as being forced to retire at that age. The proportion of men classed as voluntary normal retirees is 14 percent in the panel coding scheme, compared to 11 percent using the retrospective question.

Although both classifications place 36 percent of the men in the health retirement category and about 40 percent in the voluntary early category, there is some internal shifting between these two groups. Over one-fifth of the men counted as health retirees in the panel classification scheme reported later that they had retired voluntarily, while about the same proportion of those classified as voluntary early retirees on the basis of panel data later reported that they had retired for health reasons. Similarly, the proportion classified as discouraged retirees is about the same in the two coding schemes (1 in 20), but less than half of the men classified as discouraged in one coding scheme are so classified in the other. Of the men classified as discouraged because of the circumstances at the time of their retirement, about one-fifth report that they retired voluntarily and another fifth report being mandatory retirees.

There is no objective way of determining which of these sets of classifications is more "correct." The direction of the discrepancies suggests that the retrospective measure, at least in some cases, may be distorted in a way which preserves the self-image of the individual, especially among the men who were forced out of the labor market by unemployment. On the other hand, the inferences made from the presence or absence of a health problem or the fact that the individual experienced a spell of unemployment before withdrawing from the labor market may incorrectly attribute retirement to health or unemployment rather than to individual choice. Additional evidence and a more extended analysis of this issue is contained in an earlier study based on the 1976 NLS data (Parnes and Nestel, 1981).

Because of the difficulty in choosing between them,[7] we have used both measures of reason for retirement in all of our analyses. However, because of the general agreement between the two classification systems and because the findings are basically consistent irrespective of which system is used, we present the results only for analyses based on the panel criteria in order to maintain consistency between this chapter and others in this volume that have used the reason for retirement criterion. We should note, however, that the retrospective criteria, in general, produce sharper contrasts between categories of retirement than do the panel criteria.[8] Thus, the results that are shown provide rather conservative estimates of the degree of variation in well-being associated with reason for retirement.

Responses to Retirement. Table 7-1 shows distributions of retirees in 1981 on a number of questions asking for an assessment of the retirement experience, cross-classified by reason for retirement. All in all, most retirees seem fairly happy with retirement, with voluntary early retirees being particularly enthusiastic. A majority of the retirees say that retirement is about what they expected it to be, and most of the remainder say that it is better than expected. The exceptions are men who were forced out of the labor market under unfavorable circumstances, either due to poor health or inability to find a job. Almost a third of the health retirees report that retirement is worse than expected. Interestingly, the mandatory retirees are as likely as voluntary normal retirees to say that retirement is better than they expected it to be. Most retirees also say that they would retire again at the same age if they had to do it over again. This tendency, as expected, is much less pronounced among health and discouraged retirees, many of whom say that they would have worked longer if they could.[9]

The retirees were also asked to give the best and worst aspects of retirement, and to name their biggest problem. Note that, unlike the items where only one answer is possible, the proportions mentioning each possible best and worst aspect of retirement are relatively unconstrained because up to three responses were coded. Because many respondents did not give three separate answers, the percentage recorded for the several categories are virtually independent; being in one category does not preclude an individual from also being counted in any other category.[10]

The single item mentioned most often as one of the best things about retirement is simply not working. Apparently the routine of getting up and going to work is not much missed. The second most often-mentioned positive aspect of retirement is the amount of time available for one's own choice of activity, which is also an intrinsic aspect of retirement. Men who retired because of ill health are somewhat less enamored of their freedom, but these two categories are each still reported by over 40 percent of the health retirees. One-fourth of the health retirees and one-tenth of the discouraged retirees report that there is *nothing* they liked about retirement. On the other hand, one-third of all retirees, and almost half of the voluntary retirees, reported that there was nothing that they *disliked* about retirement.

The other side of the coin of freedom from work, of course, is boredom, which is cited as a negative aspect of retirement by many retired

Table 7–1
Reactions to Retirement by Reason for Retirement
(percentage distributions)

			Reason for Retirement[a]			
Responses to Retirement	Total	Mandatory	Health	Discouraged	Voluntary Early	Voluntary Normal
How does retirement compare with expectations?						
Total percent	100	100	100	100	100	100
Worse	17	12	30	22	9	9
As expected	58	65	52	54	59	67
Better	25	23	18	23	31	24
Timing of retirement[b]						
Total percent	100	—	100	100	100	100
Earlier	8	—	7	7	10	6
Later	23	—	33	43	16	11
Same	68	—	60	50	73	83
Biggest problem since retirement						
Total percent	100	100	100	100	100	100
Nothing	31	30	13	33	41	48
Health/depression	31	19	51	26	21	16
Finances	16	24	17	25	15	14
Bored	5	5	7	1	4	5
Family or personal problem	9	4	6	7	11	9
Other	8	19	5	7	8	9

Table 7–1 continued

Responses to Retirement	Total	Reason for Retirement[a]				
		Mandatory	Health	Discouraged	Voluntary Early	Voluntary Normal
Things liked most about retirement[c]						
Nothing[d]	13	7	25	11	6	7
Not working	57	64	48	60	61	64
Traveling	5	0	4	2	6	9
Visiting	5	10	5	4	5	6
Sports, hobbies	11	17	10	7	12	10
Time to self	52	55	43	47	60	53
Other	5	3	6	3	5	5
Things liked least[c]						
Nothing[d]	34	31	20	22	45	44
Health/depression	10	4	18	2	4	4
Finances	25	23	28	46	21	17
Boredom	35	39	42	36	30	31
Getting old	3	13	2	4	2	4
Family problems	2	4	3	1	1	1
Not enough time	1	2	1	e	e	2
Personal problems	4	0	8	4	2	4
Other	4	7	4	0	4	3

Note: UNIVERSE: Men who were retired in 1981 ($n = 1898$).

[a]Reason for retirement categories based on panel data.

[b]This item was not asked of mandatory retirees ($n = 1709$).

[c]Columns total to more than 100 percent. Respondents were allowed to mention up to 3 responses.

[d]"Nothing" is coded only when it was the only response to the question. "Nothing" as a second or third response was interpreted to mean "nothing else."

[e]Percent less than 0.5.

men; it is the most frequent response overall (35 percent) and for all categories except the discouraged retirees. However, boredom is mentioned as the *biggest problem* since retirement by only 1 retiree in 20.

For those in the discouraged group, the most commonly mentioned problem is finances. For all other categories, finances are the second most commonly mentioned problem. Voluntary retirees, whether early or normal, are the groups least likely to mention finances as a problem. Voluntary retirees are also more likely than the other categories of retirees to report that they have had no problems. Men who were forced to retire because of age are three times more likely than any other group to report that getting old is a problem. Their concern with aging may explain in part their reluctance to give up the work role.

Health, interestingly, is not commonly mentioned as a negative aspect of retirement. Its relative absence does not mean that retirees do not have health problems, but that poor health is not thought of as being *caused* by retirement. This interpretation is confirmed by the fact that when asked about their biggest problem since retirement three times as many retirees mentioned health as when the reference was to a disliked aspect of retirement. Over half of those who retired for health reasons report that health is their biggest problem. For mandatory retirees, health is second to finances.

Contrasts Between Retirement and Work Life

These direct assessments of the retirement experience present questions which can only be answered by men who are already retired. However, our larger question is how well retirement compares with nonretirement; that is, continued employment. We begin with simple comparisons between men who are not retired and retirees classified by reason for retirement. Table 7-2 presents several measures of current well-being.

Few of the total group of NLS respondents felt that they were worse off than other men, while one-fifth felt that they were better off. Those who retired because of poor health are less likely than other retirees to report themselves as better off, and at least twice as likely as any other group to say that they are worse off. Discouraged workers are also more likely to see themselves as worse off, or at least no better off, than their contemporaries, but the difference between them and other men in this regard is small. These differences, incidentally, are consistent with differences in objective measures of financial status (see chapter 5).

Turning to the questions about relative health, we find few differences among categories, except that poor health is more often reported by men who retired for health reasons. Even taking into account that

Table 7–2
Selected Subjective Measures of Well-Being, by Retirement Status and Reason for Retirement, 1981
(percentage distributions)

Characteristic	Total	Nonretired	Retirees, by Reason for Retirement[a]				
			Mandatory	Health	Discouraged	Voluntary Early	Voluntry Normal
Total	100	25	2	27	4	31	10
Comparison of lifestyle with other men of the same age							
Total percent	100	100	100	100	100	100	100
Better	20	21	27	17	18	23	19
Worse	6	4	4	12	6	3	3
Same	71	74	62	67	75	71	76
Don't know	3	2	6	4	1	3	2
Health compared to other men of same age							
Total percent	100	100	100	100	100	100	100
Excellent	27	36	38	9	28	33	31
Good	40	46	40	25	50	43	50
Fair	22	15	17	35	18	20	15
Poor	11	3	6	31	4	5	4
Health condition over past 5 years, 1981							
Total percent	100	100	100	100	100	100	100
Better	7	5	4	6	7	9	6
Worse	29	19	30	47	18	23	23
Same	65	76	66	47	76	68	71
Global happiness							
Total percent	100	100	100	100	100	100	100
Very happy	52	54	60	36	49	58	66
Somewhat happy	42	43	32	49	48	38	31
Somewhat unhappy	5	2	5	12	3	3	2
Very unhappy	1	1	3	3	0	1	1

Mean scores for well-being and attitude indexes

Positive attitude toward retirement	8.69	8.01	8.63	8.50	8.74	9.24	9.16
Work identity	6.23	6.19	6.10	6.30	6.29	6.17	6.30
Bradburn positive affect scale	2.80	2.78	2.92	2.41	2.69	3.10	3.02
Bradburn negative affect scale	1.06	0.86	1.02	1.62	1.23	0.85	0.66
Bradburn balance scale	1.75	1.93	1.90	0.80	1.46	2.25	2.36
Happiness scale	17.03	17.45	17.38	15.57	17.10	17.66	17.80
Extent of impairment index, 1976	3.57	1.43	1.17	8.03	1.58	2.38	1.61
Extent of impairment index, 1981	4.58	2.25	2.97	8.97	3.47	3.37	3.10

Note: UNIVERSE: Men who were inteviewed in 1981 ($n = 2,794$).

[a] Reason for retirement categories based on panel data.

nonretirees tend to be younger than retirees, we see few differences between nonretired men and retired men in the remaining retirement categories. Interestingly, no difference appears across categories, including the health category, in the proportion of men reporting that their health had improved over the past 5 years. If anything, the voluntary early retirees are more likely than other men to report health improvement. However, among all categories except the discouraged retirees, a large proportion reported deteriorating health. Almost half of the health retirees reported worsening health, but so did about one-quarter of the voluntary and mandatory retirees and one-fifth of the nonretired men.

Several of the measures of well-being were multiple-item scales, with too many values for tabular presentation. The means for these measures for different types of retirees are also shown in table 7-2. The first two scales shown are not indexes of well-being, per se, but are instead attitudes toward work and retirement which may serve as mediators between retirement and well-being. The first scale, positive attitude toward retirement, is the sum of scores on the responses to three items: (a) retirement is a pleasant time of life; (b) people who don't retire when they can afford to are foolish; and (c) older workers should retire when they can, so as to give younger people more of a chance on the job. A related measure, work identity, is the sum of two items on the degree to which the individual finds self-identity in work: (a) work is the most meaningful part of life, and (b) most people think more of someone who works than they do of someone who doesn't.[11] Nonretirees have a substantially less positive attitude toward retirement than do retirees—even those retirees who were forced out of the labor market through compulsory retirement or ill health. However, they do not seem to have a higher degree of work identity than other men. In fact the highest means on this dimension are for men who retired for health reasons or voluntarily at age 65 or later.

The overall mean for the nonretired men on the Bradburn Positive Affect Scale was 2.78 out of a maximum of 5, almost identical to the mean for the total sample. Among the retirees, it is not surprising that the health and discouraged groups had the lowest scores, while voluntary retirees had the highest. The pattern is reversed on the negative affect score, which is not as trivial as it seems, given that the two subscales have virtually zero correlation not only in this case but in most others where the Bradburn instrument has been used. The mirror imaging of the subscales results in large differences in means on the Affect Balance Scale, which nets the positive and negative indexes. The voluntary early and voluntary normal retirees have the highest means and health retirees the lowest.

The means for the happiness index repeat the general picture shown by the Affect Balance measure. Men who leave the labor market unwillingly, especially those who leave because of poor health, have the lowest happiness scores on average. Men who leave the labor force voluntarily, on the other hand, not only are happier than other retirees, but they also appear to be happier than men who are still working. The means for the impairment index show a general increase in the number of reported problems from 1976 to 1981, confirming the impression given by the subjective assessment of health. The sample as a whole reports on the average one more impairment in 1981 than was reported five years earlier, with the largest increases reported by mandatory or discouraged retirees.

Multivariate Analysis

The results that have been presented to this point are merely suggestive. For a more rigorous test of the effet of retirement on well-being we turn to a longitudinal multivariate analysis of all respondents who had never retired as of 1976. About half of these men retired over the subsequent five years.[12] The strategy is to control statistically for the 1976 characteristics and factors that are associated with both the decision to retire and the outcome variables (the indicators of well-being) and then to ascertain whether the men who had retired by 1981 differed significantly in measures of well-being from those who had not. Since some of the critical factors in well-being—notably financial and health resources— may themselves be outcomes of retirement (see figure 7-1), a second model is also used, which add controls for measures of resources in 1981 as well as for those in 1976 in order to assess the processes by which retirement affects well-being.

Before examining the multivariate models in greater detail, it is useful to note a basic limitation of the research strategy. Because the overwhelming majority of retirements depend at least to some degree on the volition of the retiree, even controlling statistically for variables thought to be associated both with the decision to retire and the outcome variables may leave unmeasured differences between the retired and the nonretired groups. The problem is exacerbated when control measures are not available precisely at the time of retirement. Thus, a finding that the postretirement health of retirees compares unfavorably with that of men who were ostensible comparable in 1976 may merely mean that a deterioration in health subsequent to 1976 on the part of those who retired was the factor *that led* to their retirement.[13] Problems of this kind cannot be entirely eliminated by any feasible research design, but the longitudinal character of the NLS can be exploited to minimize them.

In implementing the model shown in figure 7-1, we use a series of seven dependent variables purporting to measure various dimensions of physical and mental well-being in 1981: the Bradburn scales (1) positive affect, (2) negative affect, and (3) affect balance; (4) the global happiness measure; (5) the happiness index; (6) the comparative health measure (1981 compared with 1976); and (7) the impairment index.

For each of these dependent variables, four sets of regressions have been run. The first of these uses as the principal explanatory variable retirement status as of 1981 (1 retired; 0 nonretired). In addition there is a series of control variables representing the three relevant boxes shown in figure 7-1: personal attributes, work attributes, and resources. The personal attributes include age, race, and family composition. Resources include income, assets, and health (impairment index).

Use of work attributes represents one of the major advances of the present study over previous ones. Adaptation to retirement may well depend on the nature of the work from which the individual is retiring. The greater the individual's involvement with his work, the more difficult it should be for him to leave it behind. The measures used are all based on characteristics of the current or last job as of the 1976 interview. Men who work more hours per week, who are self-employed, and who are in highly skilled jobs should have more job involvement than men who work for wages, fewer hours, and at routine jobs.[14] Additional measures of employment characteristics are job satisfaction and tenure with current employer. Because continuity of employment in a particular line of work is an indicator of career orientation, a measure is introduced indicating whether the 1976 job matches the occupation of the longest job. Because postretirement employment is not uncommon and may affect well-being, dummy variables for extent of labor force participation in 1981 are also included in the model.

The second regression adds variables controlling for 1981 levels of health resources (the 1981 impairment index) and financial resources (income and assets), plus dummy variables indicating whether the respondent was working and whether he was working full time. The 1981 health resource measure is, of course, not used in those regressions in which health is the dependent variable.

The third and fourth regressions are analogous to the first and second except that instead of merely using a retired-nonretired explanatory variable, the several reason-for-retirement categories are introduced as dummy variables, with nonretired men serving as the reference group.[15]

Table 7-3 shows the regression coefficients for the retirement status variables in each of the models. Controlling for current (1981) resources goes a long way toward reducing or eliminating the apparent negative effects of retirement on well-being of men who retired for health reasons, but does not seem to have much effect on relative levels of well-being among other groups. More specifically, retirement status is associated with higher levels of positive affect, and the effect is concentrated among those who retire voluntarily and early. There is no significant effect of

Table 7–3
Indicators of Well-Being, by 1981 Retirement Status: Men Not Retired as of 1976
(OLS regression coefficients)

Outcome/Model[a]	$\overline{R}^2$ (F)	Retired[b]	Reason for Retirement (nonretired = reference group)[c]				
			Mandatory	Health	Discouraged	Voluntary Early	Voluntry Normal
Bradburn Affect Scales							
Positive affect							
A. Model with 1976 controls	.08 (5.30)	.340 (3.95)[f]					
B. Model with 1976 and 1981 controls	.09 (3.79)	.499 (4.14)[f]					
C. Model with 1976 controls	.08 (4.77)		.308 (1.01)	.137 (1.07)	−.186 (−0.80)	.442 (4.28)[f]	.101 (0.62)
D. Model with 1976 and 1981 controls	.08 (3.46)		.384 (1.20)	.270 (1.64)	−.135 (−0.54)	.480 (3.73)[f]	.152 (0.83)
Negative affect							
A. Model with 1976 controls	.06 (4.29)	.028 (0.38)					
B. Model with 1976 and 1981 controls	.15 (6.37)	−.109 (−1.13)					
C. Model with 1976 controls	.07 (4.05)		−.212 (−0.83)	.208 (1.93)[g]	.370 (1.89)[g]	−.057 (−0.66)	−.053 (−0.39)

Table 7–3 continued

Outcome/Model[a]	$\overline{R}^2$ (F)	Retired[b]	Reason for Retirement (nonretired = reference group)[c]				
			Mandatory	Health	Discouraged	Voluntary Early	Voluntry Normal
D. Model with 1976 and 1981 controls	.15 (5.98)		-.353 (-1.39)	-.190 (-1.45)	.340 (1.71)[g]	-.046 (-0.45)	-.101 (-0.69)
Affect balance							
A. Model with 1976 controls	.13 (7.92)	.313 (2.75)[f]					
B. Model with 1976 and 1981 controls	.18 (7.51)	.609 (3.93)[f]					
C. Model with 1976 controls	.13 (7.39)		.520 (1.30)	-.071 (-0.42)	-.555 (-1.81)[g]	.500 (3.68)[f]	.154 (0.72)
D. Model with 1976 and 1981 controls	.18 (6.93)		.737 (1.81)[g]	.460 (2.19)[e]	-.475 (-1.49)	.526 (3.20)[f]	.252 (1.08)
Happiness Measures							
Global happiness							
A. Model with 1976 controls	.09 (5.66)	.032 (0.94)					
B. Model with 1976 and 1981 controls	.13 (5.37)	.116 (2.47)[e]					

	(1)	(2)	(3)	(4)	(5)	(6)	(7)
C. Model with 1976 controls	.09 (5.35)		.188 (1.59)	−.070 (−1.40)	−.034 (−0.37)	.044 (1.10)	.099 (1.54)
D. Model with 1976 and 1981 controls	.12 (4.89)		.240 (1.93)[g]	.068 (1.07)	.009 (0.10)	.078 (1.56)	.140 (1.97)[e]
Happiness index							
A. Model with 1976 controls	.14 (9.02)	−.019 (−0.15)					
B. Model with 1976 and 1981 controls	.25 (10.73)	.452 (2.59)[f]					
C. Model with 1976 controls	.17 (9.47)		.078 (0.17)	−.901 (−4.63)[f]	.068 (0.19)	.457 (2.93)[f]	−.233 (−0.95)
D. Model with 1976 and 1981 controls	.25 (9.99)		.451 (0.98)	−.043 (−0.18)	.349 (0.97)	.576 (3.12)[f]	.024 (0.09)
Health Mesures[d] *Comparative health*							
A. Model with 1976 controls	.17 (10.88)	−.220 (−4.51)[f]					
B. Model with 1976 and 1981 controls	.20 (8.72)	.002 (0.03)					
C. Model with 1976 controls	.22 (12.80)		−.113 (−0.68)	−.668 (−9.46)[f]	−.185 (−1.45)	.046 (0.81)	−.146 (−1.63)
D. Model with 1976 and 1981 controls	.37 (16.85)		.107 (0.68)	−.139 (−1.71)[g]	.022 (0.18)	.150 (2.35)[e]	.050 (0.56)

Table 7–3 continued

Outcome/Model[a]	$\overline{R}^2$ (F)	Retired[b]	Reason for Retirement (nonretired = reference group)[c]				
			Mandatory	Health	Discouraged	Voluntary Early	Voluntry Normal
Impairment							
A. Model with 1976 controls	.29 (20.67)	1.37 (6.25)[f]					
B. Model with 1976 and 1981 controls	.31 (14.72)	.466 (1.54)					
C. Model with 1976 controls	.36 (24.45)		1.11 (1.51)	3.97 (12.76)[f]	.778 (1.38)	−.040 (−0.16)	.698 (1.78)[g]
D. Model with 1976 and 1981 controls	.37 (17.58)		.515 (0.68)	3.07 (8.02)[f]	−.076 (−0.13)	−.690 (−2.26)[e]	−.055 (−0.13)

Note: t-values in parentheses; UNIVERSE: Men working and never retired in 1976, interviewed in 1981. (N = 1200)

[a]Model A (1976 controls) regresses outcome variables on personal characteristics, characteristics of the job, health, income, assets, and household composition. Model B (1976 and 1981 controls) adds 1981 health, household composition, assets, and income to the base model.

[b]Coefficients in this column are for a variable indicating 1981 retirement status (1 = retired; 0 = not retired).

[c]Coefficients are derived from regressions using the same sets of predictor variables used for retirement status, but breaking retirement into dummy variables indicating reason for retirement. The reference group is men who are not retired.

[d]1981 model does not include 1981 impairment index where outcome variable is a health measure.

[e]Significant at .05 level.

[f]Significant at .01 level.

[g]Significant at .10 level.

retirement on negative affect. For the affect balance scale, which taps the degree to which positive emotional states outnumber negative ones, the scores of voluntary early retirees are significantly higher than those of nonretirees. Also, the small negative coefficient for health retirees turns to a substantial and significant positive one when 1981 resources (notably health) are included in the equation.

Retirement effects on happiness, using either the single global question or the domain-specific scale, are significant only when 1981 resources are taken into account. As expected, retired men are happier, and the effect is strongest among those who retired voluntarily. For the happiness index, health retirees score significantly lower than others in the base model, but the effect is probably due to the inclusion of an item on health in the index itself. The relationship between health-related retirement and the happiness index is eliminated when 1981 impairments are included in the model.

Controlling only for 1976 conditions, it appears that retirees are significantly more likely than nonretirees to report ill health, both in terms of extent of impairment and perceived relative health. However, even without controlling for 1981 resources, this effect is significant only among those who are categorized as retiring because of their health. Men who retired for other reasons are not significantly different from nonretirees; indeed, voluntary retirees report themselves as being healthier than nonretirees if current financial resources are taken into account.

Conclusions

All in all, retirement does not seem to produce any negative effects on well-being, at least not in the initial years. If anything, men find that retirement is better than they thought it would be. For a large proportion of retirees, the best thing about retirement, in fact, is not working.

Most of the variation in well-being among retirees can be traced fairly directly to health and income effects. Health is perceived as independent of retirement, a perception reinforced by the lack of effect of retirement on health among men who left the labor force for reasons other than ill health.

The results also show very clearly that retirees are not a homogeneous group. Reason for retirement has strong implications for the outcomes of individuals. Voluntary retirees are relatively well-off. For these men, aside from possible problems with income and health, retirement is a positive experience. The mandatory and discouraged retirees are both relatively small components of the retired population, so it is difficult to find strong relationships, but there are suggestions in the data that these men do not fare so well in retirement. Even here, it appears that most of their problems can be traced to other aspects of their situations, rather than to retirement itself.

Longitudinal multivariate analyses show that current health and financial resources must be taken into account in understanding the relationship between retirement and well-being. Retirees tend to have more situational problems—lower income and poorer health—than do nonretirees. There appears to be no great trauma associated with retirement, however, and many men apparently find fulfillment and happiness. The longitudinal analysis shows that men who retire voluntarily are happier, however happiness is measured, than are men who stay in the labor market.

The positive effects among voluntary retirees cannot all be attributed to the act of retiring, because these retirees are selectively men who could anticipate doing well in retirement. Similarly, negative effects on health associated with retirement are probably exaggerated due to inadequate controls on prior health. It may be that, in reality, retirement as an event has little to do with well-being. Anecdotal evidence suggests that some men thrive and others decline after leaving work, and the effects may cancel each other out. Future research should focus on the ways in which people adapt to the specific circumstances of their lives, rather than to such global and yet ultimately poorly specified events such as retirement. Just as changing jobs can lead to improvements or deterioration in job satisfaction, depending on the nature of the old job and the new, apparently the effect of going from work into retirement depends on the characteristics of retired life and its relationship to what has been experienced before.

Notes

1. See Andrews and McKennell, 1978, for an analysis of the affective and cognitive components of a range of commonly used well-being measures. Much of the following discussion is based on their work.

2. The instrument asks respondents to report whether they have felt any of ten emotional states "during the past few weeks." The positive affect items were as follows: "particularly excited or interested in something," "proud because someone complimented you on something you had done," "pleased about having accomplished something," "on top of the world," and "things were going your way." The negative affect items were: "so restless that you couldn't sit long in a chair," "very lonely or remote from other people," "bored," "depressed or very unhappy," and "upset because someone criticized you."

3. Andrews and McKennel (1978) have shown that items asking about the respondent's *happiness* with life tend to contain more of the affective component

of attitude, relative to the cognitive component, than items asking about *satisfaction* with life, or items containing implicit or explicit comparisons.

4. The activities asked included walking, using stairs or inclines, standing for long periods of time, sitting for long periods, stooping, kneeling or crouching, lifting or carrying weights up to ten pounds, lifting or carrying heavy weights, reaching, using hands and fingers, seeing (even with glasses), hearing, dealing with people, and a final open-ended category for other impairments. For each impairment, it was recorded whether the respondent could do the activity somewhat or whether he was prevented from doing it at all. The symptom list included pain, tiring easily, having no energy, weakness, lack of strength, aches, swelling, sick feeling, fainting spells, dizziness, nervousness, tension, anxiety, depression, shortness of breath, and trouble breathing. These items were coded only for their presence, not for their severity. For the method of scoring the index, see table 6-4, note b.

5. There is some argument about the degree to which reports of poor health by retirees reflect their objective health status or whether they are used as a normatively acceptable justification by men who wish to leave an unsatisfying job and do so by exaggerating the seriousness of their condition. Probably some respondents do overreport the extent of their impairments, but there is little doubt that subjective reports of ill health are correlated with medically definable conditions. Studies on the validity of survey measures of health find, if anything, underreporting of chronic conditions (Meltzer and Hochstin, 1970). Most of the errors seem to come from memory problems, rather than from self-presentation issues, and since our measures refer to current health rather than incidence of ill health over some period of time, the reports should be relatively accurate.

6. Mandatory retirees reported that their employers had a compulsory retirement age, and that they retired at that age; they also reported prior to retirement that they would prefer to continue working longer if allowed. Health retirees reported health problems prior to leaving the labor market. Discouraged retirees were men who reported that they left the labor market because they could not find employment. Voluntary retirees were divided into two groups, early and normal, according to whether they retired before or after reaching age 65. For a fuller description, see chapter 5.

7. On one hand, the panel criteria are measured prior to, or at the time of, retirement, and so should more accurately reflect conditions at the time of retirement, especially for men who have been retired for some time. On the other hand, even though the post hoc reconstructions that men provide of the circumstances of their retirement can distort the actual reason for retirement, the perception of choice for leaving the labor force is perhaps more important than the "actual" reason for leaving. In particular, the perception by the individual that he had control over the conditions of his retirement should be associated with positive psychological states (Walker, Kimmel, and Price, 1980-81). In the last analysis, it is not clear which of the two sets of definitions is more valid. The behavioral measures require making inferences about decision processes which may or not be correct for any given individual. The differences in circumstances surrounding the retirement decision embedded in the panel-based definitions are particularly troublesome in the analysis of the reasons for variation in well-being

among categories of retirees, because they are confounded with some of the situational predictors. In particular, self-reported health prior to retirement is a factor in defining retirement for health reasons. The retrospective measure at least has the virtue of allowing an estimator of health to be assessed separately from the estimator of reason for retirement.

8. A notable exception to this generalization is the fact that the panel criteria tend to show larger differences than the retrospective data in reported well-being between voluntary early and voluntary normal retirees. This pattern may stem from the inclusion in the panel-defined voluntary normal retirees of men who perceive themselves to be mandatory retirees. To the extent that perceived control is a major factor in determining well-being, mandatory retirees should be less well-off than voluntary retirees; thus, the inclusion in the voluntary group of men who regard themselves as mandatory retirees would serve to mute the effect of voluntary retirement.

9. Mandatory retirees were asked only if they would prefer to have retired later or at the same time as they had actually retired, so the data from this group are not presented in the table. The vast majority of mandatory retirees, however, report that they would again retire at the same age.

10. The one exception to this independence is the report that there is "nothing" liked best or least about retirement. This category is scored only if it is the sole response to the question, so that none of these respondents are counted in any of the other categories.

11. Respondents were asked to indicate their extent of agreement with each statement on a 4-point scale. Possible scores on the first variable range from 3 to 12; on the second between 2 and 8. These 5 items were originally part of the same series of questions. Factor analysis revealed the 2 separate dimensions.

12. A multivariate cross-sectional analysis was also performed for the total sample in 1981, using retirement status and reason for retirement as explanatory variables. The results were broadly consistent with those of the longitudinal analysis, and are therefore not presented, since the latter constitute a more definitive test of the *causal* effect of retirement on well-being.

13. My thanks to my colleague Herbert S. Parnes for helping to articulate this intuitive notion.

14. Skill level is derived from the Dictionary of Occupational Titles, and measured as the Specific Vocational Preparation (SVP) level assigned to the three-digit Census code for the 1976 survey week occupation. The SVP estimates the amount of on-the-job training needed to learn a particular job. SVP is used instead of the Duncan index because it is a more direct measure of the skill level of the job, and because income and education, two major components of prestige, are included in the equation separately.

15. The complete regression results are available from the author. In general, results are as expected: men with more favorable circumstances have higher levels of well-being.

References

Andrews, F.M., and McKennel, A.C. 1978. "Measures of Self-Reported Well Being: Their Affective, Cognitive, and Other Components." Institute for Social Research, University of Michigan, Working paper series.

Bradburn, N.M. 1969. *The Structure of Psychological Well-being*. Chicago, Aldine.

Carp, F.M.; Carp, A.; and Millsap, R. 1982. "Equity and Satisfaction Among the Elderly." *International Journal of Aging and Human Development* 15(2): 151-166.

Elwell, F., and Maltbie-Crannell, A.D. 1981. "The Impact of Role Loss Upon Coping Resources and Life Satisfaction of the Elderly." *Journal of Gerontology* 36(2): 223-232.

Larson, R. 1978. "Thirty Years of Research on the Subjective Well-Being of Older Americans." *Journal of Gerontology* 33(1): 109-125.

Meltzer, J.W., and Hochstin, J.R. 1970. "Reliability and Validity of Survey Data on Physical Health. *Public Health Reports*, vol. 85, pp. 1075-1086.

Ostrom, T.M. 1969. "The Relationship Between the Affective, Behavioral, and Cognitive Components of Attitude." *Journal of Experimental Social Psychology* 5: 12-30.

Palmore, E.B.; Fillenbaum, G.G.; and George, L.K. 1984. "Consequences of Retirement." *Journal of Gerontology* 39(1): 109-116.

Parnes, H.S., and Nestel, G. 1981. "The Retirement Experience." In H.S. Parnes, ed., *Work and Retirement: A Longitudinal Study of Men*. MIT, pp. 155-197.

Stock, W.A., and Okun, M.A. 1982. "The Construct Validity of Life Satisfaction Among the Elderly." *Journal of Gerontology* 37(5): 625-627.

Thompson, W.E., and Streib, G.F. 1958. "Situational Determinants: Health and Economic Deprivation in Retirement." *Journal of Social Issues* 14(2): 18—34.

Walker, J.W.; Kimmel, D.C.; and Price, K.F. 1980-1981. "Retirement Style and Retirement Satisfaction: Retirees Aren't All Alike." *International Aging and Human Development* 12(4): 267-281.

8
Shunning Retirement: The Experience of Full-Time Workers

Herbert S. Parnes
Lawrence J. Less

Introduction

We have seen in chapter 5 that a small minority of men who retire nevertheless continue to work full-time at other jobs. This was true of somewhat over five percent of the men in our sample who had retired by 1979. In this chapter our interest focuses on a more comprehensive group of full-time workers—all men beyond retirement age who have continued to work full-time, whether or not they have previously "retired." Who are these men? What is the nature of their work experience compared with that of younger men and with their own earlier experience? This information will be useful if public policy is directed at keeping larger numbers of older men in the labor market.

We know that these men are highly unrepresentative of their age group, most of whom are not working or working only part-time. We can safely guess that they will enjoy above average health compared with other members of the cohort and that they found retirement uncongenial from either a financial or a psychological point of view. In any case, we must keep in mind that this subsample is characterized by what is technically known as selectivity bias, so we expect to find relationships that are different from those prevailing in the total population of men in this age group.

It is more difficult now than it was two or three decades ago to decide how to define "retirement-age workers." In her study using that phrase as a title, Rix (1980) focuses on persons 65 and older, a logical choice both because 65 has long been regarded as the convential age of retirement and also because published labor force statistics frequently differentiate between persons age 60-64 and those 65 and older. Nevertheless she acknowledges that "the typical worker withdraws from the labor force before the so-called normal retirement age of 65." It may be noted that the labor force participation rate in the summer of 1981 stood at 72 percent for men age 60, 54 percent at age 62, 48 percent at age

63, and 33 percent at age 65 (U.S. Department of Labor, 1981). We have opted to use age 62 as the boundary line in this chapter, but to present data for men age 65-69 and 70-74 as well as for the total group age 62-74. Men age 60-61, who are ineligible for Social Security retirement benefits, are the reference group.

The dividing line between full-time and part-time work is also to some extent arbitrary. Here we translate the Bureau of Labor Statistics full-time, full-year worker concept (at least 35 hours per week and 50 weeks per year) into an equivalent number of hours, and take as our criterion for full-time work at least 1,750 hours of employment in the 12 months preceding the 1981 survey. We have also required labor force participation in the 1981 survey week. Thus our postretirement full-time workers are men age 62 to 74 in 1981 who were working or looking for work during the week before the survey and who had worked for wages or salaries or had been self-employed for at least 1,750 hours in the preceding 12 months.

The Number and Distribution of Full-Time Workers, 60-74

Of the approximately 11.1 million males in the United States in mid-1981 who were between the ages of 60 and 74, 39 percent (about 4.3 million) were in the labor force at the 1981 survey. Of these, 2.9 million—66 percent of those in the labor force and 26 percent of the total age cohort—were full-time workers by the criterion just described. Over one-third of the full-time workers were preretirement age, but an almost equal proportion were age 62 to 64 and 29 percent were age 65 to 74. Most of the latter group were between 65 and 69 years old; men 70 to 74 years of age comprised only one-tenth of all full-time workers in the total age cohort. The vast majority of full-time workers in each age category had never retired; yet over 1 in 5 of those age 62-74 had reported being retired at some point during the 15-year period covered by the surveys, and this proportion was 3 out of 10 among the men age 65-74.

Correlates of Full-Time Work by Retirement-Age Men

Of the total cohort of men who had achieved the minimum retirement age under Social Security by the time of the 1981 interview, 18.4 percent were still in the labor force and had worked full-time during the preceding 12 months. Virtually all of these—98 percent—were working at least 36 hours per week in the job they held in the survey week of 1981. Table 8-1 presents the results of a multiple classification analysis designed to ascertain the net relationship between their working full-time and a variety of personal and labor market characteristics.

Table 8–1
Percentage of Retirement-Age Men Who Work Full-Time, by Selected Characteristics, 1981
(MCA[a] Results)

Characteristic	Sample n	Unadjusted Percentage	Adjusted[a] Percentage (F-ratio)
Total Sample	2,383	18.4	18.4
Race			(0.006)
White	1,728	18.6	18.4
Black	655	15.8	18.2
Age, 1981			(103.262)[e]
62–64	656	36.8	35.1[d]
65–69	963	13.4	13.5[d]
70–74	764	9.3	10.5[d]
Marital status			(1.922)
Married: wife worked past 12 months	522	25.8	20.7[f]
Married: wife did not work	1,378	16.1	17.0[e]
Not married	466	17.1	20.3
Extent of impairment,[b] 1981			(28.008)[d]
None	584	30.4	27.5[d]
Minor	265	29.5	27.8[d]
Moderate	214	22.5	22.2[f]
Substantial	309	17.3	19.4
Severe	966	6.9	8.6[e]
Education			(3.421)[d]
Less than 9	1,017	14.2	18.0
9–11	409	13.9	14.9[e]
12	507	20.9	17.8
13–15	179	22.1	20.2
16 or more	215	30.9	25.7[d]
Family income, except respondent's earnings or pensions, 1980			(0.850)
$5,000 or less	953	16.6	18.6
$5,001–$10,000	225	17.9	16.7
$10,001–$15,000	134	19.0	15.5
Over $15,000	154	22.3	16.2

Table 8–1 continued

Characteristic	Sample n	Unadjusted Percentage	Adjusted[a] Percentage (F-ratio)
Eligibility for retirement income			(6.930)[d]
None	45	4.6	10.1
Social Security only	1,087	14.3	16.9[f]
Other pension only	54	30.2	0.5[d]
Social Security and other pension	1,111	23.6	21.2[d]
Attitude toward retirement (1978)			(27.613)[d]
Favorable	625	11.3	10.4[d]
Ambivalent	925	16.7	16.8[f]
Unfavorable	626	27.8	27.7[d]
Commitment to work (1966)			(6.011)[e]
Would work even if unnecessary	1,748	20.5	19.4[e]
Would not work if unnecessary	544	14.2	16.8
R^2 (adjusted)			.19

[a]For a description of Multiple Classification Analysis, see "A Note on the Tables and Graphs."
[b]For construction of index, see table 6–4, note c.
[c]Includes respondents who were undecided.
[d]Significant at the .01 level.
[e]Significant at the .05 level.
[f]Significant at the .10 level.

Demographic Characteristics

Even with such characteristics as pension eligibility and health controlled, age differences are as pronounced as in the unadjusted data. These differences doubtless reflect the influence of age-related factors not included in the analysis, especially the *amount* of retirement income an individual might expect in the absence of earnings, but it would be surprising if age discrimination and cultural norms about age and work were not also operating.

Race is not significantly related to the likelihood of full-time work on the part of men beyond the age of retirement. Although the marital status variable as a whole does not achieve statistical significance, married men with working wives are more likely to be full-time workers than those whose wives do not work—another piece of evidence of the complementarity of husbands' and wives' leisure time (see chap. 5, table 5-1). As expected, physical or mental impairment is strongly and virtually monotonically related to the likelihood of being a full-time worker: other things being equal, men with severe impairments are only one-third as likely as those with only minor or no problems to be engaged in full-time labor market activity.

Education bears a statistically significant J-shaped relationship with the likelihood of full-time work. Men who have not attended high school have higher percentages of being full-time workers than those who have. The highest rate, however—significantly above average—is for the men who hold college degrees. This pattern probably reflects the push of financial necessity on the least well-educated and the pull of attractive opportunities on those with the most education.

Economic Factors

Conventional economic theory holds that, other things being equal, the amount of labor supplied by an individual will be inversely related to the amount of income he would have in the absence of work. Where the measure of resources is total family income exclusive of the respondent's earnings and pension receipts, the pattern observed here is basically consistent with this expected relationship, but it does not achieve statistical significance. Ideally, it would have been desirable to include as an additional measure of financial resources the *potential* pension income of the men had they chosen not to work, but use of this variable was precluded by the large number of cases in which respondents were unable to provide pension information. As a substitute, we simply differentiated among the men on the basis of their *eligibility* for various types of pension income. Although it is statistically significant, the relationship is contrary to what was expected: men eligible for both Social Security and another pension are *more* likely than men eligible for only one or the other to be full-time workers.[1]

Attitudinal Factors

Deep-seated attitudes toward work and retirement apparently have a great deal to do with whether older men choose to work full-time. As early as the initial interview in 1966 respondents were asked: "If, by some chance, you were to get enough money to live comfortably without working, do you think that you would work anyway?" About three-fourths (weighted) of the men currently under consideration responded affirmatively, while over one-fifth were either undecided or said that they would not (the remaining 3 percent did not answer). As figure 8-1 shows, those who registered high commitment to work were more likely in 1981 to be full-time workers. The generalized measure of attitude toward work and retirement that was introduced in the 1978 survey shows an even stronger relationship. Other things equal, those with favorable attitudes toward retirement were less likely by 17 percentage points to be working full-time than those whose attitudes toward retirement were unfavorable.

Preretirement-Age Versus Retirement-Age Full-Time Workers

How do the personal and labor market characteristics of men who continue to work full-time after reaching retirement age compare with those of full-time workers who are approaching that age? Our definition of a "retirement-age" worker is in some degree arbitrary: many would not place men 62-64 in that category, irrespective of the provisions of the Social Security law; fewer would quarrel with age 65 as the boundary line; but we suspect that no one willing to accept the concept of "retirement age" would deny that a 70-year-old man had attained it.

For purposes of the interage comparisons, we retain the distinction between the total group of full-time workers age 62-74 and those age 60-61. However, the retirement age group is further subdivided into ages 62-64, 65-69, and 70-74, and the total group is differentiated according to whether the individual had ever "retired." These categories permit us to explore cross-sectional age differences *within* the retirement-age group—and they also permit readers to select a different set of "retirement-age" workers if they prefer to do so.

Education and Health

Were age the only factor operating, we would expect retirement-age men to have poorer health than the younger group simply because of the ravages of age, and to be less well-educated because of the secular trend in educational attainment. When attention is confined to full-time workers, however, these simple relationships do not prevail (figure 8-1). In the case of health, whether we use as the criterion the existence of a work-limiting health problem or the presence and severity of impairments, the retirement-age group as a whole appears to be at least as well-off as the men in their very early 60s. *Within* the retirement-age group the relationship between health and age is in the expected direction, but it is not at all pronounced. For instance, the 70-74-year group has as

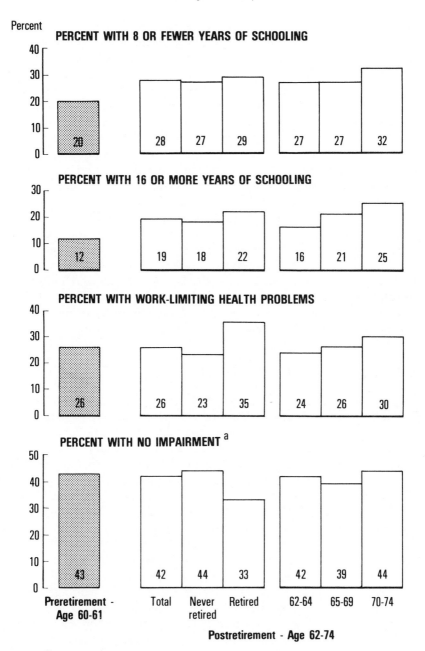

Figure 8–1. Education and Health Characteristics of Full-Time Workers, by Age and Retirement Status, 1981

large a proportion as the 62-64-year group with only minor or no impairments. Apparently there is a "survival of the fittest" phenomenon at work.

The relationship between educational attainment and age among the full-time workers is more complex. Using as the criterion the proportion with very little education (fewer than 9 years), the retirement-age workers are at a disadvantage—almost 3 out of 10 of them as compared with 2 out of 10 of the preretirement-age group fall into that category. On the other hand, the retirement-age group contains a higher proportion of college graduates (19 vs. 12 percent), and the proportion rises with age within the group, reaching 25 percent among those age 70-74. The overrepresentation of the better educated among the retirement-age workers reflects the more attractive work opportunities available to them.

The retirement-age men who returned to full-time work after retiring differ from those who had never retired from the standpoint of both health and education. The never-retired group is considerably healthier than the erstwhile retirees; on the other hand, the men who had returned to full-time work from retirement include a larger proportion of college graduates, for whom work tends to be less physically demanding than for those in other educational categories.

Employment Characteristics

Occupation, Industry, and Type of Worker. The difference in occupational distribution between preretirement- and retirement-age men is not dramatic but regular, in the sense that differences are generally more pronounced as the age gap widens (figure 8-2). To illustrate, when the total retirement-age group is compared with men in their very early 60s, the former show larger percentages of managers, salesmen, and farmworkers and lower proportions of clerical workers, craftsmen and operatives, but the difference in no case exceeds 4 percentage points. However, when one compares the 70-74-year men with the younger group, the differences are almost invariably larger, reaching 11 points in the case of managers and 12 points in the case of craftsmen.

Industrial differences are more pronounced, and, as in the case of occupation, become wider as older groups of retirement-age men are considered (figure 8-3). Retirement-age men are less likely than the younger group to be employed in manufacturing and in transportation and utilities, but more likely to be found in agriculture, finance, and miscellaneous services. The fact that the retirement age group is overrepresented in sales occupations but underrepresented in trade is on the surface perplexing, but it results from the large number in real estate sales.

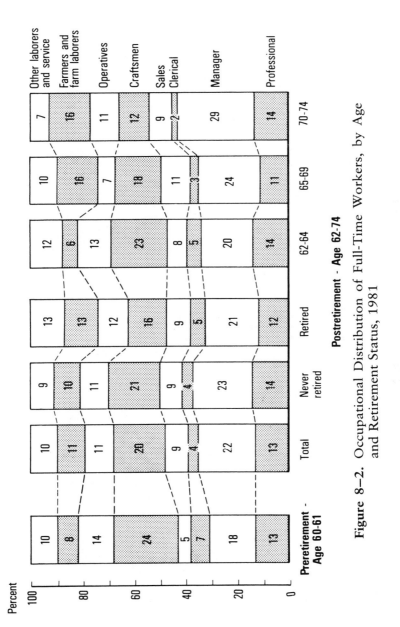

Figure 8–2. Occupational Distribution of Full-Time Workers, by Age and Retirement Status, 1981

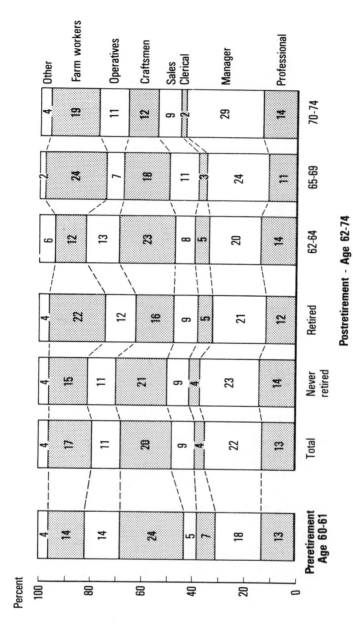

Figure 8–3. Industrial Distribution of Full-Time Workers, by Age and Retirement Status, 1981

A much larger proportion of the retirement-age than of the younger men are self-employed, and this difference grows as older age groups are considered. Self-employment accounts for 14 percent of those age 60-61, but for one-fourth of the retirement-age men as a whole and 48 percent of those age 70-74.

Within the retirement-age group the ex-retirees differ from those who had never retired. They are less likely to be in professional, managerial, or craft assignments, and more likely to be serving as farm or nonfarm laborers. Industrially, they are more frequently found in trade, and less frequently found in manufacturing and construction. They are considerably more likely than the never-retired to be self-employed (36 vs. 28 percent). In short, the men who have returned to full-time work from retirement ostensibly have less desirable employment situations, on the average, than men who had never retired.

Our findings about occupational and industrial composition of employment differ somewhat from those of Rones (1978), who reported that relative to younger men, those age 65 and older are markedly underrepresented in manufacturing, construction, transportation, utilities, and mining and overrepresented in agriculture, trade, finance, insurance, real estate, and miscellaneous services. Rones's study did not differentiate between part-time and full-time workers, and, as he observes, part of the age difference in occupational and industrial composition is attributable to (a) the greater likelihood of part-time work among older than younger workers and (b) the greater opportunities for part-time work in some occupations and industries. To illustrate, our data relating only to full-time workers show a somewhat *smaller* proportion of older than of younger workers in trade, and virtually no difference in the proportions in construction. In most cases, the differences are in the same direction as those reported by Rones, but of smaller magnitude, reflecting the influence of the additional factors that he cites as affecting age differences in employment among industries and occupations—namely, extent of pension coverage, physical demands of the jobs, income and Social Security benefits, and the rate of employment growth (Rones, 1978, p. 7).[2]

Tenure. Because they are older, retirement-age men obviously have the potential for longer tenure in their jobs than men in their early 60s. However, to the extent that they make career changes as they approach or reach retirement age, one would expect shorter tenure on their part. Actually, both of these counteracting influences are at work, so that there is very little net difference in the distributions of the two groups by length of service with the employer they served (or in the self-employed status they held) in 1981. About half of each group had been in their jobs at least 20 years, the median being 19.6 years for the preretirement-age workers and 18.1 years for the retirement-age men. As might be expected, however, there is a dramatic difference within the latter group between men who had previously been retired and those who had not. The median tenure of the latter was 22.6 years—about 6 years longer than the preretirement-age group—while the median for the erstwhile retirees was less than 9 years.

Earnings. We use two measures of earnings, one applicable to wage and salary earners only and the other applicable both to them and to the self-employed. The first of these is the respondent's report of "how much (he) usually earns . . . before deductions" at his survey week job. The second is annual age and salary and/or (net) self-employment income. It is not possible readily to convert one into the other, because although all respondents are asked about usual hours worked per week and number of weeks worked, the reference period for these questions is the 12 months preceding the survey while the income accounting period is the preceding calendar year.

Both measures are summarized in figure 8-4. Retirement-age workers are compensated, on the average, less well than the younger age group of men, but the difference is attributable exclusively to the lower earnings of the ex-retirees. By each measure, the median for the never-retired men age 62-74 is actually somewhat higher than that of men age 60-61. The median average hourly earnings of full-time workers age 60-62 is $8.10, 4 percent above that of the total older group. Moreover, within the retirement age group, the median decreases monotonically as age increases, and particularly sharply for men age 70-74. In the case of median annual earnings (of wage and salary workers and the self-employed combined), the same relationship with age prevails, albeit much less pronounced than in the average hourly earnings figures. In the latter case the differential between the reference group and men age 70-74 is 51 percent; the corresponding differential in median annual earnings is 13 percent. The inclusion of the self-employed, in other words, tends to make the earnings of the several age groups less unequal. The reason is not difficult to discern: comparison of the self-employed with wage and salary earners (not shown here) indicates that the former are disproportionately represented in the upper age groups and among the more highly educated.

In both distributions, examination of the structure of wage rates within the several age categories reveals that the behavior of the medians is at least in part a reflection of increasing dispersion of average earnings as age increases. While both the first and the third quartiles of the distribution of hourly earnings decline with advancing age, the relative decrease in the first quartile is larger than in the third—54 versus 20 percent

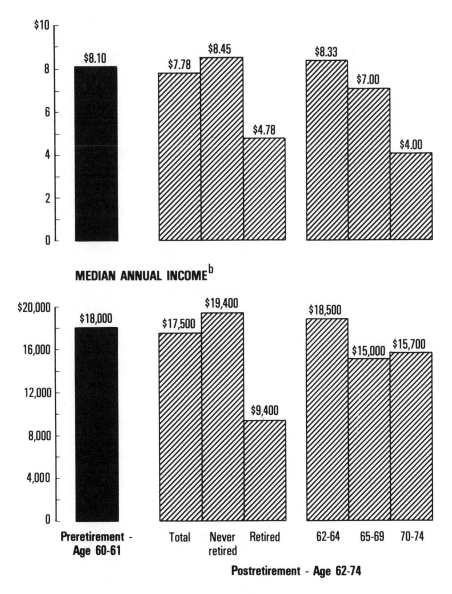

MEDIAN HOURLY EARNINGS [a]

MEDIAN ANNUAL INCOME [b]

Preretirement - Age 60-61

Total / Never retired / Retired

62-64 / 65-69 / 70-74

Postretirement - Age 62-74

[a] Wage and salary workers only

[b] Wage and salary and self-employment income

Figure 8–4. Median Average Hourly Earnings (1981) and Annual Earned Income (1980) of Full-Time Workers, by Age and Retirement Status

between men age 60-61 and age 70-74. In the case of *annual* earnings, the third quartile is actually 23 percent *higher* for the older than the younger group. The fact that the retirement-age workers have a higher proportion of poorly educated men and that this proportion increases with age helps to explain the decrease in the first quartile with advancing age. The difference between hourly and annual earnings in the behavior of the third quartile is doubtless attributable to the observed fact that self-employed individuals tend to be disproportionately older *and* better educated. To pursue this matter further, we turn to a multivariate analysis of the earnings variables (table 8-2).

Although we are primarily concerned with the age variable in table 8-2, note how the control variables affect the earnings of these men. Education bears the expected strong monotonic relationship both to the average hourly earnings of wage and salary workers and the annual earnings of the entire sample. The behavior of the retirement status and tenure variables is especially enlightening. To begin with, length of service in current job bears the expected strong positive relationship with both average hourly earnings and total unearned income. Retirement status also makes a difference, at least in the case of total earned income. The annual earnings advantage of the never-retired over the previously retired men is 26 percent—a highly significant difference. In the hourly earnings of wage and salary workers the differential is smaller (8 percent) and fails to achieve statistical significance. When we ran the analysis without the tenure variables (not shown), the corresponding differentials between the never-retired and the former retirees were 20 percent and 30 percent, respectively—both highly significant. We conclude that the earnings advantage of the never-retired men is in part—but not entirely—attributable to the fact that they have accumulated longer seniority with their employers.

Net differences appear in compensation across industries, but these are more pronounced in the average hourly earnings than in the annual earnings data, largely because the self-employed are considerably over-rrepresented (as proprietors) in three low-wage industries—trade, service, and agriculture. Surprisingly, the impairment variable is not a significant determinant of average hourly earnings among full-time wage and salary workers; but it does bear a significant relationship—at least at the extremes—with annual earnings.[3] Finally, black wage and salary workers suffer a net disadvantage of 14 percent in average hourly earnings; for the total sample of whites and blacks the corresponding differential in annual earnings is 23 percent.

With all the foregoing variables controlled, no significant systematic variation by age appears in the annual earnings of full-time workers— wage and salary workers and self-employed combined. The situation is entirely different, however, for the average hourly earnings of wage and

Table 8–2
Average Hourly Earnings of Full-Time Wage and Salary Earners and Annual Earned Income[a] of All Full-Time Workers, by Selected Characteristics, 1980–1981 (MCA[b] Results)

Characteristic	Average Hourly Earnings,[c] 1981			Total Earned Income, 1980		
	n	*Unadjusted*	*Adjusted[b] (F-ratio)*	*n*	*Unadjusted*	*Adjusted[b] (F-ratio)*
Total sample	459	$8.62	$8.62	577	$21,106	$21,106
Race			(4.141)[h]			(5.478)[h]
White	332	8.83	8.72[i]	444	21,608	21,414[h]
Black	127	6.28	7.52[i]	133	13,673	16,507[h]
Age			(4.383)[i]			(1.741)
60–61	188	9.17	9.04[h]	216	22,334	21,869
62–64	165	8.79	8.72	203	21,443	21,656
65–69	78	7.67	8.03	109	19,417	18,791[h]
70–74	28	6.46	6.76[i]	49	18,002	20,442
Years of schooling			(34.792)[i]			(19.330)[i]
Less than 9	141	6.24	6.32[i]	175	14,361	15,208[i]
9–11	82	7.44	7.45[i]	97	20,645	20,380
12	130	8.62	8.35	156	20,465	19,951
13–15	38	10.34	10.58[i]	56	23,085	23,454
16 or more	64	12.56	12.82[i]	78	30,562	30,558[i]
Extent of impairment,[d] 1981			(1.425)			(3.084)[i]
None	200	8.49	8.33	246	21,155	20,583
Minor	77	9.06	9.22[i]	94	25,135	25,168[i]
Moderate	42	9.26	9.01	59	20,628	21,001
Substantial	60	8.83	9.03	79	20,397	20,787
Severe	77	7.92	8.12	96	17,728	18,534[h]

Table 8–2 continued

Characteristic	Average Hourly Earnings,[c] 1981			Total Earned Income, 1980		
	n	*Unadjusted*	*Adjusted[f] (F-ratio)*	*n*	*Unadjusted*	*Adjusted[b] (F-ratio)*
Industry			(9.040)[i]			(4.509)[i]
Agriculture	17	e	e	54	12,255	14,606[i]
Mining	6	e	e	6	e	e
Construction	29	8.86	10.23	40	19,454	22,553
Manufacturing	172	9.27	9.01[i]	173	22,153	21,927
Transportation, utilities	41	10.31	10.70[i]	45	23,059	23,816
Trade	50	7.03	7.34[i]	79	22,798	22,259
Finance, insurance, real estate	17	e	e	29	27,414	26,574[h]
Service	81	7.22	6.59[i]	105	19,163	17,656[i]
Public administration	40	9.99	10.06[h]	39	20,121	21,032
Tenure			(12.393)[i]			(5.232)[i]
Less than 1 year	12	d	d	13	d	d
1–4 years	59	6.84	7.12[i]	73	15,460	16,196[i]
5–9 years	60	6.65	6.82[i]	72	17,632	18,022[h]
10–19 years	125	8.50	8.76	141	20,848	20,875
20 or more years	196	10.03	9.66[i]	268	23,534	23,361[i]
Hours of work, 1981						(2.010)
1,750–2,079	f	f	f	86	18,812	20,530
2,080	f	f	f	286	20,568	20,110[i]
2,081–2,600	f	f	f	122	22,157	21,849
2,601 or more	f	f	f	83	23,412	23,539[i]
Retirement status[g]			(2.007)			(10.870)[i]
Never retired	396	8.95	8.72	485	22,485	21,876[i]
Previously retired	63	6.72	8.06	92	14,523	17,429[i]

Type of worker						
Wage and salary	f	f		475	21,727	(1.298) 21,238
Self-employed	f	f		97	17,618	20.170
R^2 (adjusted)			.41			.26

[a]Includes wage and salary and net self-employment income in calendar year 1980.
[b]For a description of Multiple Classification Analysis see "A Note on the Tables and Graphs."
[c]Survey week, 1981.
[d]For construction of index, see table 6–4, note c.
[e]Figure not shown if based on fewer than 20 sample cases.
[f]Not entered in analysis.
[g]According to the subjective criterion. See chapter 3.
[h]Significant at .05 level.
[i]Significant at .01 level.
[j]Significant at .10 level.

salary workers. Here, although the gross differentials are somewhat reduced, the net differences remain significant at the 1-percent level. Men age 70-74 have hourly earnings only three-fourths as high as those of men in their very early sixties. The difference in the relationship of age to the two earnings measures is apparently attributable to the lesser degree of inequality by age among the self-employed. Another Multiple Classification Analysis of annual earnings for wage and salary workers only (not shown) produced a statistically significant relationship with age similar to that obtained in the case of average hourly earnings.

Job Satisfaction. Differences in hourly compensation of the wage and salary workers are not reflected in the degree of satisfaction the men express with their jobs. Indeed, both for the wage and salary earners and for the total sample, the relationship of age to job satisfaction is just the reverse of its relationship to wages. The retirement-age men are, on the average, at least as highly satisfied as the workers in their very early sixties, and within the former group the proportion of men highly satisfied with their jobs increases substantially and monotonically with increasing age. However, men who had previously been retired are less satisfied than the never-retired group.

Labor Market Attachment. All the men in our sample were full-time workers (by our criterion) in the 12-month period preceding the 1981 survey. Are there differences among them, however, in the continuity of full-time work in the past or in the likelihood of its continuation in the future? During the 15-year period covered by the surveys, there is relatively little difference between the retirement-age men and the younger group in regularity of full-time work, and that small difference is exclusively attributable to the minority of men who returned to full-time work after retirement. Among the never-retired group, between 93 and 98 percent were full-time workers in previous years—proportions as high or higher than those for the 60-61-year group in all reference years.

So far as *prospective attachment* is concerned, a somewhat larger proportion of the retirement-age than of the younger men expect to retire within two years—27 versus 19 percent. However, the retirement-age group also has a larger proportion of individuals who expect to remain with their jobs for at least 5 years (43 vs. 39 percent), and a much larger percentage who expect never to retire (34 vs. 19 percent). Within the retirement-age group, the proportion who expect to "die with their boots on" increases with age—accounting for three-fourths of those 70-74 years of age—and it is higher among previously retired men than among those who have never retired (54 vs. 28 percent).

Social Security and Other Pension Income

In 1980 recipients of Social Security benefits who were under age 72 were subject to a maximum annual earnings limitation.[4] ($5,000 for men age 65-71 and $3,720 for those age 62-64) beyond which $1.00 of benefits was lost for each two additional dollars of earnings. One-fifth of the retirement-age men received either Social Security or other pension income in 1980 despite their full-time work, the proportion ranging between 11 percent of those age 62-64 and 59 percent of those in their early 70s. Among recipients, the median income from these sources was close to $5,000—higher among those age 62-64 and 70-74 than among those age 65-69. Receipt of Social Security benefits was slightly more common than receipt of other pension income (12 vs. 10 percent) and was much more variable among the several age groups. The proportion of Social Security recipients ranged from 2 percent of the men age 62-64 to 54 percent of those age 70-74, whereas the proportion of pension recipients was almost invariable by age. As might be expected, receipt of any retirement benefits is much less common among the never-retired group than among the men who had at one time retired (10 vs. 67 percent); virtually none (2 percent) of the never-retired were receiving pensions other than Social Security (table 8-3).

Total Family Income

The median family income of retirement-age full-time workers in 1980 was $22,900, about 15 percent below that of the full-time workers in their very early 60s. Age differences within the former group are not as pronounced as those just described for annual earnings because differences in pension income tend to compensate to some degree. To illustrate, median earnings of those age 70-74 were 52 percent below those of the men age 62-64, whereas the corresponding differential in total family income was 24 percent. Nevertheless, because of the dominating influence of earned income, total family income displays an increasing dispersion with advancing age, albeit less pronounced than that discernible in the case of earnings (table 8-3).

Black-White Differences

The relatively small number of black men in our sample—a total of 98 between the ages of 62 and 74—has precluded an examination of racial differences in the detailed data presented up to this point. On a more aggregated basis, however, it is useful to make a racial comparison of the total group of retirement-age full-time workers (table 8-4). The black

Table 8–3
Selected Income Measures of Full-Time Workers, by Age and Retirement Status

Characteristic	Preretirement-Age	Postretirement-Age					
		62–74				62–74	
	60–61	Total	62–64	65–69	70–74	Never Retired	Retired
Sample n	238	422	229	124	69	330	92
Population n	1,015	1,732	941	505	286	1,393	339
Percent eligible for Social Security	90	99	98	100	b	99	100
Percent eligible for other pension	59	44	53	36	31	42	47
Wife's earnings							
Percent with earnings	42	26	29	28	13	26	24
Median ($000s)[a]	6.5	6.8	7.0	6.0	3.7	6.0	7.8
Social security benefits							
Percent receiving benefits	0	12	2	15	54	8	30
Median ($000s)[a]	—	4.6	4.6	4.1	5.9	5.9	4.1
Other pensions							
Percent receiving pension	8	10	10	11	10	2	37
Median ($000s)[a]	7.5	5.1	5.1	1.5	10.0	1.1	5.1
Social Security and/or other pensions							
Percent receiving benefits	5	20	11	23	59	10	63
Median ($000s)[a]	7.4	4.8	5.1	2.6	6.2	5.9	4.6
Total family income ($000s)							
Median	27.0	22.9	24.2	24.6	18.4	24.3	21.1
First quartile	17.9	13.9	16.2	11.4	11.2	15.0	10.8
Third quartile	40.0	35.9	35.7	36.8	28.5	36.3	30.0

[a]Includes recipients only.
[b]Over 99.5 percent.

Table 8–4
Selected Characteristics of Retirement-Age Full-Time Workers, by Race, 1981

Characteristic	Whites	Blacks
Sample *n*	324	98
Population (thousands)	1,619	113
Age (Percentage distribution)		
Total percent	100	100
62–64	54	59
65–69	29	27
70–74	17	13
Percent with health limitation	26	27
Percent with minor or no impairment	61	60
Percent with substantial or severe impairment	27	29
Percent employed as professionals, managers	38	8
Percent employed in service occupations	5	25
Percent employed as nonfarm laborers	3	11
Percent employed in agriculture	12	8
Percent self-employed	26	17
Percent employed 1,750 hours, 1976	89	87
Percent employed 1,750 hours, 1971	94	89
Percent employed 1,750 hours, 1966	96	84
Percent with same employer, 1966/1981	54	57
Median annual earnings, 1980 ($000s)	19.0	14.0
Percent very satisfied with job	58	65
Percent ever-retired	24	14
Percent eligible for pension other than Social Security	44	26
Percent receiving Social Security	13	9
Percent receiving other pension	9	2
Median annual Social Security benefit of recipients, 1980 ($000s)	4.8	3.9
Median annual Social Security and/or other pension of recipients, 1980 ($000s)	4.8	4.0
Median total family income, 1980 ($000s)	24.6	13.7

men are somewhat younger than the whites, being underrepresented in the 70-74-year age category and overrepresented among the 62-64-group. Despite this age difference, the white men enjoy somewhat better health, although the differences are small.

Occupational differences between the black and white retirement-age workers are what would be expected in light of what is known about racial differences in labor market status in the United States, with black men greatly underrepresented in professional and managerial positions and greatly overrepresented in the service and laborer categories. Self-employment is also much less common among blacks than among whites. The white men have more regular full-time employment records over the 15 years covered by the surveys than the blacks, although the differences are moderate when the differences in type of employment are kept in mind. The proportion of whites who worked full-time in 1976, 1971, and 1966 was roughly within the 90-95-percent range, while the corresponding range for the blacks was in the neighborhood of 85-90 percent. The proportions who remained with the same employer (or in the same self-employed status) over the 15-year period were very similar—57 percent of the black men and 54 percent of the whites.

Median earnings of black men in calendar year 1980 were slightly under three-fourths as high as those of whites—$14,000 versus $19,000. A larger proportion of white than of black men were receiving Social Security benefits (13 vs. 9 percent), and the median annual benefit payment to black recipients was only four-fifths of the corresponding figure for whites. Pension eligibility is substantially more frequent among the white men—44 versus 26 percent—but the racial difference in the proportion of actual recipients is smaller—9 percent of the whites and 2 percent of the blacks.

When all sources of income are included, the differential between white and black families is considerably greater than the differential in the men's earnings. Median family income of the black full-time workers in 1980 was $13,700, 44 percent below the $24,600 median for the white men.

The Longitudinal Record, 1966-1981

The longitudinal nature of our data makes it possible not only to compare retirement-age with younger workers at a point in time, as has been done for the year 1981 in the preceding section, but to compare the 1981 status of the retirement-age workers with their own situations at earlier stages of their careers—at least over the 15 years covered by the NLS. Moreover, the profiles for the 15-year-period developed for the retirement-age workers can be compared with those of the reference group—men who as of 1981 had not yet attained age 62.

For the retirement-age group as a whole, we examine the characteristics of the men at 5-year intervals, beginning with 1966 when they were 47-59 years of age; within this group those who were 62-64 in 1981 are differentiated from those age 65-74. For each facet of experience that is examined, therefore, we present profiles for four age categories: the total retirement-age group and its two components plus the reference group of men 60-61 years of age in 1981. Within each age category the data also differentiate between the total group of full-time workers and the subset thereof who had never retired.

Labor Force Participation and Unemployment

Labor force participation over the 15-year period differed little between the retirement-age and the younger groups, and the small differences were entirely attributable to the subset of men who re-entered full-time work after a period of retirement. In none of the 4 years is the difference between the retirement-age and the reference groups in the proportion of men with more than 3 weeks out of the labor force greater than 6 percentage points. When only the never-retired are considered, the maximum difference is only 2 points.

The unemployment records of the retirement age men and the reference group are virtually indistinguishable; in none of the years did more than 6 percent of either group experience any unemployment, and by 1981 this percentage had dropped to 2. Within the retirement age group, the youngest (age 62-64) have been more likely than those age 65-74 to have experienced unemployment, doubtless because a larger proportion of the older group are self-employed and the younger group are more likely to be mobile, as we will see.

Occupational and Industrial Assignments

Our cross-sectional analysis has revealed differences in occupational and industrial affiliations between retirement-age and younger full-time workers, as well as differences within the former group according to age. These data admit of at least two interpretations: (1) that workers shift into more congenial (or receptive) occupations and industries as they grow older, or (2) that workers who happen to be in (or have purposefully chosen) jobs that are more congenial (or receptive to) older workers are more likely to continue full-time employment.

The longitudinal data for selected occupational and industrial categories that are shown in figure 8-5 help to shed some light on this issue. To begin with a case in which age differences are pronounced and the pattern is clear, consider the proportion of full-time workers in 1981 who were employed in manufacturing in each of the survey years between 1966 and 1981. In 1981 there was an 8-percentage-point spread between retirement-age workers and the reference group who were in manufacturing—27 versus 35 percent. This differential in 1966 had been only 2 points larger, and the change over the 15-year period was attributable as much to the behavior of the reference group as to that of the retirement-age workers. The downward trend in the proportion of man-

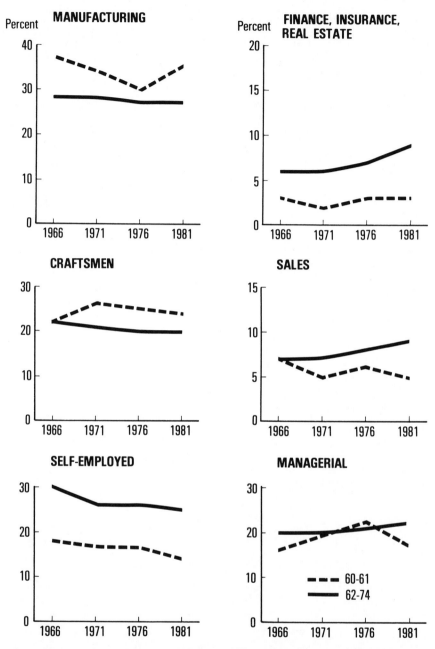

Figure 8–5. Proportions of Full-Time Workers in Selected Occupations, Industry and Type-of-Worker Categories, by Age in 1981, 1966–1981

ufacturing workers between 1966 and 1981 among men who had reached retirement age in the latter year was only 1 percentage point. Thus, the below-average proportion of retirement-age workers in manufacturing in 1981 was attributable not to a shift out of manufacturing as the men grew older, but to the below-average tendency of men originally employed in manufacturing to continue full-time employment.

In the finance, insurance, and real estate industries the relative influence of these two causal forces is somewhat different. Of the 6-percentage point differential in 1981 between the reference and retirement-age groups, half is attributable to a difference that prevailed at the beginning of the period.

Occupational differences in 1981 tend to be not as great as differences in industrial distribution. The most pronounced is in the craftsman category, which accounts for 24 percent of the reference group but only 20 percent of the retirement-age workers. In this case there was a downward drift of 2 percentage points among the latter group over the 15-year period. The sales category is the only one in which the above-average number of retirement-age workers in 1981 reflects an influx over the 15-year period.

The most unambiguous trends occur in type-of-worker distribution. The positive relationship between age and the likelihood of self-employment results exclusively from the greater tendency of the self-employed to remain in full-time employment rather than from shifts of full-time workers into that category. Both among retirement-age and younger men, the incidence of self-employment decreased between 1966 and 1981—by 5 and 4 points, respectively. The 12-point differential in favor of the older group was thus almost constant over the 15-year period. This steadiness among full-time workers is especially interesting because the well-established tendency of the self-employed to delay retirement has generally been attributed to their greater ability to shift to part-time work.

Interfirm and Occupational Mobility, 1966-1981

Surprisingly little difference appears over the 15-year period in interfirm and occupational mobility between the retirement-age full-time workers and the men in their very early 60s. Whatever differences are discernible are primarily attributable to the larger proportion of erstwhile retirees among the older group. The proportion of men with different employers in the 2 years was 42 percent for the group age 60-61 and 46 percent for the retirement-age men, but when only the never-retired are considered, these percentages are 38 and 39. *Within* the older group, those age 65-74 who had never retired had an interfirm mobility rate of 34 percent as compared with 42 percent for those age 62-64.

The proportions of men who made upward and downward occupational moves between 1966 and 1981 were almost invariant by age when only the never-retired are considered. The upwardly mobile ranged from 26 percent of the 65-74-year cohort to 29 percent of those age 60-61, while the proportion of downwardly mobile was 19 percent for the youngest age category and 22 percent for each of the others. When the men who had once been retired are included, however, as many as 30 percent of the 65-74-year-old group had slipped down the occupational ladder; among the erstwhile retirees in this group, almost half (46 percent) had done so.

Interfirm movement increases the probability of occupational change. The men who changed employers were more likely than those who did not to experience both upward and downward occupational change, but the increase in the likelihood of downward shifts is more pronounced. These generalizations are remarkably invariant among the several age groups.

Real Earnings

Real average hourly earnings of the men who were wage and salary workers and real annual wage and salary and self-employment income for the total sample are shown in figure 8-6. In interpreting this figure, keep in mind what was happening to real average earnings in the economy as a whole over the 15-year period. Using average hourly earnings in the total nonagricultural private economy as the criterion, we see virtually no change between 1966 and 1981. After an increase of 8.1 percent between 1966 and 1971 and no change between then and 1976, real average hourly earnings dropped by 6.7 percent between 1976 and 1981, for a rise of under 1 percent for the total period.

The patterns shown by figure 8-6 for average hourly earnings and annual wage and salary and self-employment income are fairly similar; we focus on the annual earnings series because it is more inclusive. Between 1966 and 1971 there was an increase in median earnings for both the reference group and the retirement-age men, more pronounced for the latter than the former. Between 1971 and 1976, however, median earnings for the reference group continued to climb (by 4 percent), while those of the retirement age group dropped by 13 percent—most precipitously among those age 65-74 (20 percent). During the final 5-year period, the median declined for both groups by about 10 percent. Whereas at the beginning of the 15-year period the older group enjoyed a $100 advantage in median income, by its end the differential had become $500 in the opposite direction. Although not shown, the change in relative position was much more dramatic for the men who had attained age 65-

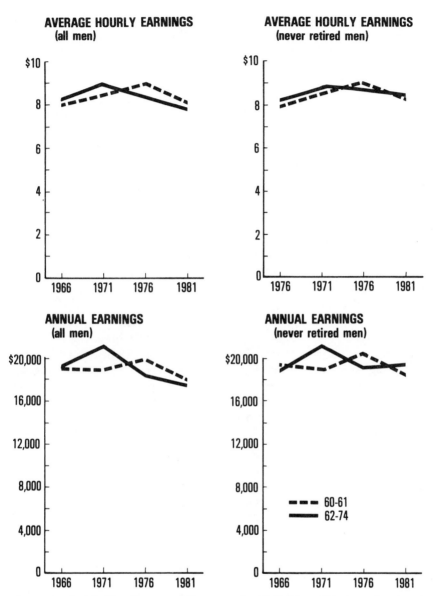

Figure 8–6. Median Income Measures for Full-Time Workers by Age in 1981 and by Retirement Status, 1966–1981 (1980 dollars)

74 by 1981. At the beginning of the period their median was $800 lower than that of the younger men; at its end the differential had grown to $6,000.

Our findings on cross-sectional earnings differences as well as those in the preceding section relating to mobility lead to the suspicion that the age differences in earnings trends are primarily attributable to differences in earnings experience between men who reentered full-time employment after a period of retirement and those who never retired. To test this hypothesis, we have run an ordinary least squares regression of 1980 annual earnings on (1) 1965 annual earnings, (2) retirement and mobility status, (3) race, and (4) change in hours worked between 1966 and 1981. The regression coefficients permit us to estimate how the earnings experience over the 15-year period differed among men who retired and those who did not and, within the latter group, between those remaining with the same employer and those who changed employers (table 8-5).

Relative to men who had retired and reentered full-time employment, the never-retired men who were with the same employer (or in the same self-employed status) in 1966 and 1981 enjoyed a 1980 earnings advantage of almost $9,500; the figure for those who had changed employers ($13,600) was even higher, but the difference between the two mobility categories of never-retired men is not statistically significant.

Another way of approaching the same question is to compare the change in median earnings between 1966 and 1981 for the never-retired men with the total sample within each age group (figure 8-6). The differences in pattern are dramatic. Among the never-retired the retirement-age men actually fare better than the reference group both in earnings gain between 1966 and 1981 and in the level of earnings in the latter year. It is clear that men who continue to work without interruption beyond retirement age have earnings experience that, on the average, is

Table 8–5
Change in Real Earnings (1980 Dollars), 1966–1981, of Never-Retired Men Age 65–74 Relative to Those Who Reentered Full-Time Work after Retirement
(OLS results)[a]

Characteristic	Coefficient
Never-retired men who were with same employer in 1966 and 1981	+$ 9,489[b]
Never-retired men who changed employers between 1966 and 1981	+$13,633[b]

[a]Regression of real 1980 earnings on (1) 1966 earnings (in 1980 dollars); (2) race; (3) arithmetic change in annual hours worked, 1966–1981; and (4) retirement and mobility status (men who were erstwhile retirees are reference group). The other coefficients are: 1966 earnings = .3625[b]; white = $5,565 ($t = 1.30$); change in hours = .62.

[b]Significant at .01 level. While both categories of never-retired men have significantly higher 1981 earnings than the men who had retired, the difference between those who changed employers and those who did not is not statistically significant ($t = 1.15$).

as good as or better than that of men who are only approaching retirement age.

Some Prototypical Cases

The generalizations yielded by the statistics in the preceding sections can perhaps be made more real by a few actual examples. Studying the detailed records of the retirement-age workers is as frustrating as it is interesting, for while they yield insights that the bare statistics do not afford, they nevertheless leave a great deal unexplained. The data produced by a large-scale survey like the NLS permit descriptions of events in a respondent's life, but little in the way of interpretations of why things happened as they did or how the man felt about them. One frequently longs for a conversation in which questions of these kinds can be explored in depth! The following case histories, in which purely fictitious names are used for convenience, will illustrate some of the variations underlying our analysis.

The Never-Retired

As has been seen, most of the men who work full-time beyond the conventional retirement age have never retired in any sense, yet even among them there are different patterns. The most common is continuation in a job (or self-employed status) that the individual has held for a long time. However, some of the men shift among jobs in much the same way that they had at younger ages.

Continuous Employment. Examples of continuous service in a job from youth or middle-age into one's late 60s or early 70s are most numerous among the self-employed and among salaried managers and professionals. Illustrative of the latter is a person who we shall call Robert Jensen, a 67-year-old white man with 15 years of schooling. Since leaving school he has served with the same steamship line, where he held an executive position when first interviewed in 1966. Over the 15 years covered by the surveys his real earnings (expressed in terms of 1980 dollars)[5] rose from $36,000 in 1965 to $53,600 in 1973, then dropped back to $35,000 in 1980, 4 percent below their level 15 years earlier. Aside from a hearing deficiency, Jensen reported no health limitations in 1981; nonetheless, he was expecting to retire the following year, when he would begin to receive an annual Social Security benefit of about $12,000.

Continuation of full-time *self-employment* into old age is found in a variety of occupational settings. At the professional level, Henry Martin is a 65-year-old physician who expects to retire at age 68. His hours of work have decreased significantly over the 15-year period—from 4500 in 1966 to 2,600 in 1981. His annual income, in excess of $110,000 in 1966, was not reported in subsequent interviews. David Burton, an attorney, is 68 years old and has practiced law for 37 years. Since 1976 the number of hours devoted to his practice has not fallen below 2,600. His real net earnings were $47,000 in 1965, peaked at $67,000 in 1972, and had fallen to $26,000 in 1980. Despite a nervous condition that he acknowledges affects his work, Burton expects never to retire.

Two other long-term self-employed individuals with no intention of retiring—but working at blue-collar jobs—are John King, a 72-year-old black man with only 8 years of education, and William McKenzie, a 66-year-old white high school graduate. Both are mechanics in the automobile repair business—King for 32 years and McKenzie for 21. King, who has no health problems, has devoted at least 2,000 hours to his business in every year but one since 1966, but his net income has averaged $3,200. Including the $4,080 in Social Security benefits that were paid to him and his wife in 1980, their total income in that year was $10,780. Despite the fact that McKenzie reports health problems affecting work, he has worked longer hours than King, and his annual net income has averaged almost $9,000. In 1980, when his net earnings were only $5,000, he and his wife received $2,630 in Social Security benefits.

Finally, Gerald Michaelson is representative of farmers who continue to work into old age. With only an eighth-grade education, Michaelson has farmed for 47 years and, with no health problems, has no intention of retiring. Between 1966 and 1981 he has devoted between 3,000 and 4,400 hours a year to his farm work, for a net return ranging between $6,400 (in 1974) and $15,700 (in 1977)—$10,000 in 1980.

The Job-Shifters. In contrast with the men who remained in the same work status for most if not all of their careers, Samuel Johnson made a number of shifts even within the 15-year period covered by our surveys. A 69-year-old black man with a high school diploma, most of his career was spent as a medical technician. However, when first interviewed in 1966 and for several years thereafter he worked as a janitor in a state government agency. By 1971 he had again found work as a technician in a public health facility, but was "bumped" from this job into kitchen work in the same agency in 1981. Johnson's real annual earnings, which had been as high as $14,800 in 1972, had dropped to $10,000 in 1980. As of mid-1981 his retirement plans were uncertain.

Another example of a job-changer is Albert Smith, a 65-year-old white man with an eighth-grade education. Smith, who has never married and has no dependents, spent most of his career in sales work. Between 1956 and 1973 he was the proprietor of a shoe store, but in the latter year took a job as a household appliance salesman, as a consequence of which his hours of work dropped from about 2800 to 2080 a year, and his real earnings fell from about $16,000 to about $9,000. With no health problems of any kind, Smith expects to remain at work until age 70.

From Retirement to Full-Time Work

As has been seen, a minority of the full-time retirement-age workers returned to such jobs after at least regarding themselves as retired. Two quite different examples of this pattern are Russell Yaeger and Jack Nelson. Yaeger, a 67-year-old married man with 11 years of schooling, has spent most of his career as a manager or proprietor. When we first met him in 1966 he had been in business for himself as a real estate agent for 8 years, with 1966 earnings of about $8,000, and he continued in this capacity till 1973. In that year he took a management position within the federal government at a salary of $21,000, but by 1975 he had shifted to the personnel department of a business service organization where he advanced by 1976 to a management position paying $21,000. In the following year he retired at age 63. By 1980, however, he was again operating as a full-time self-employed real estate agent, with undisclosed net earnings for that year. Although Yaeger admits to some difficulty in walking, he has no plans to retire from his present activity. Oram Nelson's career is probably the most variegated of anyone in this category we have encountered. Most of his working life was spent as a farmer. When we first interviewed him at age 53 in 1966, however, he reported his occupation as clergyman (2,700 hours a year) at a salary of $6,000, but with self-employment farm income of $16,700. By 1969 his principal activity was selling farm equipment, with earnings of about $16,500, but in 1971 he was again devoting himself to farming. When interviewed in 1973 he reported himself unable to work, and from then until 1981—except for a very brief period in advertising sales in 1975 (500 hours)—he was retired. However, when interviewed in 1981 at age 68, he was again working full-time as a clergyman. Despite substantial health problems, Yaeger reported that he would never retire.

Conclusion

Men who continue to work full-time beyond the age at which they can collect retirement benefits are a small minority of the total population of men in that age range—18 percent if we establish ages 62-74 as the limits, and only 12 percent if we use ages 65-74. Nevertheless, even the latter group numbers over three-fourths of a million, and the population total from which they come is destined to expand very considerably over the next 35 or 40 years. Their labor market status relative to somewhat younger men and the records of their work experience as they approach, attain, and ultimately surpass the conventional age of retirement are therefore worthy of attention.

The retirement-age full-time workers are not only a minority, but they are highly unrepresentative of the age cohort to which they belong. Consequently, as the result of what is technically known as sample selection bias, one enters a kind of Alice-in-Wonderland world as one analyzes this group. Compared with somewhat younger full-time workers they are *not* less healthy, since those among the latter in relatively poor health have not yet been "selected out" by retirement. Compared with younger workers, larger proportions of the retirement-age men have college degrees, and within the group this proportion increases with increasing age. It is also true, on the other hand, that the proportion of the retirement-age group with only an elementary school education or less is larger than for men just approaching retirement—and increases with increasing age. Again, selectivity is involved: at the risk of oversimplification we can say that the men who continue full-time work into their late 60s and early 70s consist disproportionately of those who are healthy enough to do so and who either (a) have to work because of limited resources or (b) want to because they enjoy work in general or what they have been doing in particular.

This bimodality gives rise to greater income disparity within the retirement-age group than among preretirement age workers—a disparity that increases with increasing age. Still another factor operates in the same direction: erstwhile retirees who return to full-time work do not fare nearly so well as men who have not retired, and the former retirees comprise an increasing proportion as age increases.

Some of the differences in occupational and industrial affiliation between retirement-age and younger workers result from differential opportunities for part-time work, but some of the differences persist even when, as in this study, the analysis is confined to full-time workers. Among the most important of these are the below-average proportion of retirement age workers in manufacturing and transportation and their overrepresentation in finance (real estate) and miscellaneous services. Self-employment is far more common among the full-time retirement-age workers than among men in their very early 60s. These differences result to some extent from mobility as men age, but to a larger extent from the greater propensity of men in some lines of work than in others to continue to work beyond conventional retirement age.

The mobility patterns over the 15-year period covered by our data are very similar for retirement-age workers and for somewhat younger men, and become almost indistinguishable when the erstwhile retirees are excluded. The same can be said for earnings records. When the total group of retirement-age men is compared with those in their very early 60s, the younger group has, on the average, a distinctly more enviable record. However, when the erstwhile retirees are excluded, the older age groups do as well as the younger ones.

In short, the evidence of this study demonstrates that full-time labor market activity well beyond customary ages of retirement can be viable and satisfactory alternatives for significant numbers of older men. Yet this does *not* mean that the record of such workers can be used as a measure of the potential available to *all* younger men. The issue of selectivity bias must be kept in mind as the comparisons are interpreted.

Notes

1. A life-cycle approach to the decision to work beyond a certain age would have the individual make a complete assessment of the costs and benefits of additional work, taking into account such factors as foregone leisure, additional earnings, the pleasures and pains of work, and the differences in the present values of retirement benefits at different retirement ages. Our data do not permit this kind of analysis, although we do incorporate several economic variables that are relevant.

2. In his study of manufacturing industries, Parsons (1983) considers demand as well as supply factors in explaining the large differences among industries in the proportion of the labor force made up of older workers. Industries with low utilization rates of older workers tend to be characterized by large firms for which information on worker productivity is relatively more expensive to obtain. The proportion of employment in an industry accounted for by firms of 500 or more employees is negatively related to the proportion of the industry's work force age 65 or older, controlling for average schooling and the physical demands of the job. Firm size also has a significant positive effect on the provision of mandatory retirement rules. Mandatory retirement coverage, in turn, has a significant negative effect on the labor force participation of men 65-69 years of age, controlling for education, experience, union status, health, and occupation.

3. These results are consistent with those of Chirikos and Nestel (1981, p. 107) based on the 1976 NLS data for employed wage and salary workers interviewed in that year. Using an impairment index different from the one used here, they reported that "the coefficient of the impairment variable narrowly misses statistical significance" in their wage equation, although it was significantly related to labor force participation and hours of work.

4. The earnings limit is increased each year proportionately with increases in average earnings of all workers. In 1983, the maximum age for the imposition of the earnings test was lowered to seventy.

5. As in the remainder of the volume, all earnings figures in this section are expressed in terms of dollars with the purchasing power they commanded in 1980.

References

Chirikos, Thomas N., and Nestel, Gilbert. 1981. "Impairment and Labor Market Outcomes: A Cross-Sectional and Longitudinal Analysis." In H.S. Parnes, ed., *Work and Retirement: A Longitudinal Study of Men*. Cambridge, Mass.: MIT. chap. 4.

Parsons, Donald O. 1983. "The Industrial Demand for Older Workers," unpublished.

Rix, Sara E. 1980. *Retirement-Age Workers*. Washington, D.C.: American Institute for Research.

Rones, Philip. 1978. "Older Men—the Choice Between Work and Retirement." *Monthly Labor Review* 101: November, pp. 3-10.

U.S. Department of Labor. 1981. Bureau of Labor Statistics, Special Tabulation.

9
Conclusion

Herbert S. Parnes

T he National Longitudinal Surveys have afforded a unique opportunity to exercise surveillance over a nationally representative sample of men during a 15-year period as they passed from
middle- into old age. Instead of the series of "snapshots" that emerge
from conventional periodic surveys of population samples, we have in
effect a "motion picture" of the same individuals over time, which permits analyses that can be made in no other way. To cite but two examples, longitudinal data provide a more accurate basis than cross-
sectional data for measuring the effect of age (and work experience) on
earnings, because cross-sectional data purporting to show the relationship between age and earnings are confounded by cohort differences—
for instance, the fact that older men tend to be less well educated than
younger men. Again, cross-sectional data in which attitudes and behavior
are observed simultaneously do not allow unambiguous conclusions, because it is usually not clear whether the attitudes condition, or merely
reflect, the behavior. However, when an attitude measured in a given
year is found to be associated with *subsequent* behavior, there is considerably less uncertainty about direction of causation, although it is admittedly possible that the relationship simply reflects the effect of an
unmeasured characteristic on *both* the attitude *and* the behavior.

This book is the latest in a series of six reports that follow and
analyze many aspects of the work experience of the NLS cohort of men,
beginning in the mid 1960s, when they were in their late 40s and their
50s, and when virtually all of them were employed. These 6 reports
contain only a small part of the relevant research findings, however,
because an additional 500 or more articles, monographs, and disserta-
tions have been based upon the same data set (Sproat, Churchill, and
Sheets, 1985). In view of all of this prior research on the same sample
(in much of which I have been personally involved), it seems fitting that
the final chapter of this 15-year report should go beyond the findings of
the present book and attempt a grand synthesis of the major conclusions

I am indebted to my coauthors and to Kezia Sproat for their useful comments on an
earlier draft.

that are supported by all the research based on the data set. To keep the task manageable I will have to paint with an exceedingly broad brush, and even then be highly selective. Generalizations based on the present volume will be identified by chapter number, rather than by author. Thus, what follows is a series of significant generalizations based on research findings from the National Longitudinal Surveys of Older Men, followed by a brief discussion of their bearing on major issues of public policy.

Major Research Findings

Despite the fact that the National Longitudinal Surveys of Older Men was initiated because of the potentially serious labor market problems to which older men are liable—for instance, age discrimination, skill obsolescence, and deteriorating health—a large majority of middle-aged men (45-59) suffer no special labor market disadvantage. Indeed, relative to other segments of the labor force, on the average they suffer less unemployment, and enjoy higher-level occupational assignments and higher earnings. A majority have moved up the occupational ladder during their careers; they enjoy a stable employment relationship character-ized by long tenure, and regard themselves to be in the best jobs of their careers (Parnes et al., 1970, p. 238). Even as they age, for example, by 10 years, they do not experience the decline in earnings that is suggested by cross-sectional data. During the decades when real earnings for the labor force as a whole are rising, the same will be true of men in their late forties and early fifties who remain at work (Parnes, 1981, p. 21). Indeed, even among men age 62-74 in 1981 who had never retired, real average hourly earnings were slightly higher in 1981 than they had been 15 years earlier (chap. 8).

However, although the age cohort on average enjoys an enviable labor market position, a not inconsiderable minority are plagued by unst-able employment, menial jobs and low wages. When the NLS began in 1966 1 in 12 members of the sample was an unskilled laborer, 1 in 6 had slipped down the occupational ladder since entering the labor force, and 1 in 10 earned less than $1.50 per hour (Parnes et al., 1970, p. 239). Over the decade 1966-1976, 4 percent of the men had suffered at least 66 weeks of unemployment, accounting for almost half of the unem-ployment experienced by the entire cohort (Parnes 1982, pp. 6, 8). More-over, as they age, increasing proportions of the cohort are potential victims of adversity as the result of deteriorating health. Between 1966 and 1981 the proportion of the men who reported health problems affecting their work rose from under one-fourth to over half. Even if one discounts some of the increase as rationalization to "excuse" reduced labor market participation, there is little question that a major portion of it is real (chap. 1).

Factors in Labor Market Success

The extreme variation in the labor market fortunes of middle-aged and older men invites attention to the factors that are associated with labor market success.

Education and Training. Not surprisingly, education and training have pronounced effects on the labor market experience of middle-aged men. Other things being equal, number of years of school bears a strong positive relationship to hourly and annual earnings (Adams, 1975, chap. 8), and to the probability of vertical occupational movement (Kohen, 1975). Training outside the formal educational system also has a favorable effect on the earning power of middle-aged men (Freeman, 1974). The association is clearest for training obtained earlier in life—including military vocational training that is used in one's current job (Fredland and Little, 1980)—but even in middle age certain types of training appear to have payoffs for at least some categories of men, especially for blacks who have had prior training (Adams, 1975).

Health. The labor market position of middle-aged men is also affected in important ways by the state of their health. Poor health plays a large role in explaining early withdrawal from the labor market (Kingson, 1982) and has a powerful influence on earnings and employment experience, even among men who remain in the labor force (Adams, 1975, pp. 285-90; Luft, 1975). Because the studies that have produced these findings have generally used as the indicator of poor health the respondent's report that he suffers a condition affecting the amount or kind of work he can do, they have been criticized as being in some degree tautological, especially in explaining labor force participation. Also, some have argued that men may use health conditions as an excuse for withdrawal from the labor force, especially prior to the conventional age of retirement (Myers, 1982).

Nevertheless, using indications of health problems reported *prior* to retirement as the criterion, one-third of the retirements that occurred between 1966 and 1981 appear to have been attributable to poor health, and three-fifths of these occurred before age 62 (chapter 3). Moreover, when health is measured by an index based on responses to a series of questions on physical impairments and symptoms, a strong relationship with labor force participation is discerned in a multivariate analysis, although the effect is smaller than when the work-limiting measure of health is used. Even among men who are employed, impairment has an inhibiting effect on the number of hours worked and a somewhat weaker effect on wage rates, so that a "moderately impaired" blue-collar wage earner will work 2 percent fewer hours per year and earn 1 percent less per hour than a comparable worker without impairment (Chirikos and Nestel, 1981).

At its extremes, poor health has an impact on family income and on the labor market activity of other family members. The longitudinal character of the NLS data set has made it possible to identify individuals who subsequently die and to compare the predeath experience of this group with comparable men who survive (Mott and Haurin, 1981). The nature of the effect, not surprisingly, depends upon the extent to which the man's death has been presaged by poor health. Where it has been, we see over time a substantial deterioration in income, which on the average is not replaced to any appreciable extent by increased earnings of the wife, perhaps because of the husband's need for his wife's care during his terminal illness.

Initiative. The degree of labor market success of men is affected not only by their health and vigor and the productive skills generated by education and training, but also by their motivation and initiative. The variable used to represent these characteristics in the NLS is the Rotter I-E scale, which measures variations in perceived "locus of control"—that is, the degree to which a person perceives success as being contingent upon personal effort ("internal") as opposed to believing that it is largely a matter of luck, or at least of forces not amenable to the individual's control ("external"). Other things equal, internals achieve higher earnings and occupational status and greater job satisfaction than externals. There is a reciprocal relationship, however; favorable labor market experience in turn produces later increases in degree of internality (Andrisani and Nestel, 1975).

Race. The oversampling of blacks in the NLS has allowed considerable attention to be paid to racial differences in labor market status and behavior. The dramatic differences that have been shown to prevail between whites and blacks in virtually every measure of labor market success are hardly surprising in view of the substantial disparity that exists between the two races in educational attainment and in other human capital endowments.

However, there is abundant evidence that the greater labor market rewards enjoyed by white men relative to blacks cannot be completely accounted for by their greater investments in human capital. Analyses have shown (a) a less systematic relationship between educational attainment and earnings for middle-aged black men than for their white counterparts (Adams 1975, pp. 285-90); (b) that black men reap lower returns to initiative than whites (Andrisani and Nestel, 1975, pp. 212-13); and (c) that intrafirm upward occupational mobility was less likely among middle-aged black men in the late 1960s than among equally endowed whites (Kohen, 1975, pp. 140-42). This last-mentioned racial differential in the likelihood of promotion in internal labor markets disappears, however, when attention is confined to men covered by collective bargaining (Leigh, 1979). More generally, the effect of unionism on black-white differentials has been found to depend on the type of unionism involved. Industrial unionism has generally operated to reduce racial earnings differentials, while craft unionism has tended to increase them (Leigh, 1978).

Racial discrimination is admittedly difficult to document conclusively because one can rarely be certain that all of the relevant factors affecting productivity have been adequately controlled. Nevertheless, in view of the richness of the NLS data base, to question that at least some part of the black-white difference in rewards stems from labor market discrimination goes beyond what is required by scholarly caution. There is some basis for optimism relating to this subject, however; careful examination of the relative labor market positions of white and black men between 1966 and 1976 reveals that with characteristics related to productivity controlled, the ratio of black to white earnings increased from .84 to .92 and that the differential in employment security was also reduced. The reductions in both these differences corresponded closely to changes in the level of federal expenditures on antidiscrimination programs (Daymont, 1981).

Despite the differences in rewards, the labor market behavior of black and white men are in some respects quite similar. Perhaps *because* of discrimination, black men appear to be satisifed with less, and report significantly greater job satisfaction than white men with similar personal and job characteristics (Bartel, 1981). No significant difference appears between blacks and whites in the strength of their attachment to their current employers, and the factors that influence the strength of these attachments are largely the same and operate in similar ways for whites and blacks. Nor does the probability of voluntary interfirm job change differ between blacks and whites. Other things equal, members of the two racial groups are equally mobile and tend to respond to opportunities in substantially the same way (Parnes and Nestel, 1975a).

The lower labor force participation rates of middle-aged black men relative to their white counterparts also melt away when other factors are controlled. More specifically, when account is taken of differences in age, marital status, and health; in potential wages relative to social security disability benefits and welfare payments; and in education and occupation, the black-white difference in labor force participation actually changes direction. Thus, moment-of-time differences between the participation rates of white and black men are attributable not to behavioral differences between the two races but to differences in the characteristics that condition labor force behavior. Moreover, the sharper decline in labor force participation among middle-aged blacks than whites over recent decades is explainable in terms of the same factors—specifically, the less favorable labor market opportunities faced by blacks during a period in which alternatives to work have become more attractive. The implication of this finding is that if wage rates for equally qualified whites and blacks are ultimately equalized, the difference in their labor force participation rates will disappear (Parsons, 1981).

The Operation of Labor Markets for Older Men

Even though men in their 40s and 50s are known to be less mobile than younger men, they do a considerable amount of job changing. Over one-eighth of the sample had made at least one voluntary change of employer between 1966 and 1971, and an additional one-twelfth had moved involuntarily. About one-third of the group changed occupations during the period—one-fourth across the boundaries of major occupation groups (Parnes and Nestel, 1975a, pp. 11, 120). Of the total group of men age 62-74 who had never retired and who were working full time in 1981, two-fifths had changed employers since 1966 (chapter 8).

By and large the job changes made by men in this age group appear to be advantageous. Their voluntary interfirm movement observed between 1966 and 1971, for instance, led on the average to economic gains as well as to higher levels of job satisfaction (Parnes and Nestel, 1975a, pp. 10, 111). More recent analyses have suggested, however, that the effect of voluntary movement on wage improvement is more likely when the individual quits as the result of finding a better job than as the result of dissatisfaction with his current job (Bartel and Borjas, 1981). There is also evidence that frequent job changers may have lower *lifetime* earnings than comparable men who are less mobile. Specifically, Borjas (1981) has shown that job separations among white men usually lead to wage gains in the short run, but that nonmobile workers achieve higher wages in the long run, presumably because of their greater investments in firm-specific human capital.

Effect of General Economic Conditions. One of the serendipitous aspects of the NLS is that they spanned a period encompassing substantial variation in the level of economic activity. The longitudinal data offer considerable evidence that many types of labor market processes—in addition to the level of unemployment itself—are more benign and more nearly in accord with competitive economic theory when the level of demand for labor is high than when there is slack in the economy. For example, both the propensity of middle-aged men to change jobs and the rate of actual voluntary movement were greater during the period 1967-1969, when unemployment was low, than between 1969 and 1971, when economic conditions deteriorated; moreover, the likelihood that voluntary job changes will result in a relative wage gain is greater in a buoyant than in a depressed economy (Parnes and Nestel, 1975a).

Black men fare better relative to whites when levels of economic activity are high. Most of the widening differential between the white and the black labor force participation rate over the five-year period 1967-1971 occurred between 1969 and 1971, suggesting that the loosening of the labor market in that period had a more serious effect on blacks than on whites (Parnes et al., 1975). Also, the black-white wage ratio, controlling for factors related to productivity, is higher during high levels of economic activity than when the economy is depressed (Daymont, 1981).

More generally, men who are disadvantaged in the labor market are relatively less so in good than in bad times. For example, there is evidence of upward mobility from the secondary to the primary labor market during business cycle upswings, with many workers sinking back into the secondary market, however, during slumps (Rosenberg, 1981). As another illustration, men who lost jobs between 1966 and 1969, when the national unemployment rate was relatively low, were subsequently employed at the same wage level; job losers subsequent to 1969, when unemployment rates were higher, experienced an average loss of 6 percent of predisplacement average hourly earnings (Shapiro and Sandell, 1983).

Consequences of Job Loss. Their long tenure in jobs provides above-average employment security to middle-aged male workers, with resulting low unemployment rates. Nevertheless, when such workers do lose their jobs, the duration of their unemployment tends to be longer than for younger workers. Even when one excludes agriculture and construction—industries characterized by transitory employment relationships—it is by no means rare for a middle-aged man with relatively long tenure to lose his job. Almost 1 in 10 (8 percent) of such wage and salary workers in the NLS sample who had served their 1966 employers for at least 5 years were involuntarily separated from those jobs during the next decade for reasons other than retirement. The risk of job loss does not vary across educational and occupational categories, but is lower in some industry sectors than others—public service, for example, in contrast to manufacturing and trade. While unemployment is the most obvious and immediate penalty of such displacement, there are more serious long-term impacts, both economic and psychological. Relative to otherwise comparable men who had suffered no such displacement, the displaced workers suffered deterioration in earnings and occupational status over the decade; they were also less happy both with their jobs and with life in general, and were more likely to have developed a sense of alienation, with possible adverse effects on initiative (Parnes, Gagen, and King, 1981).

Aging and Retirement

Originally planned as a five-year study, the NLS was not intended to shed much light on the processes of aging and retirement. Its repeated extensions, however, have afforded researchers an opportunity to observe the changes in the lives of men as they cross the boundary between middle and old age and as the majority of them move into retirement.

Major changes: 1966-1981 (chapter 1). As the cohort aged by 15 years, the most obvious changes in life circumstances were the increasing prevalance of health problems, the decreasing numbers of dependents, and the move into retirement. By 1981 three-fourths of the age cohort, then 60-74 years old, regarded themselves to be retired. Even though some of the retirees continued to work, the proportion of the total cohort who were neither working nor looking for work had grown from a mere 5 percent in 1966 to 61 percent in 1981.

Until retirement, real average hourly earnings were not only maintained as the men aged; they actually increased slightly, despite economy-wide trends in which real average hourly earnings rose by less than 1 percent over the entire 15-year period. However, because of the wholesale withdrawals from the labor force, median family income decreased by about one-third for the entire cohort and even more for men age 65 and older. On the other hand, because of the decreasing number of dependents, real income per family member (and per dependent) increased for the age cohort as a whole, but declined for men age 65-74.

Mortality, 1966-1981 (chapter 2). Of the original NLS sample, approximately one-fourth of the men had died by the time of the 1981 interview. The mortality rate among blacks was about half again as great as among whites. Almost all of this gross differential, however, reflects racial differences in socioeconomic status. With these characteristics controlled, there is no significant difference between the mortality rates of whites and blacks. In contrast, the gross differential in survival rates between married and nonmarried men (in favor of the former) do not disappear even when both background factors and differences in health and employment are controlled. The reasons for the marital status differential remain unclear.

The decreases in mortality that have occurred among men in their late fifties during the past decade and a half are discernible in all segments of society—among both blacks and whites, among the well- and poorly educated, and among men with and without health problems. Nevertheless, there is evidence that the most seriously ill have gained most from the secular improvements in health care; the only subset of the age cohort with significantly above-average improvement in survival rates are the men at greatest risk—those who are not in the labor force as the result of long-duration health problems.

The Volume and Pattern of Retirements 1966-1981 (chapter 3). The number of retirees at any moment in time depends on the criterion (or criteria) of retirement—curtailment or withdrawal from labor market activity, receipt of pension income, or the individual's perception (and report) of his status. It also obviously makes a difference whether one applies a "once-retired-always-retired" rule or bases the count on the individual's status in a particular year. The number of retirees age 60-74 in 1981 ranged between 6.5 and 9.5 million, depending upon one's choices among these definitions. Using the subjective criterion of retirement (i.e., the individual's report of his status) and the once-retired-always-retired rule—which constitute the definition of "retirement" used in most of the analyses in this volume—there were 8.4 million retirees, 76 percent of the age cohort.

Based on an examination of the entire longitudinal record of respondents prior to their retirement, a majority of the total number of retirements that occurred between 1966 and 1981 were in the fullest sense voluntary, while somewhat over two-fifths resulted from more or less constrained individual "choices." About one-third resulted from failing health, less than 5 percent from the unwilling removal of men from jobs by mandatory retirement rules, and a slightly larger proportion—perhaps between 5 and 10 percent—from discouragement produced by labor market adversity.

There is relatively little formal preparation for retirement. Fewer than 4 percent of men age 60-74 in 1981 had participated in a retirement preparation program. Moreover, low-income and low-status workers— who would presumably stand to gain most from such programs—appear to be the least likely to have access to them (Beck, 1983).

The Retirement Decision (chapter 4). The reasons for retirement just described carry some implications for the factors that enter the retirement decision. It is clear, in other words, that other things being equal, poor health and adequate financial resources increase the probability of retirement. A formal test of this hypothesis, based on the retirements that had occurred between 1966 and 1971, found that the likelihood of retirement prior to age 65 was positively related to the level of financial resources in the absence of work, and to the report in 1966 of (a) health problems, (b) dissatisfaction with current job, and (c) a preference of leisure to work (Parnes and Nestel, 1975b). The analysis by Reimers (1977) of both NLS and other data led her to the conclusion that poor health and job dissatisfaction are more important than financial variables in inducing early retirement.

The evidence of an increasing trend toward early retirement (prior to age 65) is clear both in the expectations reported by men of a given age and in actual retirement behavior (chap. 4). When 59-year-old men respond in each survey between 1966 and 1980 to a query about the age at which they expect to retire, the proportion reporting an age under 65 increases from 27 to 37 percent for white men and from 15 to 39 percent for blacks. Retirement expectations do not correspond very closely with actual age of retirement. In only about 30 percent of the cases did the actual age at retirement coincide with the expectations reported by respondents when they were 59 years of age. In most of the remaining cases the actual retirements occurred earlier than had been expected.

The Retirement Experience

If one is compelled to make a single generalization about retirement, perhaps the most valid would be that it is generally entered into voluntarily, found to be pleasant, and not regretted even after many years. Yet if we begin by generalizing, we must immediately add that reactions to retirement vary, and that both economic and psychological adjustments to it depend in large measure on the circumstances under which it occurs. More specifically, men who are forced into retirement by poor health are generally both less well off economically and less happy than men who retire voluntarily (chapters 5 and 7).

That retirement is not everyone's cup of tea becomes immediately evident when we see that 1 out of every 7 men age 62-74 has never retired and remains at work full-time; and that, of these, three-tenths vow they will never retire. Moreover, the labor market experience of these postretirement-age men who continue full-time work—who are highly unrepresentative of their age cohort—demonstrates that they can continue to be at least as successful as preretirement-age men and as they themselves were in their earlier years (chapter 8).

The Economic Aspects of Retirement (chapter 5). Most retirees show no interest in further work—either full- or part-time. About 1 in 5 was either working or looking for work at the time of the 1981 interview; of the remainder about one-sixth reported a definite (4 percent) or possible (12 percent) interest in a hypothetical job, while 84 percent said that they would not take a job under any circumstances. The likelihood of work activity is somewhat above average among men who had been self-employed or who had worked in professional or managerial jobs; it declines precipitously with advancing age and with increasing severity of health problems.

Nine out of 10 retirees receive Social Security (or Railroad Retirement) benefits and half receive other pensions, which on the average compensate for 44 percent of preretirement earnings. However, when other sources of income are included, median family income in 1980 was three-fifths as high (in real terms) as in the year before retirement. Men who retire for health reasons are considerably less well-off financially than the other categories of retirees: their median family income in 1980 (for married men) was 32 percent below that of the voluntary retirees. Whatever their actual income, a very large majority of retirees say they are able to get by on their income, although there are pronounced variations between nonmarried and married men (in favor of the latter), between blacks and whites, and between men who have retired for health reasons and the other groups of retirees.

Leisure Time Activities and Social Networks (chapter 6). Retirees in 1981 devoted about 2,000 hours in that year to 10 specified leisure time activities, with television viewing accounting for about two-fifths of the total. Television, visiting, and reading were the most universal activities, engaging 96 percent, 89 percent, and 87 percent of the men, respectively. Volunteer work was at the other end of the continuum, with a participation rate of only 19 percent. Retirement appears not to alter the pattern of leisure time activities, but to permit substantially more time to be devoted to them—about 44 percent overall.

The social networks of retirees are important from several perspectives, but chiefly as a means of permitting men to sustain regular social interaction outside their immediate households. Adult children are the primary but by no means the sole source of outside interaction. Friends and relatives constitute another important source, especially for black retirees and for men of both races who are not married. Variations in the size and composition of retirees' support networks appear to result primarily from differences in circumstances and opportunities for interaction rather than from differences in the attitudes and preferences of the retirees.

Psychological and Physical Well-Being (chapter 7). There are numerous indications that most retirees are satisfied with their status. Three-fourths find that retirement meets or exceeds their expectations; 70 percent say they would retire at the same age if the decision were to be made again. A majority report that the thing they like best about retirement is not having to work; one-third can think of nothing they do not like about retirement. There are differences in these reactions, however, according to the reason for retirement. By virtually every criterion, men who retired for health reasons display considerably less satisfaction than those who retired voluntarily.

The best estimate of the effect of retirement on psychological and physical well-being is derived from a longitudinal analysis of a subset of the NLS sample of whom none were retired as of 1976. Controlling for a variety of personal characteristics and comparing men who retired during the ensuing five years with those who did not according to changes in several measures of happiness and health leads to the conclusion that retirement has on average no adverse effect on happiness—with a negative effect for men who retired for health reasons being counterbalanced by a positive effect for men who retired voluntarily.

The health condition of retirees suffered greater deterioration, on the average, than that of men who did not retire—but exclusively because of the experience of men who had retired for health reasons. No other group of retirees showed the same pattern. These findings suggest the strong possibility that even for the health retirees some (if not all) of the deterioration in physical condition had taken place *prior* to retirement—especially because health was controlled as of 1976, whereas retirement might have occurred at any time up to 1981.

Policy Implications

Research findings alone never provide definitive guidelines for policy prescription, because policy decisions involve choices among values as well as knowledge about the way in which the world operates. Nevertheless, the NLS evidence is relevant to a number of policy issues relating to work and retirement, and a brief discussion of these constitutes a fitting conclusion to this volume. Not surprisingly, these observations differ very little from those offered in the concluding chapter of the ten-year report on the NLS surveys of the older men (Parnes, 1981b, pp. 266-270).

The Role of Full Employment

Analysis of NLS data has provided abundant evidence that high levels of employment are an indispensable prerequisite to the achievement of many social objectives relating to the labor market. Improving the earnings and economic security of blacks relative to whites is much easier in periods of low than of high unemployment. As another example, the impact of job loss on middle-aged men is less severe when high levels of employment opportunities prevail. This well-established principle can be stated in general terms: workers who are disadvantaged—for whatever reason—experience an improvement in relative position when the overall demand for labor is high. A society that wishes to equalize opportunities, therefore, must give high priority to the pursuit of full employment.

Health

In addition to forcing many men into early retirement, poor health has other serious consequences for the welfare of middle-aged men and their families. The impact on the worker's family is especially severe when a long illness is followed by death before the worker reaches retirement age. Improvement in the health of the labor force, therefore, will significantly reduce labor market disadvantage and public dependency; thus, research on effective methods of influencing the health-related behavior of individuals early in life has potentially high payoffs—not only on humanitarian grounds, but also because bad health robs the economy of otherwise willing human resources.

Discrimination

The evidence is clear that even when factors related to productivity are controlled, middle-aged black men fare less well in the labor market than their white counterparts. It is also clear, however, that the relative disadvantage of black men in this regard has diminished, and that the improvement has been associated—directly or indirectly—with government expenditures on antidiscrimination programs. Thus, the means of pursuing greater equality of opportunity in the labor market are evidently available.

Although the issue of age discrimination has been addressed with NLS data in only a limited context (Shapiro and Sandell, 1983), our studies have shown that a far from negligible number of men lose their jobs in middle age after having built up substantial equities in them, and that such displacements result, on average, in deterioration of earnings, occupational status, and psychological well-being. Consideration might therefore be given to special programs of "reparations" for these kinds of costs. The recommendation of the National Commission on Unemployment Compensation (1980, pp. 71-72) for additional weeks of eligibility for persons age 60-64 is illustrative.

Retirement

If society is concerned about the decreasing labor force participation of older men either because of the increasing costs of supporting them in retirement or because of the fear of labor shortages, our studies point fairly clearly to the measures that can be effective in keeping older men at work. First, the elimination of mandatory retirement is not likely to be very significant in this context, however desirable it may be from the standpoint of enhancing individual freedom of choice. Only a small minority of men are forced into retirement by mandatory rules—one-tenth as many as are forced to leave the labor market by poor health.

Because early retirement has been shown to be induced by poor health, job dissatisfaction, and the level of prospective retirement income, these constitute the principal policy variables for influencing decisions. For the long term, measures that improve the health of middle-aged men and measures that enhance the quality of working life are important means of increasing labor force participation rates. In the shorter run, modification of private and public pension plans would have the most immediate and direct effect—either by imposing greater penalties on early retirement or by granting greater financial rewards for deferring receipt of pensions. A number of the 1983 amendments to the Social Security Act are illustrative.

Programs that facilitate occupational change in mid-life might also keep men in the labor force longer, particularly if they improve opportunities for workers to move into less demanding or more flexible jobs or into those with greater psychic rewards. Although most men who retire voluntarily do not regret their choice, a minority ultimately realize that they made a mistake. Effective preretirement counseling programs would permit more informed assessments of the benefits and costs of retirement and would thus be a means of reducing these kinds of errors in judgment. In addition, whatever can be done to make the retirement decision more nearly reversible would be helpful.

Even if social policy is directed at inducing healthy workers to remain in the labor force longer than many are currently electing to do, the evidence that many men retire at early ages because of poor health needs to be kept in mind. These men are frequently in very difficult economic circumstances. Accordingly, a social judgment that retirement policy should become less generous for men able to work is not necessarily inconsistent with making retirement somewhat easier for those with serious impairments.

References

Adams, Arvil V. 1975. "Earnings and Employment of Middle-aged Men: A Special Study of Their Investment in Human Capital." In Herbert S. Parnes et al., *The Pre-Retirement Years*, vol. 4. U.S. Department of Labor, Manpower R & D Monograph 15. Washington, D.C.: Government Printing Office.

Andrisani, Paul J., and Nestel, Gilbert. 1975. "Internal-External Control and Labor Market Experience." In Herbert S. Parnes et al., *The Pre-Retirement Years*, Vol. 4. U.S. Department of Labor R & D Monograph 15. Washington, D.C.: Government Printing Office.

Bartel, Ann P. 1981. "Race Differences in Job Satisfaction: A Reappraisal." *Journal of Human Resources* 16: 294-303.

Bartel, Ann P., and Borjas, George J. 1981. "Wage Growth and Job Turnover: An Empirical Analysis. In Sherwin Rosen, ed., *Studies in Labor Markets*. Chicago, Ill.: University of Chicago Press.

Beck, Scott H. 1983. "Retirement Preparation Programs: Differentials in Opportunities and Use." Presentation at the 1983 Meeting of the Gerontological Society of America, San Francisco, November, 1983.

Borjas, George J. 1981. "Job Mobility and Earnings Over the Life Cycle." *Industrial and Labor Relations Review* 34: 365-376.

Chirikos, Thomas N., and Nestel, Gilbert. 1981. "Impairment and Labor Market Outcomes: A Cross-sectional and Longitudinal Analysis." In Herbert S. Parnes. ed.. *Work and Retirement: A Longitudinal Study of Men*. Cambridge, Mass.: MIT.

Daymont, Thomas N. 1981. "Changes in Black-White Labor Market Opportunities, 1966-1976." In Herbert S. Parnes, ed., *Work and Retirement: A Longitudinal Study of Men*. Cambridge, Mass.: MIT.

Fredland, J. Eric, and Little, Roger D. 1980. "Long Term Returns to Vocational Training: Evidence from Military Services." *The Journal of Human Resources* 15: 49-66.

Freeman, Richard B. 1974. "Occupational Training in Proprietary Schools and Technical Institutes." *Review of Economics and Statistics* 56: 310-318.

Kingson, Eric R. 1982. "The Health of Very Early Retirees." *Social Security Bulletin* 45 (September): 3-9.

Kohen, Andrew I. 1975. "Occupational Mobility Among Middle-aged Men." In Herbert S. Parnes et al., *The Pre-Retirement Years*, Vol. 4. U.S. Department of Labor R & D Monograph 15. Washington, D.C.: Government Printing Office.

Leigh, Duane E. 1978. "Racial Discrimination and Labor Unions: Evidence from the NLS Sample of Middle-aged Men." *Journal of Human Resources* 13: 568-577.

———. 1979. "Unions and Nonwage Racial Discrimination." *Industrial and Labor Relations Review* 32: 439-450.

Luft, Harold S. 1975. "The Impact of Poor Health on Earnings." *Review of Economics and Statistics* 57: 43-57.

Mott, Frank L., and Haurin, R. Jean. 1981. "The Impact of Health Problems and Mortality on Family Well-being." In Herbert S. Parnes, ed., *Work and Retirement: A Longitudinal Study of Men*. Cambridge, Mass.: MIT.

Myers, Robert J. 1982. "Why do People Retire from Work Early?" *Social Security Bulletin* (September): pp. 10-14.

National Commission on Unemployment Compensation. 1980. *Unemployment*

Compensation: Final Report. Washington, D.C.: Government Printing Office.

Parnes, Herbert S. 1981a. "Introduction and Overview." In Herbert S. Parnes, ed., *Work and Retirement: A Longitudinal Study of Men.* Cambridge, Mass.: MIT.

———. 1981b. "Summary and Conclusions." In Herbert S. Parnes, ed., *Work and Retirement: A Longitudinal Study of Men.* Cambridge, Mass.: MIT.

———. 1982. *Unemployment Experience of Individuals Over a Decade: Variations by Sex, Race, and Age.* Kalamazoo, Mich.: The W.E. Upjohn Institute for Employment Research.

——— et al. 1968. *The Pre-Retirement Years,* vol. 1. U.S. Department of Labor R & D Monograph 15. Washington, D.C.: Government Printing Office.

———. 1970. *The Pre-Retirement Years,* vol. 2. U.S. Department of Labor R & D Monograph 15. Washington, D.C.: Government Printing Office.

———. 1973. *The Pre-Retirement Years,* vol. 3. U.S. Department of Labor R & D Monograph 15. Washington, D.C.: Government Printing Office.

——— and Nestel, Gilbert. 1975a. "Middle-aged Job Changers." In Herbert S. Parnes et al., *The Pre-Retirement Years,* vol. 4. U.S. Department of Labor R & D Monograph 15. Washington, D.C.: Government Printing Office.

———. 1975b. "Early Retirement." In Herbert S. Parnes et al., *The Pre-Retirement Years,* vol. 4. U.S. Department of Labor R & D Monograph 15. Washington, D.C.: Government Printing Office.

———. 1981. "The Retirement Experience." In Herbert S. Parnes, ed., *Work and Retirement: A Longitudinal Study of Men.* Cambridge, Mass.: MIT.

———; Gagen, Mary G.; and King, Randall H. 1981. "Job Loss Among Long Service Workers." In Herbert S. Parnes, ed., *Work and Retirement: A Longitudinal Study of Men.* Cambridge, Mass.: MIT.

Parsons, Donald O. 1981. "Black-White Differences in Labor Force Participation of Older Males." In Herbert S. Parnes, ed., *Work and Retirement: A Longitudinal Study of Men.* Cambridge, Mass.: MIT.

Reimers, Cordelia W. 1977. *The Timing of Retirement Among American Men.* Ph.D. diss. Columbia U.P., New York.

Rosenberg, Sam. 1981. "Occupational Mobility and Short Cycles." In Frank Wilkinson. ed., *The Dynamics of Labor Market Segmentation,* New York: Academic.

Shapiro, David and Sandell, Steven H. 1983. *Age Discrimination and Labor Market Problems of Displaced Male Workers.* National Commission for Employment Policy Research Report Series, RR-83-10. Washington, D.C.: National Commission for Employment Policy, processed.

Sproat, Kezia V.; Churchill, Helene; and Sheets, Carol. 1985. *The National Longitudinal Surveys of Labor Market Experience: An Annotated Bibliography of Research.* Lexington, Mass.: Heath.

Index

About the Authors

Herbert S. Parnes, professor (emeritus) of economics at The Ohio State University, is founder of the National Longitudinal Surveys (NLS). After receiving his M.A. in economics from the University of Pittsburgh in 1941, he served in the military during World War II, then taught economics at The Ohio State University from 1947 to 1980, having earned his Ph.D. in 1950. When he first retired in 1980, he became professor of industrial relations and human resources at Rutgers University; in 1983 he "retired" again, to write a textbook and the present book (see chapter 8). Professor Parnes had visiting professorships at Princeton University in 1954-1955 and at the University of Minnesota in 1959. In 1961-1962 he served as consultant for the Organization for Economic Cooperation and Development in Paris, where he developed a methodology for educational planning. Currently he consults at the Center for Human Resource Research and the National Center for Vocational and Technical Education at The Ohio State University. Professor Parnes has written over twenty books and monographs and more than forty articles. His earlier book based on ten years of data on the NLS men's cohort, *Work and Retirement: A Longitudinal Study of Men* (Cambridge: MIT, 1981) was selected as one of ten "Outstanding Books in Industrial Relations and Labor Economics in 1981," by Princeton University Industrial Relations Section. His textbook on human resources, *Peoplepower: Elements of Human Resource Policy* (Beverly Hills, Calif.: Sage Publications) appeared in 1984.

Frank L. Mott holds a Ph.D. in sociology from Brown University. He is a senior research scientist at The Ohio State University Center for Human Resource Research and associate project director of the NLS. He has worked with these data since 1975. He is principal author of two volumes about the young women's cohort: *The Employment Revolution* (MIT, 1982) and *Women, Work and Family* (Lexington, 1978).

Joan E. Crowley received her Ph.D. in social psychology from the University of Michigan in 1978. A senior research associate at The Ohio State University Center for Human Resource Research since 1979, she contributed to two studies of the NLS youth cohort by M.E. Borus:

Tomorrow's Workers, (Lexington, 1983), and *Youth and the Labor Market* (Upjohn, 1984).

R. Jean Haurin received her M.A. in sociology from The Ohio State University, and is a research associate at the Center for Human Resource Research. She began working on the NLS in 1975. She and Frank Mott coauthored chapters in *The Employment Revolution* and *Work and Retirement*. She is currently pursuing a Ph.D. in sociology.

Lawrence J. Less received his M.A. in economics from The Ohio State University, and served as Professor Parnes' research assistant at the Center for Human Resource Research from 1979 to 1984. He is currently employed in the Labor Market Information section of the Ohio Bureau of Employment Services.

William R. Morgan received his Ph.D. in sociology from the University of Chicago. He is a research scientist at The Ohio State University Center for Human Resource Research. He has been analyzing NLS data since 1981. He contributed a chapter on schooling to *Youth and the Labor Market*.

Gilbert Nestel holds an M.S. in mathematical statistics from the University of Michigan. He is a research scientist at The Ohio State University Center for Human Resource Research. He has worked with the NLS since 1969. Among the many NLS-based volumes he has contributed to are *Work and Retirement* and *Unplanned Careers* by Lois B. Shaw (Lexington, 1983).